Texts of Power

Texts of Power

Emerging Disciplines in Colonial Bengal

Partha Chatterjee, editor

Published in conjunction with
the Centre for Studies in Social Sciences, Calcutta, India,
as part of its Perspectives in Social Sciences Series

University of Minnesota Press
Minneapolis
London

Published by the University of Minnesota Press
111 Third Avenue South, Suite 290, Minneapolis, MN 55401-2520
Printed in the United States of America on acid-free paper

Library of Congress Cataloging-in-Publication Data

Texts of power : emerging disciplines in colonial Bengal / Partha Chatterjee, editor.
p. cm.
"Published in conjunction with the Centre for Studies in Social Sciences, Calcutta, India."
Includes bibliographical references and index.
ISBN 0-8166-2686-3 (alk. paper). — ISBN 0-8166-2687-1 (pbk. : alk. paper)
1. Bengal (India)—Intellectual life. 2. Bangladesh—Intellectual life. I. Chatterjee, Partha, 1947– . II. Centre for Studies in Social Sciences.
DS485.B44T49 1995
954′.1403—dc20 95-11205

In honor of Professor Asok Sen

Contents

Illustrations and Tables

Figures

Tables

Preface

The present volume is the product of collaborative work carried out mainly in 1992 at the Centre for Studies in Social Sciences, Calcutta. It grew out of a long series of weekly meetings at which the authors of these chapters discussed many of the new theoretical questions that had appeared in historical and cultural studies in the last decade or so. Those discussions soon seemed to lead to new ways of approaching familiar materials from Indian intellectual and cultural history. The result is this collection of exploratory studies into the genealogy of our own contemporary intellectual modernity in India. Each chapter has drawn upon the author's current research interest; however, all of the chapters were written, and subsequently put through several revisions, specifically for the purpose of producing this volume.

Needless to say, the authors of these chapters are greatly and mutually indebted to one another for help, criticism, and support. Other colleagues at the centre who frequently joined our discussions, some at the formative stage and others at the concluding phase of this work, include Vivek Dhareshwar, Amitav Ghosh, Anjan Ghosh, and Manas Ray. Asok Sen has been a constant source of encouragement; we are especially happy to dedicate this book to him. We thank Amiya Kumar Bagchi, Gautam Bhadra, Dipesh Chakrabarty, and three anonymous readers for their comments on an earlier version of this manuscript.

We thank the staff of the centre for their unstinting cooperation. In particular, we thank Rita Banerjee for her help with many of the computations,

Anjusri Chakrabarti for drawing the maps, and Rajkumar Mahato for his unfailing support in the production of the manuscript in the computer room.

Finally, we thank Janaki Bakhle of the University of Minnesota Press for her enthusiasm, efficiency, and persistence in the cause of publishing this volume.

Calcutta
12 September 1994

1 / The Disciplines in Colonial Bengal

Partha Chatterjee

A Center of Empire

When the gods arrived in Calcutta in 1880, they were met by a weeping Gaṅgā. The only available account of this visit tells us that Gaṅgā complained bitterly to the gods about the indignities she was being forced to suffer at the hands of the English, the new rulers of the country.[1] As he heard this tale of woe from his long-lost daughter, Brahmā, the creator of the world, was greatly distressed. Looking up, he surveyed the shore and realized to his utter amazement that this was not how he had created the world. Clearly, someone had intervened. The river was so thick with boats, large and small, of all descriptions that the water was hardly visible. The air was heavy with the sounds of horns, sirens, and whistles emanating from the vessels. There were English sailors perched on the masts of the large ships. On the opposite bank of the river, bathers had lined up like rows of ants on the ghats (riverbank steps). Beyond them, in a line stretching from one end of the horizon to the other, stood the great mansions of the city, interspersed at points by huge chimneys belching smoke into the sky.

Puzzled by this unexpected sight, Brahmā said to his daughter, "Gaṅgā, you are the mother of the world, the greatest of rivers! Have the English made you so contented that you have forgotten even your old father? Their ships float on your waters, their city adorns your bank. Does this please you so much that you cannot get away from this place even for a moment?"

Gaṅgā turned to her waves and said, "Look, that old man standing there weeping is my father. Next to him are Indra, king of the gods, Varuṇa, the rain god, and Nārāyaṇa himself, from whose feet I sprang to life. They all look so crestfallen. It breaks my heart to see them like this, unattended. If a son of the empress of India, or if even the governor, were to come here, imagine what a scramble there would be. All the great men of the city would assemble to receive him. Schoolboys would line up with flags in their hands. Shopkeepers would close their businesses for the day and crowd around to watch. And by now the guns would sound in the fort. But no matter! Run along quickly and wash their feet."

The ablutions over, Gaṅgā proceeded to tell her father about her present condition. "I have been bound and gagged," she said. "Look over there. See how they have put me in chains." Brahmā turned his gaze up the river and saw the bridge. He stared at it long and hard, and his eyes were filled with astonishment. Varuṇa, whose annual visits during the monsoons had made him familiar with the changes in this part of the world, decided that he ought to explain. "When they first put it up," he said, "we did try to destroy it. We even sent a cyclone for the purpose. But it withdrew after a while, fearing the damage it would cause to the rest of Bengal. The bridge connects Calcutta to Howrah. It's the only floating bridge of its kind. It cost them eighteen lakhs of rupees to build. It is one thousand five hundred and thirty feet long and forty-eight feet wide. It was opened in October 1874."

Gaṅgā in the meantime had begun to catalogue her woes. "Father," she said, "no one, god, demon, or human, is as unfortunate as me. The new rulers of the country are not content with having me bound in chains. They force me like a slave to carry their huge ships. If I say it's too hard for me, they tug the boats all over me. There are carriages and men crossing that bridge at all times of day and night. I don't have a minute's rest. And now they've put up all kinds of factories on my banks: the noise and the smoke are unbearable. I've never seen rulers like these in my life. When they need land, they grab it from me. Just look how far they have filled up the land near the mint. They tax the boats, they tax the fish, they tax the corpses, they even tax my waters."

Brahmā, we can imagine, was both moved and embarrassed by his daughter's plight. He felt it necessary to console her. "Daughter," he said, "don't worry. Your days of sorrow will soon be over. As soon as possible, I will arrange to take you back to heaven. When you left my care, I had told you that when towns become forests and forests towns, when you are forced in places to flood your banks and at others to dry up, when people lose faith in you, it is then that you will return to heaven. I see that the time has come. Be patient for another ten or fifteen years. I will take you back to heaven."

Although the report on the visit does not tell us this, we know that these were empty words. Even in his dotage, perhaps Brahmā, too, knew it. For when the gods took their leave of Gaṅgā and proceeded to cross the bridge into the city, they were struck with awe by the power and inventiveness of the British. Brahmā had to strain to the utmost his failing memory in order to recall another instance when the waters had been stilled so as to float a bridge. "I've seen this only once before, in the Tretā age, when Rāma made the crossing to Laṅkā."[2]

During their wanderings through the city over the next few days, with Varuṇa as their guide, the gods saw many more examples of this awesome power of the new rulers of the country. They saw the great public buildings, the massive offices of government, the High Court, the municipal office, the museum, all recently built. They saw the banks, the shops, the new municipal market, the racecourse, and Presidency Jail. They went up the Ochterlony Monument, from where the cows looked like goats and the women like little dolls. They went around the fort and saw the 999 guns on the ramparts (one less than planned: someone made a mistake with the count). They visited the police headquarters in Lalbazar (from which they beat a hasty retreat when they discovered that the officers of the law were empowered to impose fines on even such everyday necessities as relieving oneself on the side of the street). Varuṇa, the rain god, was particularly voluble on the subject of the new waterworks and the system of supplying water through pipes, which he regarded as an encroachment on his jurisdiction. To Brahmā, however, this again confirmed his assessment of the spectacular powers of the British. Finally, when they managed to enter Government House (because the viceroy was away) and to see for themselves the pomp and splendor of imperial power, Indra, king of the gods, made a confession: "This *lāṭsāheb* must be the happiest man in the world. Before him, my own powers fade into insignificance. Who knows how many crores of years of meditation are necessary to get someone a post like this?"[3]

What the gods did not know, because their followers on earth had not endowed them with a modern historical consciousness, was that the wonderful inventiveness of the British was not unrelated to the humiliations they were inflicting on the gods as well as on the people of the country. Had they received proper historical advice, the gods would surely have discovered that power on earth was no longer the gift of a divine providence; it was now produced by a diligent practice of the new disciplines of knowledge. Perhaps

Table 1.1. Population of Calcutta, 1876–1921

	Old Town		Calcutta Municipal Area	
	Population	Decadal increase (%)	Population	Decadal increase (%)
1876	429,535			
1881	433,219			
1891	468,552	8.16	681,560	
1901			847,796	24.39
1911			896,067	5.69
1921			907,851	1.32

Note: The municipal limits of the city were expanded in 1888. The 1891 census is considered unreliable; hence, the increase in population between 1891 and 1901 is probably an overestimate.
Source: Data from Bagchi, "Wealth and Work," pp. 212–23.

then they would have been less baffled by the strange goings-on in the capital city of the new rulers of India.

The city had in fact grown, and in the last decades of the nineteenth century was still growing, according to a historical pattern that was quintessentially colonial. The division of the city into white town, intermediate town, and Indian town was still in place.[4] The population had increased five times during the course of the nineteenth century, and yet, or so at least the available records show, the number of houses rose by only 14 percent.[5] The overcrowding was mostly in the intermediate zone and in the Indian town to the north. Building activity, it seems, picked up significantly in the last decades of the century. Still, whereas the number of brick-built houses went up between 1891 and 1901 by 55 percent, this was overtaken by the rate of increase in the number of *kutcha* houses with mud walls and thatched roofs—67 percent.[6] Large parts of the city outside the white town had by then taken recognizable shape as the infamous slums of Calcutta. The population growth especially quickened in the period between 1881 and 1901 with the rise of industries in the northern suburbs and across the river in Howrah (see Table 1.1).

But increase in population was not a uniform feature of every locality of the city, nor indeed was the density of population the same. While the population in the northern wards of Shyampukur, Bartola, Jorabagan, Jorasanko, and Sukea's Street rose steadily in this period, southern wards, such as Kalinga, Park Street, Victoria Terrace, Hastings, and Alipur, did not see any population increase at all. Between 1881 and 1921, the northern wards became twice as densely populated as before, the average density in 1921 being in the region of two hundred per acre, whereas in southern wards with European concentrations the average density remained steady at around thirty per acre.[7]

There was a large element of conscious intervention in all these urban developments. The apparent chaos in the city today has produced a widespread impression of Calcutta being an "unplanned city," or even "an overgrown village." The truth is that those who founded the city as the capital of their empire also devoted considerable attention, both administrative and scientific, to its orderly growth.[8] From the early decades of the nineteenth century, a succession of committees was appointed by the colonial government to suggest measures for the improvement of the city. Physical intervention began in earnest in the 1820s, when the so-called Lottery Committee took charge. It was this committee that supervised the construction of a roadway cutting straight through the middle of the Indian town from north to south and named it in sections after stalwarts of empire—such as Cornwallis, Wellington, and Wellesley. More significant was the laying out of the area just south of Park Street where the scattered slums, shrubland, and narrow gullies, bearing names like Anis Barber's Lane and Misser Khansama's Lane, had to make way for a new, far more ordered residential area into which the European population would begin to move. The Lottery Committee died an inglorious death in 1836 because the political authorities in Britain found it morally indefensible that money should be raised for municipal improvements by encouraging the dubious public passion for gambling. In 1856, three paid commissioners were appointed to a new corporation that was given funds and the responsibility for "the conservancy and improvement" of the city. Soon, a health officer and an official engineer were appointed, and under this regime, in which the commissioner of police was the leading figure (one should not be surprised: we are talking of the capital city of a colonial empire), new services were inaugurated: the metalling of roads, the installation of gas lighting on the streets, a major sewerage works, and a system of filtered water supply. A historian of colonial Calcutta was later to record the obstacles that had to be overcome:

> In the matter of the water-supply infinite tact and patience were required to meet the initial difficulty occasioned by the prejudices of religion. Orthodox Hindoos debated whether they would, without loss of caste, drink water that had come through infidel pipes. But their scruples were gradually overcome. The claims of conscience were met halfway by the mingling of a little of the muddy but holy Ganges water with the pure fluid from the municipal standpost: and finally they were ignored altogether.[9]

While the civilizing mission was thus making some headway in the native quarters, considerable reorganization was also taking place within the central space. The decade of the 1870s in particular saw the physical consolidation of the principal offices of both the imperial and provincial governments within an area centered on Dalhousie Square, with Writers' Buildings to the north and Government House to the south. Several new buildings were put up—the High Court, the Imperial Secretariat Building, the General Post Office, the Central Telegraph Office, the Customs House—and existing buildings were extended and renovated, notably Writers' Buildings and the Treasury Building. The stretch between the Strand and Dalhousie Square that was "covered with native dwellings of the very worst type" was cleared. It was this newly refurbished capital, with its distinctly Victorian look, that so dazzled Brahmā and Indra when they toured Calcutta in 1880.

In 1875, diagonally across the Maidan from Government House, near the point where Park Street today disgorges its traffic into Chowringhee, the massive Indian Museum was built to house "collections illustrative of Indian Archaeology and of the several branches of Natural History." The museum soon became the nucleus for an entire campus devoted to the pursuit of colonial knowledge. The offices of the Geological Survey of India were housed there, as was the new School of Art and the Government Art Gallery. South of the museum, at the corner of Park Street, the venerable Asiatic Society continued to flourish. A little way down Park Street new buildings arose for the offices of the Surveyor-General of India. Directly north of these citadels of science, another massive redbrick building was constructed for the offices of the municipal corporation. From there, the "improvement" of the city would henceforth be supervised. Further north, at the point where the line running northward along Chowringhee Road and Bentinck Street met Bowbazar Street, running east from Dalhousie Square—the point of origin, in geometric parlance, of the axes of power on the one side and of knowledge on the other—stood Lalbazar, the headquarters of the Calcutta police (Fig. 1.1).

A third axis gave to the colonial edifice its solidity, representing as it did the original cause of empire. If we project this axis on to a map of Calcutta from the turn of the century, we find it extends northward from Dalhousie Square along a street named after the very founder of the empire in Bengal: Clive. The corner of Clive Street and New China Bazar Street was where the Bengal Chamber of Commerce, the premier association of British commercial interests in Calcutta, was located. The same building also housed the Royal Exchange, with its six hundred or so members at that time. Farther north, on both sides of Clive Street, were the offices of the numerous managing agencies and banks. This was the hub of colonial economic activity,

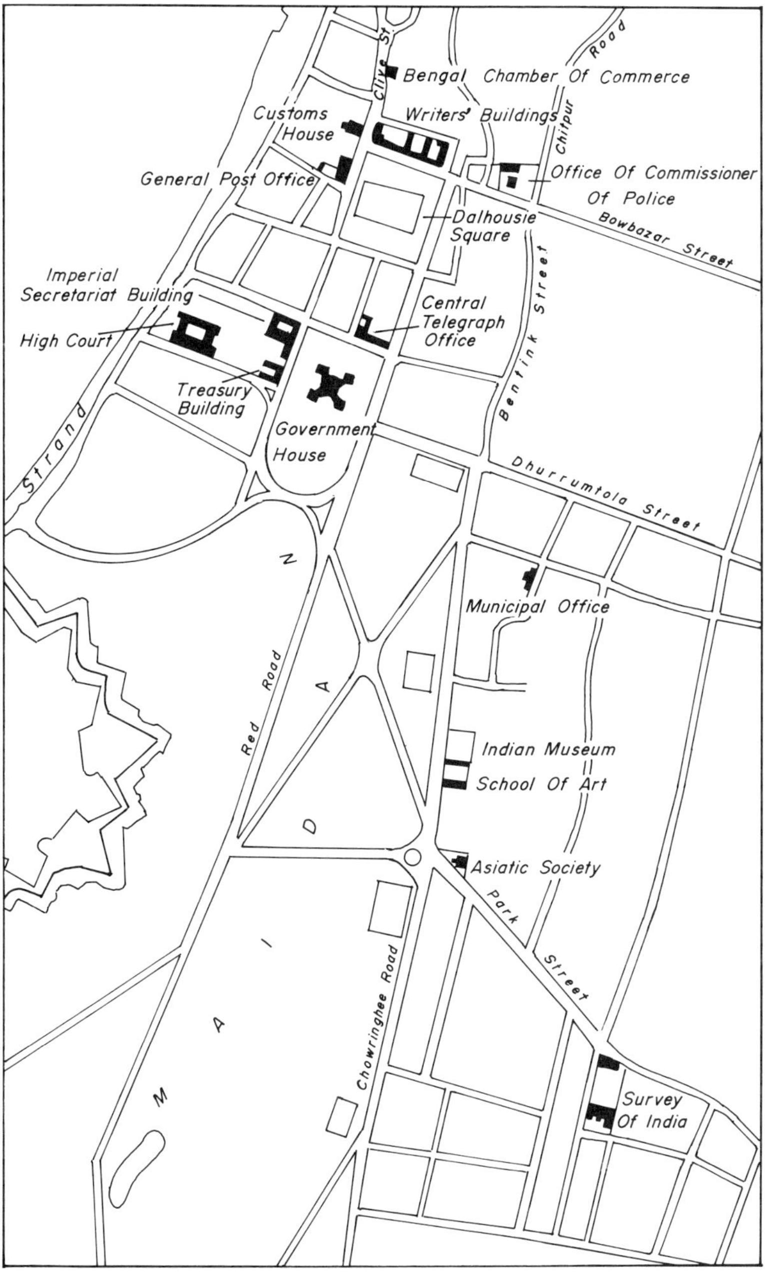

Fig. 1.1. Complex of knowledge and power in Calcutta

which by the turn of the century had expanded from its original mercantile function to become the leading force in both industrial manufacturing and finance.

Our recent understanding of the modern regime of disciplinary power tends toward persuading us that power no longer has a center and that older forms of political authority, radiating outward from singular institutions or zones, or even bodies of sovereignty, are dissolved and dissipated by modern disciplinary practices into capillary forms of power. These forms pervade every part and exist at every point of the social body. We must remind ourselves, however, that although the fully developed colonial regime of the Victorian period was precisely the agency that supervised the introduction into India of most of the institutions characteristic of modern disciplinary power, the project of modernity was insurmountably limited by the nature of colonial rule itself. Thus, whereas the superior reach and effectiveness of modern power would justify the introduction into colonial governance of appropriate disciplinary institutions and practices, they would at the same time be compromised, and even subverted, by the need to maintain a specifically colonial form of power. Indeed, since it could continue to exist only by reproducing the difference between colonizer and colonized, the colonial state was necessarily incapable of fulfilling the criterion of representativeness—the fundamental condition that makes modern power a matter of interiorized self-discipline, rather than external coercion.[10] We should not be surprised, therefore, to find the connections between colonial power and colonial knowledge displayed so clearly, and yet confined within such a carefully protected zone of physical exclusiveness, as in late-nineteenth-century Calcutta.

But if this was the end of modernity's journey in colonial India, we would have had no nationalism, no independence, and indeed none of our postcolonial confusions and miseries. Fortunately for history, modern power and the scientific practices of the disciplines spilled over their colonial embankments to proliferate in the native quarters. Energized by the desires and strategies of entirely different political agencies, the intellectual project of modernity found new sustenance in those densely populated parts; and in the process it took on completely new forms. That is the process we will look at in this book. Notwithstanding the mocking remarks of the colonial historian, we will find that it was not as though the "pure fluid" of European enlightenment was merely mingled with a few drops of the "muddy but holy Ganges water"; the "claims of conscience," as indeed the strategies of power, opened to question some of the very procedures of the practice of modernity.

English, the Classical Language of Bengal

The formative role of English-language education in the rise of the new intelligentsia, and through it in the emergence of modernizing movements and nationalism in India, has been commented upon innumerable times.[11] As far as the involvement in all this of the colonial state is concerned, the debate in the early nineteenth century between Orientalists and Anglicists, and the acceptance by the government in 1835 of Macaulay's minute recommending the spread of Western learning through the medium of the English language, are usually regarded as crucial. Also seen as important is Wood's dispatch of 1854, which argued that government should involve itself in higher education only to the extent that it be given to the upper classes of Indian society, from whom the effects of Western knowledge would filter down to the masses.[12]

In fact, the role of the colonial government in the spread of education was quite limited. There was undoubtedly an attempt, especially from the middle decades of the nineteenth century, to organize a system of liberal education so as to spread Western knowledge. This was shown particularly in the establishment of the first Indian universities in 1857. It was expected that the new class of Indians, literate in English and schooled in the various branches of European knowledge, would pass on the results of their schooling to other Indians in the Indian languages. The colonial government itself would confine its role mainly to that of assisting private enterprise in education. The assessment made in 1853 by John Marshman, a missionary long associated with vernacular education and journalism in Bengal, was prescient:

> It is impossible to extinguish the language of 30,000,000 of people; English will, doubtless in the course of time, become the classical language of Bengal, and every native of respectability will endeavour to give a knowledge of it to his children; but at the same time, the vernacular language of Bengal . . . and of the other provinces throughout India, will continue to be used and to be cultivated to an increasing degree.[13]

As it happened, there was a rapid expansion, especially from the 1880s, of secondary and higher education in Bengal, as indeed in other parts of India, principally as a result of private initiative. Between 1881-82 and 1901-2, during which time only one new government college was set up in all of India, the number of private colleges with government aid increased from twenty-one to fifty-five and that of private unaided colleges went up from eleven to fifty-three. The growth of English secondary schools in the same period reflects a similar trend: government, 562 to 696; private aided, 1,080 to 1,573; and private unaided, 491 to 828. Most of this expansion of education in the private sector was in Bengal. Government high schools in Calcutta had 1,750 students in 1883, whereas the city's unaided schools had 8,088 students.[14] Some of the older private institutions were run by European missionaries, almost all of them with government aid; the unaided schools and colleges were invariably set up and run by Indians. In 1881-82, of the twenty-three arts colleges in all of India run by private organizations, only five were managed by Indians, the rest belonging to missionary organizations; by 1901-2 forty-two colleges were run by Indians, compared with thirty-seven by the missionaries.[15]

On the whole, the expansion in higher education was most rapid in Bengal. In 1901-2, the province had forty-four colleges, government and private, compared with forty in Madras, twenty-six in the United Provinces, and ten in Bombay.[16] Literacy in English increased by 100 percent between 1891 and 1901, by 50 percent in the next decade, and by 50 percent again in the next. In 1921, while the figure for literacy stood at 18 percent in Bengal, 3.4 percent of the population was literate in English.[17] By 1918, Calcutta University, with twenty-seven thousand students, was the largest university in the world, and the proportion of literate people taking full-time university courses was the same as in the United Kingdom.[18] But the proliferation was only in the liberal arts. Just as official policy on vocational education was merely to train Indians for the lower grades of the government's technical services, so also was there a lack of enthusiasm among Indians to initiate professional or technical education. There seemed to be little demand for it. In 1901-2, compared with 140 arts colleges in India with some seventeen thousand students, there were thirty law colleges with about twenty-seven hundred students, and only 4 colleges each for medicine and engineering.[19] Not surprisingly, the bulk of the university graduates were employed in government service, education, and law: of 1,378 graduates of Calcutta University between 1858 and 1881 on whom information was available, 44.48 percent were in legal occupations, 25.91 percent in government service excluding education, and 23.66 percent in teaching. This left a mere 6 percent engaged elsewhere.[20]

There is substance, of course, in the argument that the colonial influence on modern education in India had sources other than the direct role of the government in setting up schools and colleges. One of the most important of these was the choice of curriculum. Bringing Western education to India did not mean the mere replication of a course of instruction that might have been offered at a British school or university. Much thought and effort was spent in the nineteenth century in determining a suitable content of Western education under colonial conditions. The emphasis clearly was on providing a general humanistic education; advanced courses in the sciences were largely unavailable until the last decades of the century. Religious instruction was carefully avoided, but in its place, as Gauri Viswanathan has shown, an entire academic discipline was invented for the teaching of English literature as the formative spiritual influence on a colonized elite.[21] The consequences were far-reaching for the emergence of the new literary and aesthetic disciplines in the modern Indian languages.

Another focus of colonial influence was, of course, the institutions of school, college, and university themselves, and their characteristic disciplinary practices. Contrary pulls operated in this area. On the one hand, the government was happy to let Indian managements take the initiative in opening schools and colleges, since the expectation was that the very content of the new education and the rigors of the institutional system would correct the deficiencies in knowledge and character inherited by the students from their native culture. As Alfred Croft, a senior educational officer in Bengal, put it, in 1886:

> It is in the school-room alone that habits of obedience and discipline are at the present time systematically taught. School discipline is now the one force that does not conspire with, but actively combats and counteracts, those other and far stronger influences that are apparently at work in Bengali society.[22]

On the other hand, there existed in official thinking a parallel concern that mere humanistic enlightenment and school discipline might not be enough to contain disloyalty or to generate active consent among the educated. Soon, with the rise of nationalist political agitation in the last decades of the century, a demand went up in official circles for more direct government control over education. With the turn of the century, Curzon made a determined attempt to reorder the system; his reforms, however, failed almost entirely to achieve the objective of establishing greater control.[23] Indeed, educational institutions, especially in Bengal, had by then largely passed into a disciplinary domain where the discursive forms of a specifically nationalist modernity were already in command.

Curiously, even as nationalism was in the process of constructing its sovereignty over this crucial area of cultural hegemony, it continued to harbor suspicions about the alienness of these institutions of learning. The nationalist cultural project of producing disciplined citizens for the new nation took root in the inner spaces of the community, especially in the restructured everyday life of the new family, not in the public institutions of civil society. Seeking zealously to protect that inner space from colonial incursion, the nationalist tended to see the school as a source of alien cultural influence and moral corruption. Virtually as a mirror image of the colonial view of the school as the only reliable disciplinary institution for counteracting the unhealthy influences of a native culture, the nationalist thought of the home as the proper domain where the "spiritual character" of the new citizen of the nation would be cleansed of outside, corrupting influences.[24] And as the contest over this disciplinary space intensified, the official view tended to construct the schoolroom as an extension of the state, while the nationalist sought to bring it under the domain of family and community.

Societies of Learning

The oldest and most prestigious institution of colonial knowledge was the Asiatic Society of Bengal. Set up in 1784 at the initiative of William Jones, then a brilliant young member of the Indian judiciary, the society pioneered the formation of the different branches of Indological scholarship. About its journal, it was said in 1833 that "the *Asiatick Researches* comprehended the sum of our knowledge of the classical literature of India; the European inquirer into that literature began and ended his investigations with this work."[25] Indeed, the main achievement of the society was to make available for modern European scholarship the materials of an oriental civilization. Not surprisingly, it was not until the second half of the nineteenth century that there was any serious participation by Indians in the intellectual activities of the society. In the first hundred years of its existence, only five Indians figured in the list of officeholders of the society, and of these only Rajendralal Mitra could be said to be a leading scholar. In the same period, among nearly a thousand contributors to the journals and proceedings of the society, there were only forty-eight Indians; of these, only the polymath Rajendralal was a regular contributor.[26]

In the meantime, there had come up in Calcutta other institutions through which a new Indian intelligentsia was already engaging with the modern disciplines of knowledge. The activities of these learned societies provide an account of not only the transformation in a colonial situation of the nineteenth-century European sciences, but also of the emergence in that situation of the civil-social institutions characteristic of the new public sphere.[27]

Of the dozen or so literary and learned societies in Calcutta in which Indians took the leading part in the middle of the nineteenth century, the four most important were the Society for the Acquisition of General Knowledge (established 1838), the Tattvabodhini Sabha (established 1839), the Bethune Society (established 1851), and the Bengal Social Science Association (established 1867). The appeal that was circulated by the founders of the first of these four began with a significant observation: "Countrymen," it said, "though humiliating be the confession, yet we cannot, for a moment, deny the truth of the remark so often made by many able and intelligent Europeans, who are, by no means, inimical to the cause of native improvement, that in no one department of learning are our acquirements otherwise than extremely superficial." School education, it continued, could hardly do more than lay "the ground-work of our mental improvement," but this was not enough. It had become necessary to set up a society "to create in ourselves a determined and well regulated love of study, which will lead us to dive deeper than the mere surface learning, and enable us to acquire a respectable knowledge on matters of general and more especially, of local interest." That this was a matter of self-interest as well as patriotic duty was also emphasized: "We cannot believe that in such a cause, coldness will be manifested by any person that entertains the least regard for his own improvement, or breathes any love for his own country."[28]

The leading lights of the Society for the Acquisition of General Knowledge were former students of Hindu College, and several of them had been members of "Young Bengal," a celebrated circle of radicals that had formed in the 1820s around the freethinking rationalist Henry Derozio. Although the Young Bengal radicals were renowned (and reviled) for their overtly Westernized views and manners, the society, it seems, allowed papers to be presented not just in English but in Bengali, too.[29] More interesting is an account of how it sought to establish and defend its autonomy as a civil-social institution. In 1843, at a meeting of the society held at the Hindu College, a paper was being read on "The Present State of the East India Company's Criminal Judicature and Police." D. L. Richardson, a well-known teacher of English literature at the college, got up and, according to the record of proceedings, angrily maintained that

> to stand up in a hall which the government had erected and in the heart of a city which was the focus of enlightenment, and there to denounce, as oppressors and robbers, the men who governed the country, did . . . amount to treason. . . . The College would never have been in existence, but for the solicitude the Government felt in the mental improvement of the natives of India. He could not permit it, therefore, to be converted into a den of treason, and must close the doors against all such meetings.

At this, Tarachand Chakrabarti, himself a former student of Hindu College, who was chairing the meeting, rebuked Richardson:

> I consider your conduct as an insult to the society . . . if you do not retract what you have said and make due apology, we shall represent the matter to the Committee of the Hindoo College, and if necessary to the Government itself. We have obtained the use of this public hall, by leave applied for and received from the Committee, and not through your personal favour. You are only a visitor on this occasion, and possess no right to interrupt a member of this society in the utterance of his opinions.[30]

This episode, usually recounted in the standard histories as an example of early nationalist feelings among the new intelligentsia of Bengal, is significant. But the significance does not lie in the obvious drama of an educated Indian confronting his British teacher; rather, it is in the separation between the domain of government and that of "this society," and the insistence that as long as the required procedures had been followed the rights of the members of the society to express their opinions, no matter how critical of government, could not be violated. This represented, one might say, the founding moment of modernity, where a liberal theory of power, namely, the freedom of the members of civil society, could declare itself as the enabling condition for rational knowledge, namely, the condition of freedom of speech and unhindered access to discourse. It is interesting to see the argument being deployed in this fashion so early in our history of the emergence of the scientific disciplines in India.

The moment held the possibility of alternative developments. Either the liberal distinction of state and society could have stayed in place, with freedom of speech and unhindered access becoming established in the institutions of civil society: in this case, there would have been no need for a specifically "nationalist" modernity. Or (and this is what actually happened) the domain of civil society could split, one part being inhabited by the colonizers and the other by the colonized, with the rights of the latter regarded by the colonial state as inferior to those of the former. The nationalist response to this would be to declare the domain of intellect and culture—the "spiritual" domain—its sovereign territory from which the colonial power was excluded. This would become the nation's own "civil society," with the crucial proviso that, within that sovereign zone, there would be no distinction between the political and the social, between "national state" and "national society": they would lie enmeshed in the moral and institutional life of the nation as community. As to the pursuit of knowledge, there would emerge a curious ambivalence: on the one hand, a persistent complaint at being excluded from or discriminated against in the matter of equal access to the supposedly universal institutions of knowledge; and on the other hand, an insistence on a distinctly Indian form of modern knowledge. We will encounter this ambivalence in the rest of this history.

The Bethune Society and the Bengal Social Science Association were in some ways a continuation of the first possibility, by which learned bodies were still seen as representing an unfractured civil society in which rational men, irrespective of race or creed, could unite in the pursuit of knowledge and defend their right to do so. Indeed, the Bethune Society congratulated itself in 1861 for its success "in bringing together—for mutual intellectual culture and rational recreation, the very elite of the educated native community and blending them in friendly union with leading members of the Civil, Military and Medical services of Government, of the Calcutta bar, of the Missionary body, and other non-official classes."[31]

In some ways, the Tattvabodhini Sabha was the first learned society to pose squarely the problem of propagating a knowledge that was both modern and national. It conducted its affairs exclusively in Bengali and, along with its journal *Tattvabodhinī Patrikā*, which was edited for the most part by the redoubtable Akshaykumar Datta (1820-86), could be said to have founded the modern discourse of science and rational philosophy in that language. In particular, it faced up to the question of finding a rational and modern way of talking about the religion and culture of the people of the country. Not surprisingly, a historian of nineteenth-century intellectual history has concluded that the reason for the spectacular success of the Tattvabodhini Sabha—its membership reached eight hundred within a few years and every major writer of the period contributed to its journal—was its avowal of Western modernity without, as in the case of Young Bengal, declaring war on Indian religion.[32]

Science was undoubtedly the most revered idea in the deliberations of these societies. Even on social and cultural questions, a scientific viewpoint and method were considered essential. The variety of subjects on which learned discussions were held is remarkable. A list of lectures delivered at the Bethune Society, for instance, shows that a talk in English and Bengali "on the Sanskrit Language and Literature by Pundit Isser Chandra Vidya Sagar" was followed by one "on the Practical Working and Varieties of the Electric Telegraph by Mr. Woodrow"; "Pizzaro, the Conqueror of Peru," by the Rev. C. H. A. Dall, was followed by a lecture entitled "On the Nature of the Evidences on Which the Truth of Phrenology Is Founded," by Babu Kali Kumar Das.[33] Also significant are the speed and seriousness with which the latest advances in European knowledge were followed. Social philosophy in particular is a case in point, and the utilitarianism of Bentham and

Mill, Comtean positivism, and the social evolutionism of Huxley and Spencer were keenly debated.[34] Empirical investigations on social matters, using schedules and questionnaires, were pursued, especially at the initiative of James Long, an Irish missionary, in the Bethune Society and the Bengal Social Science Association.[35]

In the social and cultural disciplines, however, the most persistent methodological problem arose out of the awareness of cultural difference. Did the fact of the birth of the modern sciences of society in Europe rule out their applicability in societies that were fundamentally different? Could their methods be used in Indian conditions without modification? Were their fundamental concepts applicable to India? Was it necessary to devise alternative theories? Or was science itself inappropriate in discussing matters of Indian society and culture? These are, of course, questions that pervade the entire literature on modernity in India, and they acquired their problematic and contested disciplinary forms even at the time of their birth in the deliberations of the nineteenth-century learned societies.

The Cultivation of Science

The curricula in the educational institutions in the nineteenth century were, as mentioned earlier in this chapter, heavily biased toward the liberal arts. When the resources of the natural sciences were deployed for the acquisition of colonial knowledge, it was done outside the universities and colleges, in specialized technical services set up and controlled by the government. In fact, it would not be an exaggeration to say that virtually all scientific personnel engaged in research in India in the nineteenth century were employed by the government. There were nearly a dozen such scientific organizations: the Survey of India, the Geological Survey, the Botanical Survey, the Zoological Survey, the Archeological Survey, the Agricultural Service, the Forest Service, the Medical and Bacteriological Service, the Munitions Board, the Meteorological Department, and the Veterinary Department. The senior personnel in these organizations were predominantly European; even as late as 1920, when there were 195 European scientific officers in senior grades in the various services, including those in select government colleges with research laboratories, Indians of equal rank numbered only 18.[36]

Thus, Indians participated little in scientific research in the nineteenth century. What did occur, however, was a massive program of translation of the results of modern science into the Indian languages. This was particularly true in Bengal: between 1875 and 1896, 776 books were published in

Bengali on medicine, mathematics, and the natural sciences, representing more than one-third of all books on science published in Indian languages in that period.[37] All the major Bengali journals of the time—*Tattvabodhinī*, *Rahasya sandarbha*, *Baṅgadarśan*, *Āryadarśan*, *Bhāratī*, *Bāmābodhinī*—regularly carried articles on scientific subjects, and *Bibidhārtha saṃgraha* and *Bijñāndarśan* were almost exclusively devoted to the cause of popularizing science.

The main point of debate in this writing on the natural sciences, unlike the literature on social theory and philosophy, was not the content or methods of science but the problem of translation. From the time when the School Book Society in Calcutta decided, in 1819, to bring out a Bengali textbook on geography, the debate began on whether to retain approximate equivalents of scientific terms, if these were commonly used in the local language, or whether to coin new words by drawing upon Sanskrit, or whether, indeed, merely to transliterate the English terms. There were those who pointed out the advantages of popularization if local terms were used; others complained of the imprecision and lack of standardization of such a local terminology. In 1877, Rajendralal Mitra made a reasoned intervention: he suggested a flexible scheme in which, depending on specific criteria, commonly used Bengali terms could, in certain cases, be retained; in other cases, new terms could be constructed by using root words from the Sanskrit; in still other cases, European terms had to be adopted. Even today, Rajendralal's overall strategy will be regarded as unexceptionable; and yet, more than a hundred years after his suggestions, the problem of translation of scientific terms in Bengali continues to be a vexed question.[38]

The reason for this, it is obvious, is the absence, despite the attempts at popularization, of any participation of the Indian languages in the formation of scientific discourse. From the early decades of the twentieth century, when the science departments in the Indian universities began to flourish, English has been the professional language of Indian scientists. The function of science writing in the Indian languages has been to make available at the lower educational levels and to the general reading public the materials of a "translated science." The engagement with the discursive process of scientific research, which alone can give to a scientific terminology its consensual fixity, has not been available to any Indian language. The point can be well illustrated by looking at the history of medical education in the Bengali language.

In 1851, a Bengali section was opened at the Calcutta Medical College in order to train Indian students in Western medicine without requiring them first to go through a course of secondary education in English. The licentiate and apothecary courses were a great success. Beginning with a mere 22 students in its first year, this stream overtook the English section in 1864, and in 1873 it had 772 students, compared with 445 in the English section. That year, the Bengali section was transferred to newly established medical schools in Calcutta and Dacca. Largely because of the demand from students, nearly seven hundred medical books were published in Bengali between 1867 and 1900.[39]

But while the courses remained popular, complaints began to be heard from around the 1870s about the quality of training given to the students in the vernacular sections. It was alleged that their lack of facility in English made them unsuitable for the positions of assistants to European doctors in public hospitals. This was at a time when a hospital system had begun to be put in place in Bengal and professional controls were being enforced in the form of supervision by the General Medical Council in London. From the turn of the century, with the institutionalization of the professional practices of medicine in the form of hospitals, medical councils, and patented drugs, the Bengali section in the medical schools died a quick death. From 1916, the licentiate courses were taught exclusively in English.[40]

Curiously, this move came at a time when, propelled by nationalist concerns, organized efforts were afoot to give to the ayurvedic and yunani systems of medicine a new disciplinary form. The All India Ayurveda Mahasammelan, which is still the apex body of ayurvedic practitioners, was set up in 1907. The movement that this organization represented sought to systematize the knowledge of ayurvedic clinical methods. It produced standard editions of classical and recent texts, formalized the college system leading to a degree, standardized medicines, and even promoted the commercial production of standard drugs by pharmaceutical manufacturers.[41] There have been debates within the movement about the extent and form of "integration" of indigenous and Western medicine in ayurvedic curricula, but even the proponents of *shuddha* (pure) ayurveda agree that the course should have "the benefit of equipment or the methods used by other systems of medicine . . . since, consistent with its fundamental principles, no system of medicine can ever be morally debarred from drawing upon any other branch of science, . . . unless one denies the universal nature of scientific truths."[42]

The very idea of the universality of science is being used in the above quote to carve out a separate space for ayurvedic medicine, defined according to the principles of a "pure" tradition, and yet reorganized as a modern scientific and professional discipline. This is one of several strategies one encounters in the emergence of the disciplines in colonial society. The claim is not that the field of knowledge is marked out into separate domains by the fact of cultural difference; it is not being suggested that ayurveda is the appropriate system of medicine for "Indian diseases"; it is, rather, a claim for an alternative science directed at the same objects of knowledge.

Thus we see that it is not only on the grounds of the different cultural constitution of the objects of knowledge that there will be claims for disciplinary difference. It will not do to say that the disciplines of the natural sciences are more resistant to the play of cultural difference than the social and cultural disciplines. It is not simply because of the fact that clinical procedures are liable to be influenced by cultural conditions that it was possible to sustain a nationalist agenda for the revival and reorganization of indigenous medicine. Similar claims were made even on behalf of the so-called hard sciences, and not only from the lunatic fringe shouting "It's all in the Vedas"; such claims came from within the modern academic and scientific professions themselves. It was not only the will to fight against racial discrimination in the government scientific organizations or the desire to have autonomous national institutions of modern scientific research that gave rise to a movement such as Mahendralal Sarkar's Indian Association for the Cultivation of Science. The same set of nationalist desires led the eminent academic philosopher Brajendranath Seal to compile *The Positive Sciences of the Ancient Hindus* and the scientist Prafulla Chandra Ray to write *A History of Hindu Chemistry*.[43] The same desires also guided Jagadischandra Bose, Fellow of the Royal Society, into a research program, regarded by most scientists as of dubious validity, to demonstrate that inanimate life "was merely the shadow of human life."[44] Even for the natural sciences, then, there was a struggle to nibble away at the edges of the supposedly hard disciplines, to carve out spaces that would be no less "disciplinized" but where national identity would be implicated in defining the position of the scientist. As Jagadischandra asked, "When science is universal, can there be in the world of science a place which will remain vacant without an Indian devotee?"

Dissemination, Hybridization, and Agency

In a recent paper, Gyan Prakash has argued that while science acted as a crucial force authorizing the new discourse in nineteenth-century India of modernity and reform, "its very functioning and the demonstration of its power as a transformative force required the ground of cultural difference, producing the dissemination and hybridization of its authority."[45] The posing of the difference between enlightened rationality and "ignorant and bigoted superstition" was essential for science to become a justification for social reform. Yet the fact that this difference was implicated in the political relations between colonizer and colonized meant that the purported culture of rationality could never be allowed wholly to replace that of indigenous tradition, since the erasure of all difference is also the erasure of identity. Science therefore had to be "translated" from one culture to another: just as indigenous tradition (or so at least the argument went) needed to be adequately supplemented by modern science, so did the European enlightenment need to be naturalized in India. "The position of science could not but be dislocated by the process of translation and negotiation in which its functioning was situated."

What resulted was a hybrid. The process of translation and negotiation did not define a dialectic; science did not negate tradition and produce a new and higher unity. Rather, translation became a process of dissemination and hybridization in which science's authority was "renegotiated and relocated." Science no longer possessed "a language independent of the place and event of its enunciation"; it was subjected to discrete, local strategies of redeployment.

The trouble with this characterization is not that it is incorrect. As Homi Bhabha has pointed out in an oft-cited article, the advantage of looking at the effect of colonial power as the *production* of hybridization is that one does not have to narrate this history as "the noisy command of colonialist authority or the silent repression of native traditions."[46] Nor does one have to name the new formations in their entirety with negative qualifiers such as semi-, quasi-, or non-, or with the negative chronological indicators pre- or post-. The field can be said to be structured variously, according to local and entirely contingent strategic conditions.

The trouble is that the characterization remains insufficient. In spite of making a plea for acknowledging variableness and contingency, it manages to impose, paradoxically, a quality of sameness upon all products of dissemination. How are we to distinguish between hybrid and hybrid? How do we pin down the location of the local? How define the discreteness of the discrete? Instead of negative qualifying prefixes, one now has recourse to metaphors of spatial transference such as realignment and relocation, but can we devise a language to describe the new topographies?[47] Can we, in other words, find the means to distinguish, spatially as well as in time, between the products of dissemination? Can we then identify the specific genealogies of the formation of each of the separate "hybrid" disciplines?

The argument around which the chapters in this volume are knit suggests that the distinctions can be best made by focusing on the institutional sites where the new discourse of modernity was produced. We will, consequently, look for instruments of dissemination, for attempts to enforce disciplinary norms through institutional practices, and, most crucially, for the evidence of contests over these practices. Home, school, university, bureaucracy, literary society, journals, books—each of these became a site for the definition of disciplinary practices; their institutional reach defined the boundaries of disciplinary enforcement. By focusing on the histories of these contests over institutional sites, we hope to be able to write specific histories of dissemination, distinguished by disciplinary fields.

The metaphor of hybridization is one that was familiar to the nineteenth-century pioneers of the modern disciplines. As Gyan Prakash has noted of Rajendralal Mitra, his proposal for translating scientific terms involved

> a process of aligning and realigning non-equivalent languages. . . . This process exposed scientific reason to "contamination" from the subordinated, indigenous culture in which the authority of western science was re-presented. There ensued, then, a dissemination, not a dialectic, of western science and Indian culture from which neither one nor the other could re-appear in its "original" position and meaning.[48]

This is entirely true. But Rajendralal also went on to point out that the production of hybrids depended on certain conditions; not all attempts at hybridization had equal chances of success:

> Languages of the same class can borrow freely from each other without difficulty; but from different classes they cannot do so to any large extent without serious injury. The loan becomes an incubus in the one case, and a reproductive and useful resource in the other; or, taking it as a process of hybridization, it becomes agenesic in dissimilar families, and ugenesic among similars.

He also did not fail to point out the political dimension to the question of transference between "non-equivalent" languages:

> No language on the face of the earth has borrowed more extensively, and is better able to do so, than the English; and yet I doubt very much if any person would for a moment tolerate a proposition to put into it 20,000 Manchu, or Kamschatkan, or even Greek, words in a lump. . . . The foreign matter, unless introduced in very moderate quantities, will never engraft itself on the new stocks, and is sure to be cast out as sloughy, dead substance unsuited to their constitutions, even as the Bengali and the Hindi are now casting off the Semetic elements which were forced into them by the Moslem rulers of India, and which seven centuries of intimate association did not suffice to assimilate. That an experiment of the kind with Latin, Greek, and English elements will prove more successful, I have every reason to doubt.[49]

The range and subtlety of the contestatory moves made in these passages are remarkable. Not only is it a question of translation between nonequivalent languages, but between unequal languages—languages unequal in power. English has become the world's most powerful language by borrowing extensively from other languages; as a result, it claims universal currency as the language of modern science. But if it imposes its universality on less developed languages, it does so by virtue of the superior power wielded by its political agency. However, forcible hybridization of this kind does not succeed (and the intrusion into the Indian languages of English under British rule is in this regard no different from the intrusion of "Semetic elements" under the "Moslem rulers": the fact that it acts as the vehicle of modern science does not confer upon English any special privilege). Hybridization of languages, like that of natural species, must follow certain natural laws; the crossbreeding of languages not "of the same class" must be attempted with great caution, for being "unnatural" the attempt is likely to fail.

Rajendralal is indeed deploying the metaphor of naturalness to use the very authority of science to challenge the claim of English to act as science's universal vehicle. By doing this, he is not rejecting hybridization but asserting the right to define "the native stand-point" for selecting the appropriate hybrid. It is assertions like this that constitute the materials of the emergence of the disciplines in the colonies.

To narrate them as history, we must situate them in their particular configurations of the strategies of power and the contested claims to agency. There was nothing inherent in the "pure" disciplines that determined the particular forms of this hybridization in the colony. The specific intellectual history of dissemination—the specific contingencies of power and agency—determined why and how ayurveda and yunani now flourish as parallel "disciplined" forms of medicine, whereas "Hindu chemistry" was virtually stillborn, and why the canonical principles of the novel in India remain explicitly European, whereas those of music, both classical and popular, have been successfully "disciplined" into modern, and yet recognizably Indian, forms. It is questions of this nature that we will raise and seek to answer in the chapters of this volume.

Dispersed Disciplines

It must be obvious that these questions have been largely prompted by our reading of Michel Foucault. In this, our efforts could be seen as proceeding along the same lines as recent investigations into the "disciplinarity" of various disciplines of knowledge.[50] However, there is, I think, an irrevocable historical contingency in the genealogies of the disciplines in the colonies that give rise to questions of an altogether different import. Since, for reasons of accessibility to a wider readership, we have for the most part avoided using the specialized vocabulary of Foucauldian discursive analysis in the rest of this volume, this may be the appropriate place to spell out the theoretical implications of this difference.

If one recalls the detailed and complex genealogical exercises carried out by Foucault in *The Birth of the Clinic*, in *Discipline and Punish*, or in the first volume of *The History of Sexuality*,[51] one cannot help thinking how ridiculously simple by comparison our task is in India of identifying a "moment of rupture" as the discursive event that produces a new disciplinary constellation. The various modern knowledges arrive in the colony in the nineteenth or early twentieth centuries already formed as disciplines, their objects and boundaries defined, their conceptual apparatus in place, and their authorities firmly established (in the metropolis, of course). The only interesting question here seems to be the institutional one, that is, of the specific educational, literary, cultural, or professional institutions through which the modern disciplines are transmitted in the colony and the nature of their appropriation within various nondiscursive practices. One might say that this is exactly what the "social and intellectual history" literature on Indian modernity has attempted to do for many years.

A more critical look, of the sort I have described earlier in the chapter, into the contents of the disciplines as they have been practiced in India in the last hundred years or so must suggest, however, that the matter is far from simple. We are forced to recognize, first, that, following its implantation in a different if not entirely alien field, the new discursive formation will open itself to intrusions by various elements in the preexisting linguistic or intellectual practices of the country. Perhaps the natural-topographical analogy itself becomes inappropriate here, because what happens is that the new indigenous practitioners of the disciplines actively seek out the various points of entry—equivalence, similarity, adjacency, substitutability, and so forth—through which, in a ceaseless process of translation, the new knowledges are aligned with prior knowledges. These "prior" knowledges are not those whose elements may have already gone into the formation of the discipline (such as, let us say, the Greek sciences or medieval scholasticism). These are "prior" knowledges that belong, so to speak, to an anachronistic present, knowledges that one would have assumed had been overtaken by the history of scientific progress, except for the fact that they now have to be encountered horizontally, as adjacent formations that must be engaged in the process of translation. Second, we also recognize that the relation between the discursive and the nondiscursive does not operate in one direction only: the appropriation of the new disciplines within the array of existing nondiscursive practices in the colony could result in substantial modifications in the disciplinary formations themselves.

Indeed, if we consider the rules of formation of disciplinary knowledges as Foucault attempts to set them out in the *Archaeology of Knowledge*,[52] we will find that, in the dispersal of the disciplines in the colonies, differences could appear at all four levels: in the formation of objects, in the modalities of enunciation, in concept-formation, and in the thematic choices. There are numerous examples, most frequently of course in the social and cultural disciplines but not necessarily only in those, where the objects of knowledge in a non-Western field are declared to be specifically different from the ones considered by those sciences in their "original" Western forms (thus, to take possibly the most enduring example, *caste,* as an object of sociological inquiry). As far as enunciative modalities are concerned, the questions of who is authorized to speak, from which institutional site, and from which subject-position, lead to some of the most fascinating transferences. Even as the metropolitan authorities and institutions of science come to be recognized as authoritative, there are attempts, as we will see in several of the following chapters, at setting up parallel authorities, parallel institutions, and parallel subject-positions, all claiming a privileged status by virtue of the "authenticity" of their affiliation to the indigenous tradition and yet displaying, at the same time, as many authorized tokens of "science" as possible. The differences that occur in the course of conceptual translations are perhaps the most intricate of all. This ranges from the identification of an absence in the given disciplinary forms (is the concept of *rasa* available at all in the Western aesthetic disciplines?) to pointing out a whole range of divergences between supposedly analogous concepts (is *dharma* the same as religion? Is *vyavahāra* the same as law?). By tracing these lines of divergence, it even becomes possible to define entire conceptual ensembles claiming to reorder "in the Indian context" several related disciplinary fields (such as, for example, the opposition Indian spirituality/Western materialism, as it has been used in the various social and aesthetic disciplines).

Finally, in the matter of thematic choices, several strategies can be encountered. There are attempts, first of all, to look for "possible points of diffraction"[53] in the Western scientific disciplines where two incompatible concepts or enunciations may exist in the same discursive formation as alternatives (since both *pathology* and *effective remedy* belong to the scientific clinical discourse, the latter concept could be used to proclaim the scientific legitimacy of alternative therapies based on, say, ayurveda or yunani, disregarding entirely the corresponding statements on pathology). Then there are attempts to locate authorities from within the Western discursive constellation in order to sustain the claims of indigenous knowledges (an interesting example is the encouragement given in the early twentieth century to the study of indigenous preindustrial manufacturing processes, with a view to utilizing locally available raw materials, on the political-economic grounds of industrial self-sufficiency). And, of course, most frequently of all, there are attempts to alter the rules and processes of appropriation of scientific discourse by various institutions situated in the field of nondiscursive practices.[54] There are innumerable examples here of differences in the manner of appropriation, not only in familiar disciplinary institutions such as the school or the family or the court of law, but in a host of other arenas such as religion, politics, and art. Particularly crucial here are the strategic possibilities opened up by the "positions of desire in relation to discourse." It seems possible for Foucault to say of discursive analysis in its European setting that it

> must show that neither the relation of discourse to desire, nor the process of its appropriation, nor its role among non-discursive practices is extrinsic to its unity, its characterization, and the laws of its formation. They are not disturbing elements which, superposing themselves upon its pure, neutral, atemporal, silent form, suppress its true voice and emit in its place a travestied discourse, but, on the contrary, its formative elements.[55]

In the colonial setting, discursive transformations will always appear to be the result of external intrusion by local, nondiscursive elements and thus as impurities, travesties. To take seriously the possibility of such transformations as internal to the field of scientific discourse is to introduce an entirely new source of instability into the formation of the disciplines.

This, we think, is exactly what the study of the emergence of the disciplines in the colony shows. The subsequent chapters in this volume, while focusing on individual disciplinary fields, take up many of the issues enumerated in the preceding paragraphs. More precisely, the focus is in most instances on selected texts that are used to show the marks of contestation that appear when the disciplines are translated. The basic institutional setting is, of course, provided by the technology of printing: it is through the production and circulation of printed texts—that universal commodity of "print-capitalism," as Benedict Anderson has so ingeniously named it[56]—that the discourses of modernity are disseminated in Bengal from the early nineteenth century. Print creates its own field of circulation, with new rules of exclusion, new sites of authority, new hierarchies. Tapti Roy's essay (chapter 2) shows the convergence of two distinct disciplinary authorities upon the field of Bengali literature in the nineteenth century—the colonial state and the new Bengali cultural elite. But the difference in modalities is clear from the beginning, with the latter claiming institutional sites and enunciative positions located, as it were, within the process of discursive production itself, rather than seeking prohibitory controls from outside. This difference in enunciative modalities was indicative of a fundamental characteristic of the dispersal of modernity in the colonies—the ultimate redundancy of the colonial state in the domestication of the disciplines. But the convergence of the two authorities in the launching of the disciplinary project shows early traces of the contestatory strategies that would come into operation in virtually every scientific field in the period of nationalism, namely, parallel institutions, parallel authorities, and parallel subject-positions.

These contestatory strategies become visible in an especially clear form in the aesthetic discipline of art history. Focusing on two early texts and on the institutional setting in which they were produced, Tapati Guha-Thakurta in chapter 3 describes the emergence of a modern Indian artistic discipline. The marking of differences here seem to range across every level of the disciplinary formation, from objects to enunciations to concepts to themes, leading finally to a declaration that true Indian knowledge in the field can come only from the rejection of disciplinary knowledge itself. My essay (chapter 4) on an early tract on "the science of politics" describes many of the same processes, except here the difference between West and East appears, at one moment as a lack in the latter, but at the next as a claim of superiority. Since these contestations occur in writing about politics and the state, we have here an early example of the formulation of the modern discursive strategies of the weak.

Pradip Kumar Bose's chapter 5 occupies a position of centrality in our exercise. It deals with a text that seeks directly to lay down new disciplinary principles to be followed within the institution of the family. As such, the implication of desire with discourse is revealed dramatically in the choice of disciplinary site—family rather than school, community rather than the state—as well as in the appropriation of positions of "scientific expertise" to fix a disciplinary project whose aim, however, is to produce a different individual from that of "Western man."

Keya Dasgupta, in chapter 6, deals with what might be called a failed attempt at disciplinary translation. The text she discusses encounters a difference in the formation of the very objects of a cartographic discipline and, despite an ingenious attempt to devise suitable mapping techniques, it represents a failure in the effort to make cartography available for appropriation within social and cultural practices. Ranabir Samaddar (chapter 7) deals with another marginal instance, this time of a varied collection of texts presently located in distinct discursive formations—official, legal, oral, popular—and not sharing any thematic connection. Yet, as he shows by marking in a hypothetical theme, they could very easily be turned in the future into materials for a well-formed historiography, telling the story of the struggles of a people to achieve their identity.

These exercises are meant to suggest new points of entry into textual materials that have until now been regarded either as somewhat faded souvenirs of nationalist ideology or as marginal subliterature, unworthy of serious scholarly attention. Being exploratory studies, they do not engage the existing knowledge of the conventional institutional histories of nineteenth- and twentieth-century Bengal in all the details that are suggested by our textual inquiries. Nevertheless, this is clearly an agenda that could be put on the table: to rewrite our institutional histories of modernity in the various fields of knowledge. Perhaps these studies will also show that modern discursive practices in the non-European languages are driven by similar interests and desires as in the West and that, instead of producing caricatures or travesties, they continue to represent serious attempts to produce a different modernity.

Notes

1. Durgacharan Ray, *Debgaṇer marttye āgaman.*
2. Ibid., pp. 408-14.
3. Ibid., p. 502.
4. Pradip Sinha, *Calcutta in Urban History,* p. 15.
5. A. K. Ray, *Short History of Calcutta,* pp. 140-41.
6. Ibid., Appendix III, p. 125.
7. Amiya Kumar Bagchi, "Wealth and Work," pp. 212-23. In 1931, 36.70 percent of the population in Park Street Ward was European (computed from *Census of India, 1931,* vol. VI, parts I and II, imperial table XIX, p. 178), whereas in the northern parts—"deep in those recesses of the Black Town"—a white face was, as an English resident of Calcutta observed, "a thing to scare children with." Mowson, *A Few Local Sketches* (1846), cited in Sinha, *Calcutta in Urban History,* p. 115.
8. For a short account of municipal planning in Calcutta in the nineteenth century, see Samita Gupta, "Theory and Practice," pp. 29-55. For a history of municipal administration, see Keshab Choudhuri, *Calcutta.*
9. H. E. A. Cotton, *Calcutta Old and New,* p. 181.
10. I have discussed at length the colonial state as a modern regime of power and its limitation by "the rule of colonial difference" in my *The Nation and Its Fragments,* pp. 14-34.
11. Perhaps the earliest elaboration of this argument in academic historiography is McCully,

English Education. However, liberal nationalist historiography in Bengal has long accepted this idea, from as early a work as Sibnath Sastri, *Rāmtanu lahidī o tatkālīn baṅgasamāj.*

12. For a general review of colonial policy on Indian education, see Syed Nurullah and J. P. Naik, *History of Education.*

13. J. C. Marshman before the Select Committee of the House of Commons on Indian Territories, 21 July 1853, quoted in Basu, *History of Education in India,* p. 125.

14. Nurullah and Naik, *History of Education,* p. 297; Seal, *Emergence,* pp. 21-22.

15. Aparna Basu, *Growth of Education,* p. 80; Nurullah and Naik, *History of Education,* p. 260.

16. Basu, *Growth of Education,* p. 105.

17. *Census of India 1921,* vol. V, part I, pp. 298, 394.

18. Basu, *Growth of Education,* p. 107.

19. Ibid., p. 80.

20. Computed from figures furnished in Seal, *Emergence,* p. 358.

21. Gauri Viswanathan, *Masks.*

22. Alfred Croft, director of public instruction, Bengal, quoted in McCully, *English Education,* p. 172.

23. See Basu, *Growth of Education,* pp. 32-59.

24. See Pradip Kumar Bose, "Sons of the Nation," chapter 5 in this volume.

25. Cited in O. P. Kejariwal, *Asiatic Society,* p. 154.

26. Computed from Appendix B, "List of Presidents, Vice-Presidents and Secretaries of the Asiatic Society" and Appendix D, "Index to contributions to Asiatic Researches and Journal and Proceedings of Asiatic Society (up to 1833)" in Mitra, Hoernle, and Bose, *Centenary Review,* part I, pp. 84-94 and 106-95.

27. For general histories of these learned societies, see Dutt Gupta, *Sociology in India;* Binay Ghosh, *Bāṃlār bidvatsamāj;* Rajat Sanyal, *Voluntary Associations.*

28. Appeal by Tariney Churn Banerjee, Ramgopaul Ghose, Ramtonoo Lahiry, Tara Chand Chukerbuttee, and Rajkrishna Day, 20 February 1838, reprinted in Binay Ghosh, *Bidvatsamāj,* pp. 126-28.

29. Binay Ghosh, *Bidvatsamāj,* p. 87.

30. A report on this meeting that appeared in the *Bengal Hurkaru,* 13 February 1843, is reprinted in Goutam Chattopadhyay, ed., *Awakening,* pp. 389-99.

31. Bethune Society, *Proceedings,* p. v.

32. Binay Ghosh, *Bidvatsamāj,* p. 94.

33. *Proceedings of the Bethune Society,* pp. 35-37.

34. On the influence of positivism, see Forbes, *Positivism in Bengal.*

35. See Dutt Gupta, *Sociology in India.*

36. Krishna, "Emergence," pp. 89-107.

37. Ibid.

38. For a survey of the debates over scientific terminology in Bengali in the nineteenth century, see Binaybhusan Ray, *Bijñān sādhanā,* pp. 17-57.

39. Computed from list supplied by Binaybhusan Ray, *Bijñān sādhanā,* pp. 252-77.

40. For a brief history of medical education in Bengali, see Binaybhusan Ray, *Bijñān sādhanā,* pp. 58-120. A recent study of medical education in general is Poonam Bala, *Imperialism and Medicine.* For colonial health policy in British India, see Arnold, *Colonizing the Body.*

41. For brief discussions on the recent history of the ayurvedic movement, see Brass, "Politics of Ayurvedic Education" and K. N. Panikkar, "Indigenous Medicine," pp. 283-308.

42. *Report of the Shuddha Ayurvedic Education Committee* (Delhi, 1963), cited in Brass, "Politics of Ayurvedic Education," pp. 342-71.

43. Prakash, "In the Beginning." Also see Prakash, "Science Gone Native."

44. Bose, *Researches;* Bose, "Plant Autographs"; Bose, *Manual;* Bose, *Physiology;* Bose, *Growth.*

The scientific significance of these researches has been discussed in D. M. Bose, *J. C. Bose's Plant Physiological Investigations*. The question of their cultural-historical significance has been raised in Nandy, *Alternative Sciences,* pp. 17-91.

45. Prakash, "Science between the Lines."

46. Bhabha, "Signs Taken for Wonders."

47. The difficulties become apparent from the massive overwork to which the metaphor of spatial transference has to be subjected. *Dislocation, division, realignment* (three times), *relocation* (twice), *rearrangement*: these words occur in the first few sentences of Prakash, "Science between the Lines."

48. Ibid.

49. Rajendralal Mitra, pp. 6-7. For biographical details on Rajendralal, see Alok Ray, *Rājendralāl mitra.*

50. For example, the essays in the collection Messer-Davidow, Shumway, and Sylvan, *Knowledges.*

51. Foucault, *Birth of the Clinic*; Foucault, *Discipline and Punish*; Foucault, *History of Sexuality.*

52. Foucault, *Archaeology of Knowledge.*

53. Ibid., pp. 65-66.

54. Using *nondiscursive practices* in Foucault's sense, ibid., pp. 67-68.

55. Ibid., p. 68.

56. Anderson, *Imagined Communities.*

2 / Disciplining the Printed Text: Colonial and Nationalist Surveillance of Bengali Literature

Tapti Roy

The Print Industry

In the second half of the nineteenth century, the publishing industry, comprising the writing, printing, and distribution of books and periodicals, was perhaps the largest indigenous enterprise in Calcutta. In 1911, when the six jute mills located in Calcutta employed 15,111 people, there were ninety-nine printing presses with 11,880 people working in them, making printing the second largest industry in the city.[1] However, unlike other industries, printing posed special problems of supervision and control. As is well known from examples from all over the world, the social impact of the printing of books went far beyond that of the mere triumph of technical ingenuity in the production of a commodity.[2]

The culture of publishing and reading printed texts was, like most other items of everyday modernity, introduced into India by Europeans and, in some sense, grafted to prior indigenous traditions of learning and intellectual activity. James Augustus Hicky, whose otherwise questionable career earned him the disapproval of his contemporary expatriates, was one of the pioneers of printing in Calcutta.[3] After Hicky, Nathaniel Brassey Halhed, Charles Wilkins, and the Srirampur missionaries William Carey and Joshua Marshman (and their typecasters, Panchanan Karmakar and his son-in-law Manohar Karmakar) made pioneering attempts at printing in the Bengali language. Although government presses were set up in the late eighteenth century, the year 1800 is really the most crucial date in the history of Bengali printing, because in that year Fort William College and the Srirampur Baptist Mission Press were established. Young officers of the East India Company, freshly arrived in India and unraveling the mysteries of the East at Fort William College, needed texts from which to learn the local language, and the Srirampur Baptists were keen on spreading literacy and Christianity. Together, they gave impetus to the printing and publishing of books in Bengali.[4]

Very roughly estimated, a total of 212,000 copies of books were published in forty languages between 1801 and 1832 from the Srirampur Mission.[5] During this time, Bengali entrepreneurs also came forward to try their hand at this new cultural technology. It turned out to be a roaring success. The first Bengali publisher was Gangakishor Bhattacharya, a former employee of the Srirampur press. Gangakishor set up a press entirely on his own and started a newspaper entitled *Bengali Gazette* in 1816. He also brought out printed editions of the popular eighteenth-century Bengali ballad *Bidyāsundar*, the longer *Annadāmaṅgal,* and the classical tales from *Betāl*, with woodcut illustrations.[6] A contemporary source claims that the first book published at the initiative of a Bengali was *Annadāmaṅgal*.[7] Gangakishor Bhattacharya can therefore be credited with having been a pioneer who foresaw the potential market for printed editions of popular books that were already in circulation as manuscripts or in oral performance. Nothing much, unfortunately, is known of this man; his newspaper, too, was short-lived.[8]

But Bengali entrepreneurs came into the new trade in a big way as soon as it became apparent that books could become popular as a marketed commodity. The history of these early presses is hard to reconstruct; there is little or no documentary evidence to indicate anything of the background of the printers or the life of each press. For the period between 1820 and 1830, we have the names of twenty presses, from four lists quoted in two sources.[9] As the lists are incomplete, there is no way of ascertaining when these presses were set up or how long each survived. In several cases, their locations are also not mentioned. We have thirteen place-names for seventeen of the presses: Bowbazar, Mirzapur, Sankharitola, and Arpuli were places claiming more than one press. The presses were quite widely dispersed in the Bengali settlements in the northern part of the city.

Sometime later, a major center of printing and publishing grew up along Chitpur Road, in the neighborhood of Shobhabazar, Ahiritola, and Goranhata. Exactly when this happened, it is hard to say because, except for mention of a single press in Shobhabazar, there is no indication in any of the available records of a printing center in the area until the 1830s. The exception was Bishwanath Deb's press, set up perhaps by one of the members of the Deb family of Shobhabazar. Sukumar Sen has suggested that Bishwanath began the press in 1817 or 1818 and was the first person after Gangakishor to start a press. Sometime later (once again, it is difficult to be exact), the presses in this area came to be referred to collectively as the Baṭtalā press. Sukumar Sen has declared Bishwanath Deb as the founder of the first Baṭtalā press and most scholars today accept this.[10] *Baṭtalā,* as a descriptive term for books and prints, first earned its name from this area of concentration of printing presses, although gradually it came to signify a whole range of popular productions that, in the course of the middle decades of the nineteenth century, found themselves displaced from the podium of high culture. By then, hierarchies had appeared in the domain of the printed text in Bengali and these were beginning to reflect the new social and cultural differences in Bengali literate society.

For our purposes, this sudden boom in the book trade had another very important consequence: it summoned the state to intervene and take cognizance of this rapidly proliferating industry. Ostensibly to keep itself informed about the effects of education on the native mind, the colonial state began to devise mechanisms of control and censure. The state's intervention was not without its effects on Bengal's literate society and how it set out its own criteria of classifying printed literature by quality and taste.

Colonial Controls

In order to keep tabs on indigenous printing and the publication of books in the vernacular, the colonial government periodically commissioned exhaustive catalogs of Bengali books, but the first such catalog was not an outcome of official enquiry: James Long, an Irish missionary who arrived in India in 1846, compiled the "Granthavali, An Alphabetical list of works published in Bengali," apparently prompted by his own intellectual curiosity. Published in 1852, it contained a total of 1,084 titles, arranged alphabetically but classified by subject.[11] The list was incomplete in several ways, having only the titles of books and not the names of the authors or printers. Yet this first catalog was important. It set a major precedent in classifying books by category.[12] Classification, the first step in the procedures of surveillance of printed books, allowed the state to intervene and pass judgments on the qualitative content of books, and these judgments often came to have legal implications.

Barely a year after the publication of Long's catalog, the under-secretary to the Bengal government, W. G. Young, instructed the administrators of Calcutta, the Lower Provinces, Cuttack, Chittagong, Assam, Arracan, Tenasserim, and Marta-Ban Province and the governor-general's agent in South-Western Frontier to submit returns naming the native presses in their districts, and of the publications issued therefrom during 1852.[13] The returns (on annexed forms A and B) were to be submitted annually for the government's information and were to include every printing press at which any book, pamphlet, or periodical was printed or published during the year. Young's letter said, "Magistrates will probably have no difficulty in making up the Returns, as the Printer and Publisher of every periodical work, and the owner of every Printing Press, is required, by law, to make declaration of the same before a Magistrate." Each form had seven columns and asked for the following information: place, name of press, name of each work, description of each work, number of copies of each work struck off, number of copies of each work sold, and price per copy.

The justification for the government seeking such a detailed knowledge of what was being printed was succinctly summarized by Long in a letter to the chief magistrate of Calcutta. This was a forwarding letter, submitted with the return of Bengali books published between April 1853 and March 1854. Long concludes with the remark: "That the fact of not less than 2,000,000 of Bengali books have issued from the press within the last ten years, is a loud call of effective measures being taken to create a healthy literary taste among the people by a sound vernacular Education."[14]

Long's *Descriptive Catalogue of Bengali Works,* printed in 1855, was more detailed than his earlier list. It contained "a classified list of Fourteen Hundred Bengali Books and Pamphlets which have issued from the press during the last sixty years with occasional notices of the subjects, the prices and where printed." In the preface, Long set out his purpose: "The object of this work is to be a guide to those who wish to procure Bengali Books, either for educational purposes, or for gaining an acquaintance with the Hindu manners, customs, or modes of thought. Popular Literature is an Index to the state of the Popular mind."[15]

Soon, the political implications of such intellectual curiosity became apparent. In 1859, Long prepared his third set of returns "relating to Publications in the Bengali Language in 1857." He added to this a "list of the Native Presses with the Books Printed at Each, their price and character, with a Notice of the Past Condition and Future Prospects of the Vernacular Press of Bengal and the statistics of the Bombay and Madras Vernacular Presses." There was no pretension of this being any sort of cultural or intellectual undertaking. Long himself explained the overtly political motive underlying this catalog:

> The preparing of this Report on the Native Press, a work which involved far more laborious research than the author originally expected, was suggested by the mutiny of 1857. Much at that period was written and spoken on the subject of the Native Press, and many hasty remarks were made respecting it, while some said it was so radically corrupt that it ought to be abolished. It was found that on this ground as well as for statistical purposes, it was most desirable to test the question, as far as related to the Bengal Press, by an accurate investigation of the facts of the case.[16]

If we compare the three lists, all compiled by Long but with somewhat different motivations, the differences are striking. But before we do this, let us take into account another opinion on this subject from a nonofficial colonial source. *Samācār darpaṇ* was a periodical published by the Baptist missionaries from their Srirampur Press. The period spanned by *Samācār darpaṇ*'s entries of the 1820s and Long's returns of 1859 was more than thirty years. During this time, there had been a phenomenal boom in the book trade. In its issue of 20 February 1819, *Samācār darpaṇ* wrote that in the previous ten years (1809-19) nearly ten thousand copies of books had been published. Long in 1854 estimated that not less than two million Bengali books were issued in the previous ten years (1844-54).[17] Four years later, Long observed in 1859 that "within the last quarter of a century (1834-59), the number of Bengali books printed and sold has not been less than 8,000,000."[18] The figures are very approximate and do not tally unless one assumes that two million books were printed in each of the first two decades and another four million from 1854 to 1859—a period of only five years. However, the figures do indicate that by the mid-nineteenth century the book trade had indeed become a thriving industry.

This had an obvious bearing on the changing content and quality of the books produced. In 1819, in its issue of 3 April, *Samācār darpaṇ* wrote:

> It is an auspicious sign that many different kinds of books are now being printed in this country. Just as the waters of a tiny river gradually spread through the surrounding lands finally to make the whole country fertile, in the same way have printed books reached all ranks of people in the province. Whereas in earlier times it was hard to find a palm-leaf manuscript even in a prosperous household, one expects that ordinary people with modest means will now have books in their homes.[19]

Six years later, *Samācār darpaṇ* (23 July 1825) was still very positive about the kinds of books that were being printed in Bengali. In its column entitled "New Books," the periodical said:

> In the olden days, there used to be much discussion in this country on branches of knowledge such as logic, Smṛti, astrology and the Purāṇas; there were many great scholars in these fields whose books are still in use. Later, for a time, these books became rare. But now, with the introduction of the printing press, studies on these subjects have revived. Books are now being written in languages such as Sanskrit, Bengali, Persian, and English; works on many different branches of knowledge are being published by different scholars. This is a cause of much satisfaction among the people.[20]

Darpaṇ remained full of approval and approbation at what the vernacular presses were producing. Writing in 1830 (30 January), it said: "It has only been sixteen years since men in this country first took the initiative in printing books for sale. It surprises us that in so short a time, they have achieved such progress in the field of printing."[21] Although most of these books related to the Hindu religion, *Darpaṇ* hoped that with the spread of education, various educative works would be written or translated and published.

Long's catalog of 1852 had no introductory comments; his method of classification, however, was in many ways a commentary on his opinion of Bengali books at the time. In all, he had nineteen categories, most of which were straightforward, such as history, geography, moral tales, Christian tracts, and Mahommedan, Vaishnav, and Vedic literature. For fictional works in prose, Long used four major categories: *upanyas,* meaning classical tales; *upakhyan,* meaning historical fiction; *galpa,* or stories; and *rachana,* or prose composition, which included items ranging from Bhabanicharan Bandyopadhyay's *Nababābu-bilās,* a contemporary satire, to Rammohan Roy's learned tract on *satī.* There was no hint of censure in Long's voice as he put together books under different heads. By classifying the books, however, Long moved a step forward from *Samācār darpaṇ.* On the other hand, by using categories without overt value judgments, he was yet to anticipate his future role as censor.

The contrast with Long's descriptive catalog of 1855 is striking. The later list is divided into three parts: educational, literary and miscellaneous, and theological. In his preface, Long states that a total of 1,400 "works have been noticed," of which only 489 books had been numbered, listed, and remarked upon. Under the subsection "Tales," the author sets out the criteria by which the books were selected and marked: "We shall notice in the numbered catalogue only those fit for general circulation, those out of print or unfit for general circulation are not given, they are all love tales."[22] Only nine tales were described in this section; the rest were simply mentioned. All the nine tales were translations from Sanskrit and Persian classics. As for the rest,

Long's opinion is best exemplified in his comments on *Bidyāsundar*, the highly popular ballad by Bharatchandra: "Last century we had Bharat, the Horace of his day, his themes were war, and love." He described "Vidyea Sundar" as "a book that will serve to amuse those who are but little acquainted with the Hindu system of courtship. It is perhaps the most classic poem we now possess in the Bengali language: but is disfigured in some places by licentious allusions."[23] Long's denunciation of popular songs, however, was more forthright. "The Bengali Songs," he wrote, "do not inculcate the love of wine or like the Scotch, the love of war, but are devoted to Venus and the popular deities; they are filthy and polluting." In the same section, Long described yatras as "a species of Dramatic Action, filthy, in the same style with the exhibition of Punch and Judy, or of the Penny Theatres in London, treating of licentiousness or of the amours of Krishna." Long concluded this section with the following entry: "On Erotic subjects there are various books which have passed through many editions in prose and poetry and have a wide circulation, . . . These works are beastly, equal to the worst of the French School."[24]

Interestingly, *erotic* was a new category of classification. Of the names cited as examples of books on erotic subjects in 1855, several are to be found in Long's earlier catalog of 1852.[25] There they were either marked out as tales (Adi Ras, Beshea Rahasyea, Kunjari Bilas, Prem Bilas, Rasomanjari, Prem Rahasyea, etc.) or poetry (Prem Taranga, Prem Natak, and Rasa-tarangini, among others).

Appearing between Long's two catalogs, we have a list of "Books and Pamphlets published in the Town of Calcutta in 1853-54." The list was appended to a "correspondence relating to the Vernacular Education in the Lower Provinces of Bengal."[26] This is in fact the first detailed list of presses, their locations, the books produced, description of each work, number of copies sold, and price per copy (there were ten columns, each with different kinds of information). In this list, not many books earned the infamy of being classed as erotic. "Rasamanjari," which had two different editions from two separate presses, was placed under "Erotic Poems," but others included in Long's list of erotic works came under various categories: "Rasaraj" and "Rasa-Tarangini" were classified as love songs, "Rati-Bilas" as Pauranic, and "Premtarung" as a tale. Thus it was not as though there were major changes in the content of the books produced. The changing classifications were more the result of shifting perceptions of the reporting authority. Many classical works of Sanskrit poetry were, in this process of imposition of external official surveillance, pushed to the margins of vulgar literature. Later in the century, colonial aesthetic judgments of this kind were not without their effects on the Bengali elites as they set down their standards of "good" and "bad" literature.

In 1856, the secretaries of the government directed that "one copy of each work of every description in original Bengali, published by the Native Presses of Calcutta" should be sent to the India House Library in London.

Reporting in 1859, Long outlined the role that the government increasingly was to play in the area of vernacular literature:

> In the present position of India, the Native Press as the exponent of the Native mind ought to be attended to; if the sound part of the Native Press be encouraged by the Authorities, it will become the instrument of much good; if it be left in the hands of ill-designing ignorant men, it will be the source of much evil.[27]

On the whole, however, despite his notes of concern, Long appeared quite satisfied at the "rapid improvement in the Vernacular Press" that was being employed now "as an instrument for promoting various useful objects" relating to social reforms. He calculated that approximately 600,000 Bengali books were printed for sale in Calcutta in 1857. This excluded 7,750 books printed by affluent Bengalis for gratuitous distribution and 76,950 tracts and scriptures given away by the Bible Society and the Tract Society of Calcutta.

Long then enumerated the improvements in each category of books. Writing of "Dramatic works," for instance, he observed:

> All over Bengal *Jatras* or popular Dramas in honor of the gods, with a full sprinkling of indecencies, are attended by crowds. It is pleasing to see, however, that in Calcutta and its neighbourhood many of the educated Natives patronize Dramas composed by Pundits, which in popular language and sometimes with the sarcasm of a Moliere condemn caste and polygamy.[28]

Long noticed similar improvements in other categories, too. Commenting on the total of 14,250 copies of erotic books that was found to have been on sale in that year, Long noted:

> By Erotic is meant books abounding in obscene passages. The above list represents not the entire number, but with the introduction of a better class of works, moral tales, and innocent works of fiction, the number of these is diminishing, and the terror of law against obscene publications is effecting what a regard to morality could not. The year before the Act against obscene publications was passed,[29] we knew that of one most hideously obscene book with its 20 most filthy pictures, 30,000 copies were sold in twelve months. But such books are now sold on the sly and are not obtruded on the public gaze as before.[30]

By this time, *Bidyāsundar*, described earlier in the 1855 official list as "the most popular Tale in Bengali,"[31] had come to acquire the stigma of being "the cleverly written but indecent tale" and "an amatory tale." Two other traditionally popular works were now freshly inducted in the list: "Panchalis," or popular songs, were denounced as "very licentious," "filthy," and "indecent," and "Betal Panchis" were described as fairytales "mixed up with coarse and indecent passages."

Changing Categories

Despite such strictures, Long discouraged press censorship: he felt there had been a perceptible and rapid improvement in the content of printed matter. Most of the books, he reported, were mythological and fictional until the 1850s "when the tide turned in favour of useful works"—by which he meant biographies of eminent men, translations of English classics, moral lessons, and scientific discourses.[32] Long, of course, provided detailed figures under each category and title; although he complained that "the conductors of Presses in many cases do not keep accurate accounts of all the books they print, or they are reluctant to furnish them, suspecting there may be some motive in connection with taxation in one's applying for a list."[33] Besides, in the absence of regular bookshops, books were often sold off before an official could lay hands on them.

Jatindramohan Bhattacharya, who gives Long's 1852 list, added another 950 titles of books that Long had missed.[34] From Jatindramohan's edition of Long's catalog, it is possible to trace in detail the rate of increase in the number of books printed in the period from 1801 to 1852. We have divided the period in Table 2.1 into three phases: (a) 1801 to 1817, when the number of publications did not exceed 30 in any single year, (b) 1818 to 1843, when despite a perceptible increase, the figures did not go beyond 100, and (c) 1844 to 1852, when with a few exceptions they always reached above 100. More accurately, an average of 10.24 books were printed annually between 1801 and 1817, 39.31 from 1818 to 1843, and 91.89 between 1844 and 1852.

Tables 2.1 and 2.2 make clear certain observations about changes in the types of books published in the first half century of printing in the Bengali language. In the first phase (1801-17), of the total number of books printed, 44.25 percent were claimed by scriptures and mythologies, followed by dictionaries and grammar (16.09 percent), moral tales (9.77 percent), and Christian tracts (a small 8.62 percent). Books on history accounted for 5.17 percent of the total and "musalmani" 3.45 percent. This early phase of printing

Table 2.1. Number of published titles by category, 1801-52

	1801-17			1818-43			1844-52		
	New	Reprints	Total	New	Reprints	Total	New	Reprints	Total
History	4	5	9	34	15	49	23	26	49
	(3.45)	(8.62)	(5.17)	(5.61)	(3.60)	(4.79)	(5.64)	(6.20)	(5.93)
Biography	2	2	4	9	11	20	2	7	9
	(1.72)	(3.45)	(2.30)	(1.49)	(2.64)	(1.96)	(0.49)	(1.67)	(1.09)
Classic tales	0	0	0	4	6	10	9	15	24
	(0.00)	(0.00)	(0.00)	(0.66)	(1.44)	(0.98)	(2.20)	(3.58)	(2.90)
Fiction	1	0	1	18	11	29	13	9	22
	(0.86)	(0.00)	(0.57)	(2.97)	(2.64)	(2.84)	(3.19)	(2.15)	(2.66)
Prose	1	0	1	23	13	36	16	8	24
	(0.86)	(0.00)	(0.57)	(3.80)	(3.12)	(3.52)	(3.92)	(1.91)	(2.90)
Poetry	3	0	3	26	4	30	34	31	65
	(2.59)	(0.00)	(1.72)	(4.29)	(0.96)	(2.93)	(8.33)	(7.40)	(7.86)
Moral tales	10	7	17	41	41	82	15	36	51
	(8.62)	(12.07)	(9.77)	(6.77)	(9.85)	(8.02)	(3.68)	(8.60)	(6.17)
Scriptures &	49	28	77	88	71	159	62	89	151
mythologies	(42.24)	(48.28)	(44.25)	(14.52)	(17.07)	(15.56)	(15.20)	(21.24)	(18.26)
Vedic/Vedantic	7	0	7	43	12	55	20	26	96
	(6.03)	(0.00)	(4.02)	(7.09)	(2.88)	(5.38)	(4.90)	(6.20)	(11.61)
Vaishnav	2	0	2	15	5	20	24	28	52
	(1.72)	(0.00)	(1.15)	(2.48)	(1.20)	(1.96)	(5.88)	(6.68)	(6.29)
Christian	11	4	15	103	66	169	62	33	95
	(9.48)	(6.90)	(8.62)	(17.00)	(15.86)	(16.54)	(15.20)	(7.87)	(11.49)
Musalmani	2	4	6	3	4	7	14	10	24
	(1.72)	(6.90)	(3.45)	(0.49)	(0.96)	(0.68)	(3.43)	(2.39)	(2.90)
Medicine	0	0	0	12	2	14	12	6	18
	(0.00)	(0.00)	(0.00)	(1.98)	(0.48)	(1.37)	(2.94)	(1.43)	(2.18)
Natural science	2	0	2	66	36	102	31	26	57
	(1.72)	(0.00)	(1.15)	(10.89)	(8.65)	(9.98)	(7.60)	(6.20)	(6.89)
Law	2	0	2	48	21	69	32	11	43
	(1.72)	(0.00)	(1.15)	(7.92)	(5.05)	(6.75)	(7.84)	(2.62)	(5.20)
Geography	0	0	0	8	6	14	5	3	8
	(0.00)	(0.00)	(0.00)	(1.32)	(1.44)	(1.37)	(1.23)	(0.71)	(0.97)
Dictionary &	20	8	28	65	92	157	34	55	89
grammar	(17.24)	(13.79)	(16.09)	(10.73)	(22.11)	(15.36)	(8.33)	(13.13)	(10.76)
TOTAL	116	58	174	606	416	1,022	408	419	827
Average per year			10.24			39.31			92.89

Note: Figures in brackets indicate percentage of total number of titles published.
Source: Data from Jatindramohan Bhattacharya, *Tālikā*.

Table 2.2. Average number of books per year, 1801-52

	1801-17	1818-43	1844-52
History	0.53	1.88	5.44
Biography	0.23	0.77	1.00
Classic tales	0	0.38	2.67
Fiction	0.06	1.11	2.44
Prose	0.06	1.38	2.67
Poetry	0.18	1.15	7.22
Moral tales	1.00	3.15	5.67
Scriptures/mythologies	4.53	6.11	16.78
Vedic/Vedantic	0.41	2.11	10.67
Vaishnav	0.12	0.77	5.78
Christian	0.88	6.50	10.55
Musalmani	0.35	0.27	2.67
Medicine	0	0.54	2.00
Natural science	0.12	3.92	6.33
Law	0.12	2.65	4.78
Geography	0	0.54	0.89
Dictionary & grammar	1.65	6.04	9.89
TOTAL	10.24	39.31	91.89

Source: Data from Jatindramohan Bhattacharya, *Tālikā*.

was largely associated with the activities of Fort William College and many of these books were sponsored for its curriculum, as vernacular readers. A total of 77 scriptural and mythological books were printed over the fifteen years of this period, an average of 4.53 books each year as shown in Table 2.2; "dictionary and grammar" stood second with 28 books at an annual average of 1.65 books, followed by 17 moral tales, 1 book per year. In the other categories, there was an average of less than one book published each year.

In the second phase (1818-43), associated with more active missionary enterprise, Christian tracts increased from the low average of 0.88 book per year in the first phase to 6.50 in the second. This category now exceeded that of scriptures and mythologies, which contributed an average of 6.11 books per year, to be closely followed by dictionary and grammar (6.04). Natural science and moral tales claimed far less, 3.92 and 3.15, respectively. In terms of their respective shares in the total number of books (Table 2.1), Christian tracts were 16.54 percent, scriptures and mythologies 15.56 percent, dictionary and grammars 15.36 percent, natural science 9.98 percent, and moral tales 8.02 percent. Books on law claimed 6.75 percent, history 4.79 percent. It is noteworthy that 40.70 percent of all books were reprints, denoting that a major part of publishing was still the printing of older works, rather than the commissioning of original writing. The reprint figure also reflects the great demand, compared with other categories, for dictionaries and grammars.

In the third phase (1844-52), scriptures and mythologies (18.26 percent) overtook Christian tracts (11.49 percent) as the largest category. Remarkable in this phase is the increase in the number of books on poetry: from an average of 0.18 before 1817, now 7.22 books of poetry were being produced every year, comprising 7.86 percent of all books. Vaishnav literature, too, showed a big increase: from 0.12 (1801-17) to 0.77 (1818-43) to 5.78 (1844-52). In many categories (e.g., scriptures and mythologies, moral tales, classic tales, histories, biographies, dictionaries and grammars), reprints outnumbered first editions. In biographies, for instance, there were seven reprints but only two new books.

In his 1859 report, Long also gives figures for "books printed for sale in Calcutta during the year 1857, arranged according to subjects." It is worth comparing the subject categories Long made for the 1852 and 1857 figures. Almanacs, which in 1852 were included with periodicals, in 1857 were allotted a separate slot, not without reason. As many as 135,000 copies of 19 almanacs were printed for sale in 1857; and yet Long writes:

> This estimate we feel convinced is too low; there are probably as many as 250,000 copies of Almanacs published annually. Almanacs circulate where few other Bengali books reach; just previous to the beginning of the Bengali year is a busy season with the Native Almanac sellers of Calcutta; book-hawkers in numbers may be seen issuing from the printing presses, weighted with the store of Almanacs which they carry far and wide some of which they sell at the low rate of 80 pages for one anna.[35]

The popularity of almanacs can be quantified from Long's figures, as shown in Table 2.3. An average of 7157.89 copies per almanac were printed for sale, the highest of any category in the list. In comparison, although 85 books were printed on mythology and Hinduism, the total number of copies was only 96,150, an average of 1,131.17 per book. Long used a broad category for textbooks on subjects like geography and dictionary and grammar, naming it "educational"; not surprisingly, educational books sold the second highest number of copies. Long wrote:

> The spread even of English Schools has led to an increased demand of Vernacular educational works, besides this there are three Government Normal Vernacular Schools at Calcutta, Dacca, Hooghly in operation, supplying a superior

Table 2.3. Number of books available for sale, 1857

	Number of titles	Number of copies	Average copies per title
Almanacs	19	136,000	7,157.89
Biography and history	15	20,150	1,343.33
Christian	8	9,550	1,193.75
Dramatic	8	5,250	656.26
Educational	46	145,300	3,158.70
Erotic	13	14,250	1,096.15
Fiction	28	33,050	1,180.35
Law	5	4,000	800.00
Miscellaneous	12	18,370	1,530.83
Mythology and Hinduism	85	96,150	1,131.17
Moral tales and ethics	19	39,700	2,089.47
Musulman Bengali	23	24,600	1,069.56
Natural science	9	12,250	1,361.11
Newspapers	6	2,950	491.66
Periodicals	12	8,000	666.66
Sanskrit-Bengali	14	15,000	1,071.43
TOTAL	322	571,670	1,775.37

Source: Long, "Returns."

> class of teachers to explain in the Vernacular difficult books on Euclid, Algebra, Natural Philosophy, Physical Geography. The demand is creating the supply, and the improvements in Vernacular education are producing a suitable class of books, as the want of teachers are the best criteria for the kind of supply.[36]

Long was probably happy with the increased demand for educational books; however, two new categories appeared in his 1859 list and these—"dramatic" and "erotic"—as noted before, had a lot to do with changes in Long's perceptions. The computed figures are nevertheless interesting. Eight books of drama were printed with a total of 5,250 copies, an average of 656.26 copies per book. Thirteen "erotic" books, however, had 14,250 copies, (1,196.15 copies per book). The "fiction" category (28 books) with 1180.35 copies per book totaled 33,050 copies. That year, a total of 571,670 copies of books was printed in Calcutta.[37]

Printing Presses

Long gives names of forty-six presses operating in Calcutta in 1857. The report on education of 1853-54, quoted earler in this chapter, listed the names of forty-nine presses. In view of the increasing number of books being printed, an obvious question to ask is whether these presses had come to specialize in the production of particular kinds of books. This does not, however, seem very likely, except in the cases of presses like the Baptist Mission in Calcutta and Srirampur, Bishop's College, and the School Book Society, where, predictably, most publications were Christian tracts, moral tales, and schoolbooks. Presses owned by Bengalis are difficult to identify in terms of specialization. It is possible, however, to trace the locations of these presses and to see if there were major shifts in geographical concentration over the years. From three incomplete lists in *Samācār darpaṇ* (1825, 1826, and 1830) we have the names of twenty-one presses; of these, four presses appear in more than one list.[38] Of these early presses, only Chandrika Press at Kolutola, Mahendra Lal Press at Sankharitola, and Prabhakar Press (from where the poet Iswarchandra Gupta brought out his daily newspaper *Saṃbād prabhākar*) survived into the 1850s.[39] Most of the other presses included in the list of books of 1853-54 and in Long's catalog for 1857 were relatively new, being between ten and twenty years old.

What is particularly striking about the list of 1853-54 is that out of the forty-nine presses, as many as twenty were located in the area later to be known as Baṭtalā and made synonymous with so-called low literature. Baṭtalā was a fairly large contiguous stretch, including areas bearing the names of Garanhata, Shobhabazar, Ahiritola, Chitpur, Kumartola, Shankharitola, and Banstala.[40] The other twenty-nine presses were dispersed over other northern parts of the city—Mirzapur Street, Nimtala, Radhabazar, Bowbazar, and so on (see Fig. 2.1).

It is worth pointing out that Hindu College was originally located on Garanhata Street. The later-vilified Baṭtalā was, in fact, the original center of scholarship in Calcutta. In 1825, Hindu College was shifted for want of space to the area close to Pataldanga, next to a pond known as Goldighi. Sanskrit College was set up next to Hindu College in 1826. The pond and the street adjoining it were thenceforth called College Square and College Street, this becoming the principal center of education and scholarship in the city by the middle of the century. The School Book Society started an outlet for books next to Hindu College in 1826 and Iswarchandra Vidyasagar, appreciating the potential for the trade in textbooks, opened a bookshop, named the Sanskrit Press Depository, in 1847. Although until 1857 this remained the exceptional case of a press on College Street, it marked the moving away from the traditional center of publishing to a location sanctified by contiguity to the centers of academic learning, or, in other words, adherence to the standards of "good" literature.[41]

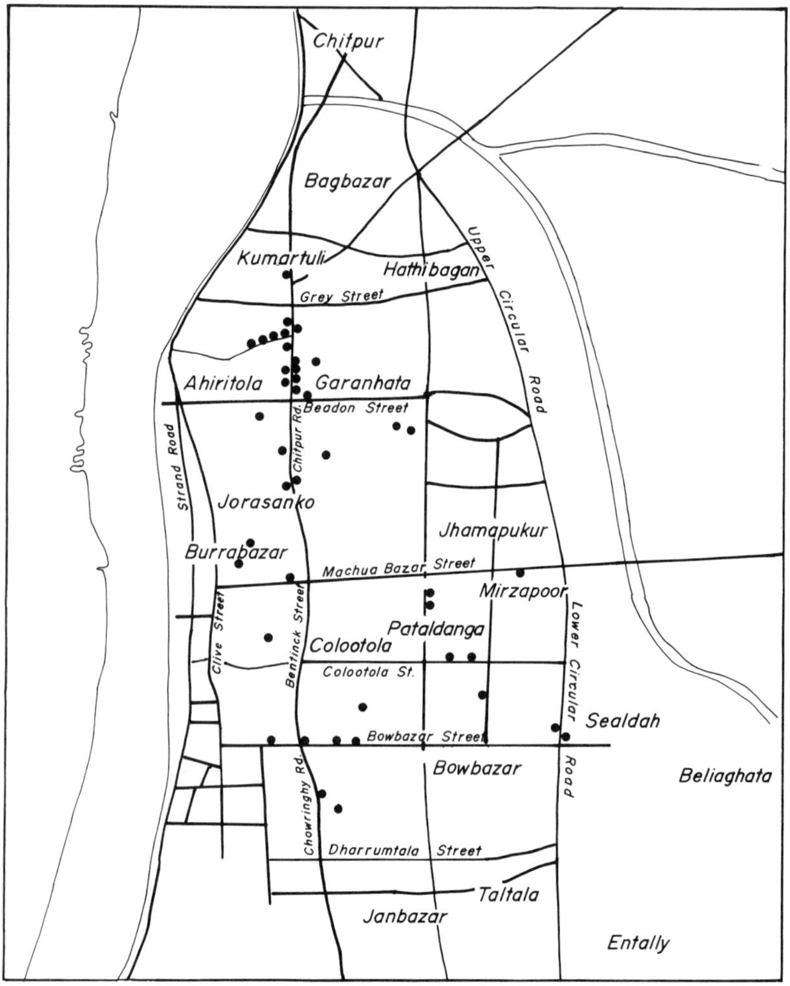

Fig. 2.1. Location of printing presses in Calcutta, 1858

One major development that Long noticed in 1857 was in the relative prices of Bengali books:

> The new Bengali works published by Natives are generally rather high priced when they are *copy-wright*, as various natives now find the composing of Bengali books profitable, and some authors draw a regular income from them. . . . Books for the masses, not copy-wright, are very cheap. We have before us a copy of a Bengali Almanac on good paper of 302 pp. in 8vo, printed at 60 pages for the anna, while some Almanacs on inferior paper are sold at 80 pages

> for the anna; this almanac sells at the rate of 6,000 copies annually. The Shishubodh or Lindlay Murray of Bengal sells 60 pages for the anna, 6 or 8 editions are published annually; the Videa Sundar, a popular tale, is sold at 61 pp. 16mo. for 1 anna.

In the footnote, Long makes a comparison between prices over a period of thirty years. "Videa Sundara" printed on bad paper sold at 1 rupee in 1825; in 1857 it was obtainable on good paper at 2 annas. "Shishu bodh," sold in 1825 at 8 annas, in 1857 was to be had at 3 pice.[42]

The increase in the scale of production and growing competition significantly brought down the price of books. The average price of books printed at the Srirampur Mission in 1821 was 7.625 rupees.[43] In 1853-54, the Baptist Mission Press in Calcutta published 15 books: 5 were distributed gratis and 1 was not priced; the rest cost an average of 7 annas.[44] Benimadhab Datta of Chandrika Press inserted a notice in the issue of 17 March 1827 of *Samācār darpaṇ* inviting subscriptions for *Caitanya caritāmṛta,* which he intended to publish in 868 pages at 10 rupees.[45] This would have been unthinkable in 1853-54, when out of a total of 222 books only 1, a textbook for the Bengali Medical Class entitled *Auṣadh byabahārak*, was priced as high as 5 rupees. Only 6 books were priced at 2 rupees; 15 books were at 1 rupee plus a few paisa, and the rest were priced in annas. For instance, "Panchali Dasarath"—printed at Chaitanya Chandroday Press in Ahiritola and the thickest book in the list of 1853-54, with 951 pages—cost only 1 rupee 2 annas. *Caitanya candroday*, a biography in 490 pages, was published by Kamaleswar Press, also at Ahiritola, at 2 rupees.[46] In fact, publishers found that printing entire epics like the Ramayana, the Mahabharata, or even large works like *Caitanya caritāmṛta* or *Caitanya-bhāgavat* in one volume, was not economical; they preferred to bring them out in parts, in slender, cheap volumes.

New Uses for Printed Books

Even as the guardians of "native morals" were encouraged by the spread of books with an educational value, it is clear that many popular volumes served entirely functional needs or were used purely for amusement and entertainment. The almanac, for instance, whose popularity we have already noticed, was, Long wrote:

> as necessary for the Bengali as his hooka or his pan, without it he cannot determine the auspicious days for marrying (22 in the year), for first feeding an infant with rice (27 days in the year), for feeding the mother with rice in the fifth

> month of gestation (12 days), for commencing the building of a house, . . . In former days a rupee a copy was paid for printed Almanacs; now the same kind are to be had for 2 annas, this cheapness has greatly reduced the profits of the old daivagyas or astrologers.[47]

In fact, in the new urban families printed almanacs took the traditional place of the astrologer. The almanac's main function was to act as a ready reckoner for the rules and timings of rituals. Little wonder, therefore, that when the Tract Society of Calcutta got together with missionaries from the Church of England to publish a more rationally organized almanac, ostensibly "to counteract the evils of the Native Almanacs," it did not sell.[48]

Printed books also made a new option available to the traditional performing arts. Books became the means for the recording and circulation of texts for new forms of urban performance. Long wrote in 1859 that "with orientals it is a common practice to be read to, and hence numbers who cannot read themselves listen to those who can. Readers (Kathaks) are often hired to recite or chant certain works, and most impressively do some of them execute this." Kathakata, a conventional form of recital of Pauranic tales accompanied by singing and theatrical performance, often carried on for several days during festivals, found a new textual medium in the printed book:

> We know a native who was for years employed by a rich Babu to read 2 hours daily to 40 or 50 females in his house. This has been a practice from time immemorial in Bengal—where "readings" as in all Eastern Countries have been so popular, and where intonation, gesture etc. make a book listened to more telling, than when simply read. Women sometimes sit in a circle round a woman, who reads a book to them. Allowing them an average of 10 hearers or readers to each book, we calculate that these 600,000 Bengali books have 2,000,000 readers or hearers.[49]

Long's enthusiasm for sociological statistics may have been excessive, but his observation does give us an idea of the new cultural uses to which the printed book was put. An official report written ten years later described a similar publicly enacted scene:

> Frequently, in this very town of Calcutta, an observant passer-by sees a large knot of natives collected round a Tailor or native grocer's shop to hear a man (the most prominent person for the time being) reading a Tale in Musalmani-Bengali, in which the auditors appear to take the most lively interest, whilst the crowd observes the utmost decorum and order, and would resent any approach to interruption; and the reader is looked upon as a prodigy of learning; the only gift perhaps which he has being a ready knowledge of the alphabet and words and fluency of reading, which is always rapid, sonorous, and musical, and must be

accompanied with rapid motions of the head and body, without which he could not go on.[50]

Clearly the printing press opened up entirely new opportunities for the proliferation of a popular culture. We will see later how this posed completely new problems of disciplining.

Further Changes in Categories

We have noticed some of the changes that took place in the first half of the nineteenth century in the types of books published: these changes became more pronounced in the middle decades of the century. We have a catalog of Bengali books available for sale in 1865 (not necessarily published in that year).[51] The figures (summarized in Table 2.4) show a total of 901 books, quite a jump from the 322 books recorded for sale by Long in 1857. There is a striking increase in works of prose fiction and drama: 114 prose fiction works, claiming 12.65 percent of the total, and 112 dramas (12.43 percent). By comparison, in 1857 there were only 8 dramas and 28 fiction works, and in the nine years from 1844 to 1852 there were only 24 prose works and 22 fiction. Dramas were not even listed as a separate category in the period ending 1852. Scriptures and mythologies plummeted in 1865 to only 60 titles; Christian tracts dropped to a mere 10 (1.11 percent of the total). School readers increased to an impressive 105 (11.65 percent). Vocabularies and dictionaries fell to 31 titles; Brahmo tracts, a relatively new category, accounted for 51 (5.66 percent).

This catalog also showed that by 1865 original prose compositions had clearly overtaken reprints or translations of older works as the staple of the publishing industry. There was a new variety of fictional writing—the short skit, based on contemporary subjects. The catalog described them as "little books . . . humorous, and some very coarse. For their size they are very dear." They were often spoofs and caricatures of new urban lifestyles and mores, with titles such as *Kalir bau ghar bhāṅgāni* (A modern daughter-in-law who ruined a home), *Rāṅḍ, bhāṅḍ, mithyākathā, tin laye kalikātā* (Whores, rogues, and lies make up Calcutta). Nineteen such "little books" were printed at the Anglo-Indian Union Press, located at 92 Goranhutta Street, with prices ranging from 1 anna to 8 annas.[52] This press, established in 1844, was one of the nine presses listed in 1859 that survived until 1865. Other presses (e.g., Seal and Brothers, Sahas Bidyaratna, and Sucharu) were also churning out these "little books" in increasing numbers.

We have another source, making it possible to trace changes in the num-

Table 2.4. Bengali titles available for sale in 1865

	Number	Percent
Poetry	62	6.88
Poetry (religious)	12	1.33
Drama	112	12.43
Prose fiction	114	12.65
Social tracts	14	1.55
Other prose	53	5.88
Brahmo tracts	51	5.66
Christian tracts	10	1.11
Scripture/mythology	60	6.66
Law	72	7.99
Medical	22	2.44
Educational: School Book Society/Vernacular Lit. Dept.	67	7.44
Vocabularies/dictionaries	31	3.44
Grammar	28	3.11
Readers	105	11.65
Geography/astronomy	27	3.00
History/geography	42	4.66
Mathematics	19	2.11
TOTAL	901	

Source: Wenger, "Catalogue."

bers and variety of books until 1867: the recently published second volume of Jatindramohan's catalog. This covers the period 1853 to 1867.[53] This is a list of the books printed in a particular year, not of all books available for sale; hence, the figures are not strictly comparable to those from Long's or Wenger's lists. Table 2.5 summarizes Jatindramohan's figures. Clearly, there was a general increase in the average number of books every year after 1852. The figures always stood above 150. In 1857, the year of the founding of the University of Calcutta, a remarkable number of books was published—291, more than double the number for the previous year. In 1863 more than 300 books were published and in 1865 more than 400.

Compared with Long's and Wenger's lists, Jatindramohan's catalog has a much more detailed breakdown of books, listing 81 categories (Table 2.6). Only nine of the categories claimed more than a hundred books. Predictably, the largest number was Bengali poetry (250), followed by Bengali plays (225), and education (187). Enumerated by year, subject listings show that 59 plays were printed in 1863, the largest number on a single subject in any single year. The number of poetry books was consistently high. Jatindramohan also lists 180 publishers and printing presses; of these, 89 have ad-

Table 2.5. Number of titles printed between 1853 and 1867

	New	Reprints & Editions	Total
1853	116	47	163
1854	119	49	168
1855	106	83	189
1856	71	55	126
1857	240	51	291
1858	94	64	158
1859	116	44	160
1860	107	69	176
1861	132	70	202
1862	172	85	257
1863	244	97	341
1864	160	84	244
1865	219	185	404
1866	95	67	162
1867	177	114	291

Source: Data from Jatindramohan Bhattacharya, *Pañjī.*

dresses, 29 of which were in the Baṭtalā area. This was the largest single concentration in the city (see Fig. 2.2).[54]

This massive spate of new books in the 1860s prompted the government to put in place a comprehensive machinery for the surveillance of Bengali publications. An act (no. XXV) was passed in 1867 "for the regulation of printing-presses and Newspapers, for the preservation of copies of books printed in British India, and for the registration of such books."[55] In effect, it meant that every book printed anywhere in India had to be officially registered. A year later, in 1868, the Bengal Library Catalogue was started and a copy of each book listed therein was sent to the India Office Library, London, and the Imperial Library, Calcutta. From this time, too, the *Calcutta Gazette* listed, every quarter, all books and periodicals published by the native Bengali press.

These collections and catalogs, even with gaps in their coverage, confirm the trend already noticed in the 1865 figures, except that dramas significantly came to outnumber prose fiction. In the collection of Bengali books at the India Office Library up to 1900, 55.4 percent are classified as literature. This compares with 22.5 percent theology, 12.4 percent arts and sciences, and 12 percent books for schools. Of the literature titles, 33.2 percent were dramas, 37.7 percent poetry, and only 18.3 percent prose fiction.[56] In a single year (1878), when 105 dramas were registered in Bengal, 12 were recorded as printed in the North-Western Provinces, and only 5 in Bombay.[57]

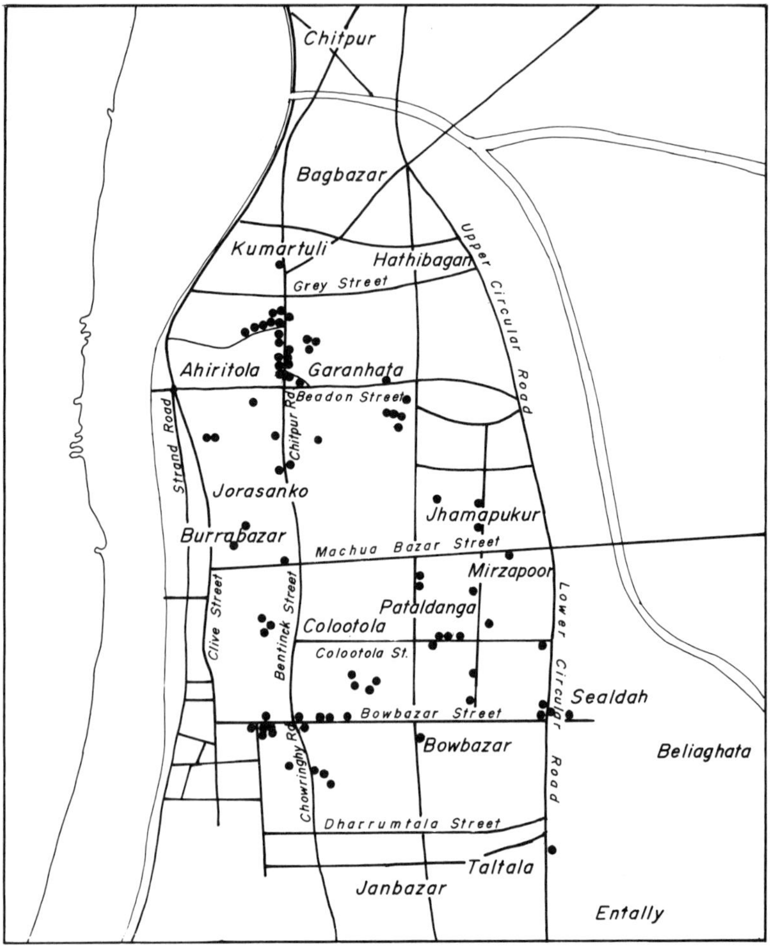

Fig. 2.2. Location of printing presses in Calcutta, 1867

The phenomenal rise in the popularity of drama and its emergence in the late nineteenth century as the most prolific form of literary production has not been adequately investigated in the history of Bengali literature. It was related not only to the spread of vernacular education and the emergence of a reading public but also to

> the success of native theatres in Calcutta (as may be evinced by the numerous posters and placards posted about the walls of the town) and the Mofussal, coupled with the fact that many of the Bengalis hitherto wrapped in ignorance are by reason of their vernacular education now beginning to come in contact

Table 2.6. Number of titles published, by subject, 1853-67

Dictionaries	35	Economics	8
Law	133	English tales	34
English poetry	3	English drama	8
English grammar	3	Italian tales	1
History	105	Muhammadan religion	43
Nature studies/botany	5	Upanishad	4
Urdu poetry	1	Kalidasa	8
Agriculture	11	Sports	4
Christian religion	138	Ganga	3
Home science	3	Ballads	5
Bibliography	2	Greek poetry	3
Medicine	57	Art	3
Rhetoric	5	Biography	56
Genealogy	26	Astronomy	6
Astrology	6	Tantra	5
Philosophy & moral science	93	Religion	24
Aesthetics	1	Norwegian tales	9
Letter writing	6	Physics	10
Arithmetic	17	Purana	43
Technical education	3	Natural calamities	13
Zoology	8	French tales	1
Persian tales	22	Persian poetry	4
Lectures/speeches	3	Bible	55
Bengali tales	140	Bengali poetry	250
Bengali humor, sketches, parody	13	Bengali drama	225
Bengali essays	11	Bengali proverbs	3
Bengali grammar	49	Bengali language	3
Trade	1	Science	8
Algebra	3	Brahmo religion	87
Bhagavat Gita	2	Indian Hindu philosophy	33
Linguistics	3	Geography/travel	42
Mahabharata	19	Chemistry	1
Ramayana	18	Folktales	14
Education	187	Sanskrit tales	8
Sanskrit poetry	37	Sanskrit ballad	1
Sanskrit grammar	14	Sanskrit language & literature	3
Music	52	Associations	23
Social issues	113	General knowledge/miscellaneous	18
Shakespearean literature	3	Smriti	20
Hindi poetry	4	Hindu religion	174
Unspecified	162		

Source: Data from Jatindramohan Bhattacharya, *Pañjī.*

> with the superior dramas and romances in the English language and with the classical dramas in the Sanskrita.

This observation, in the annual report on the Bengal Library for the year 1878, was made by C. W. Bolton, an undersecretary of the Bengal government who was charged with keeping an eye on what was being published by local presses. Bolton's comments on the general standard of literary productions, especially fiction and drama, were scathing—much harsher than Long's. He called them "flimsy and silly," noticing that over the preceding two years there had been a "large and rapid increase" in the number of dramas.

> It is a fact worthy of notice that in fiction, as well as in this branch of composition, a really abnormal development has taken place in Bengali. . . . That the native authors should have so kindly taken to the drama and to fiction, and in a manner have ignored the very important branches of science and history, may be accounted for by the shallowness of the current popular education, the facility and ease with which imitations can be made of the original works, and the difficulty which authors of such calibre would find in attempting any successful treatment of a historical or scientific subject.

Bolton regretted that "the education which so liberal a Government as the British bestows on the Bengalis, especially at so immense a cost, should be thus as it were frittered away and diverted into a channel other than that for the benefit of . . . poorer and more ignorant countrymen." The undersecretary's illustration of education being "frittered away" was as follows:

> Among those plays written to depict the state of society at the present time, there appeared a drama called Sabhyata-sopan, or stepping-stone to civilization and enlightenment, a powerful satire on the Bengalis, where, had the injudicious writer but have stopped, it would have been well, and his desire to ameliorate the debased condition of his fellow-countrymen might have been appreciated, nay, even applauded, but he preferred going on and attacking the administration of criminal justice in this country by Europeans at the present time, especially trial by jury; he spared not also the relations subsisting between the Europeans and natives, thus tending not only to widen the existing breach between these two classes, whom every earnest Christian should try and bring together, but to mislead his readers, who are his own fellow-countrymen.

Bolton thought it important that the government keep a close watch on the vernacular press. He reiterated Long's complaint that, despite the 1867 act, books were "often not sent in for registration" as was mandated, within a month of issue from the press. Bolton described how he had "procured from itinerant hawkers on the roads" copies of works that had not been sent to the library. Bolton suggested that

> if the Government really thinks it worth while having the provisions of Act XXV strictly carried out, it would be as well to appoint a Bengali Inspector to visit the Calcutta presses regularly. Such an officer could bring any default or omission of the printers and publishers to the notice of the Inspector General of Registration.[58]

Discipline Internalized

Colonial surveillance of the proliferating publishing arena in Bengali was always from a position of externality. Even when it sought detailed knowledge of this world, the colonial power did so as an outside observer; when it attempted to exercise legal or administrative controls, it was in this external capacity.

But uncontrolled proliferation of printed texts was a problem not only for the colonial state, situated as it was outside the cultural world of producers and readers of Bengali books; it set a crucial task for the new Bengali elite seeking cultural hegemony. Curiously, in some of the early examples of its awareness of this task, the new intellectuals can be seen to be demanding controls not unlike those sought by the government; indeed, they often demanded state intervention. Thus, in its issue of 23 October 1865, *Baṅgabidyā prakāśikā*, a weekly, carried a short entry of two columns under the heading "Useless Writers should be Punished":

> It is true that the Bengali language has no guardian. The Bengali language is like the dough for making *luchi*. People give it whatever shape they wish. In the absence of a guardian, there is no one to prevent this.
>
> With the setting up of the printing press, there have been unexpected improvements in the Bengali language. That we are now able to read books and newspapers that satisfy our minds is entirely due to the printing machines; it deserves our thanks. Especially, the presses in Baṭtalā have made things really easy. Finding the rates cheap, people are writing and publishing whatever they please. We do not say that only useless and trivial books are printed in Baṭtalā. A number of Puranas have also been printed there, but they too smack of their Baṭtalā connections.
>
> The more books are published in Bengali, the more propitious it would be for the language. However, some foolish men, lacking foresight but with a great desire to become famous, have taken to writing books. They do not have enough sense to discern whether the books are good or bad. In fact, these books have become like weeds in the Bengali language.

Having stated the problem, *Baṅgabidyā prakāśikā* went on, despite the metaphorical mixing of dough and weeds, to suggest the remedy:

> The Bengali language is yet to secure strong roots. If now, by using the language in a thoughtless fashion, its growth is distorted, then its branches will also be stunted. Later, when the Bengali language will assume its fully developed form and will be endowed with richness, people reading these books will certainly criticize the present administration.
>
> It is a crime to express contempt for a language by writing vulgar books. Our government, unfortunately, does not punish such crimes. Therefore, the number of vulgar books is increasing every day. There is a law against obscene writings, but no one respects it. If the books described above are examined for their contents, they will certainly be proved obscene. Nowhere in these books is decent respectable language used, and not a single purpose for which authors write books are served by them. Only some people presumably get satisfaction from them. The authors of all such books should be punished.[59]

The concerns here seem to be little different from those expressed by contemporary colonial observers. We see the same issues raised, of taste, of public decency, and of the waste—the "frittering away"—of a powerful instrument of education and cultural improvement. But despite this apparent similarity, the position from which a journal like *Baṅgabidyā prakāśikā* would make its complaint about the need to watch and control what was being printed in Bengali was, in fact, quite different from that of a Bolton or even of a James Long. Although, in 1865, this journal is still demanding the intervention of the colonial government to clear up unsavory aspects of indigenous cultural life, much in the manner of the social reformers of the first half of the century, this was no longer to be the dominant trend. Increasingly, the new intellectual elite sought to demarcate a cultural zone that would be regulated by normative practices laid down and enforced by institutions set up and run by the dominant practitioners of that culture, not by an external colonial government. The new elite, in other words, sought to discipline the world of the printed text from within, by trying to enforce a set of normative literary practices.

A major institution for the laying down and enforcement of norms was the literary review.[60] From the 1860s, there began to appear Bengali journals that were quite conscious of their roles as creators and guardians of literary taste, and that were in fact mutually supportive in this task. Thus they managed to demarcate in institutional terms what qualified as good literature and what did not. When *Bāndhab*, a monthly literary journal containing essays and criticism, was started in 1874 from Dhaka by Kaliprasanna Ghosh, it received laudatory reviews from its contemporaries. *Sādhāraṇī* commented that *Bāndhab* had proved that East Bengal had been able to arrest the flood of vulgar writings.[61] *Rahasya sandarbha*, another Calcutta-based journal, declared its optimism and support for the intended purpose with which *Bāmābodhinī patrikā* was begun in order to spread awareness and knowledge among women.[62] The condemnation by such quality journals of what was "vulgar" and "unrefined" was equally consensual and forthright.

In the 1870s, Bankim Chandra Chattopadhyaya, the first Bengali novelist and perhaps the leading literary figure of his time, became the prime spokesman of refinement in literary taste. *Baṅgadarśan*, the journal he edited from 1872, embarked on a relentless, uncompromising campaign against what it considered to be bad writing. Its criticism of contemporary literature was scathing. "It is distressing to review the rubbish which accumulates in our office . . . nothing can be more distressing than having to read the books we receive." Quite often, *Baṅgadarśan* would tear a work to pieces with comments like "this has no merit . . . it is unreadable . . . it displays the most abominable taste . . . true there is a vulgar side to the human character, but if one does not know what to reject and what to accept one should not write books."[63]

It was not simply that new canons of taste and respectability were sought in order to impose and define a high culture of enlightened modernity; this campaign was also seen as the culmination of a history of the development of the Bengali language. In this new narrative, the decisive criterion of literary quality was the test of "lasting value." All the contributions that were supposed to define the story of Bengali literature—the high points—had withstood the test of time and the same standard was applied to contemporary productions. Most did not pass the test. Ramgati Nyayaratna, for instance, who wrote in 1872 the first formal history of Bengali language and literature, had this to say about the contemporary period:

> Readers are aware that for the past few years the number of Bengali books has been increasing daily. If these were really worthwhile books, then we might have regarded the present situation propitious for the development of the Bengali language. But this not so. It seems that some people have developed a disease of writing and publishing anything at all, irrespective of merit or value. . . . Books which are being churned out in this manner will not be read by ordinary people nor will they last long; they will cease to exist after a few days. There are some among these which, in fact, smell of the gutter. Readers, please do not think that we will even touch them.[64]

The National and the Popular

What were the new canons? How were they derived? Almost from the moment that this task was formulated, there seemed to be two approved sources of the new "high" literature. One was the "classical" source of ancient Indian civilization, especially the Sanskrit language and literature. The other was the "modern" example of English. The two sources were united into a conception of a high culture by their supposed relation to the building of a "nation." The argument was elaborated with varying degrees of sophistication and subtlety by nineteenth-century writers, but, even at the most commonsensical level, the project was widely understood. The journal *Bāndhab*, in setting out its objectives in its first editorial, added a passage on the state of the Bengali language:

> All knowledgeable persons will admit that the enrichment of the mother-tongue is closely associated with the overall development and enrichment of the whole nation. Greece and Rome have lost their political glory but the wealth stored in the coffers of their languages have not yet been exhausted. . . . One hardly has left any traces of the world's oldest civilization, that of the Aryans. Yet even today, the manner in which it serves to benefit the country is evident to all. Learned men feel that one of the major reasons for the recent development of the English nation is the enrichment of its language. In every instance does the enrichment of a language raise the standard of the nation.[65]

But even as the general terms of the project were understood, and largely accepted, it did not lead to an easy resolution of the debates over precisely where and how to apply those criteria. Bankim's *Baṅgadarśan* was perhaps the one organ that carried out the most clarified and sustained campaign to enforce literary and aesthetic standards derived directly from modern European examples. In an article in one of its early issues, it described the possibilities that had opened up for the new Bengali literature:

> Of all the provinces of India, Bengal is now certainly the most advanced in learning and in the progress of civilization. Consequently, its literature too has reached high standards of excellence and seems to resemble European literature. Bengalis today have abandoned the endless repetitions of the mythological tales from the Puranas and immature, vulgar and obscene stories. Instead, they are now writing blank verse, plays, travelogue, history, science, poetry, essays and so on.[66]

But the citation of a modern European example was not necessarily a good justification for upholding a norm. It could, in fact, be turned into its very opposite, and rejected on the grounds of being alien and inauthentic. Indeed, whereas European literature was often held up for pedagogical purposes as the mark of all that Bengali literature still needed to achieve, in the performance of that task the norms underwent considerable changes. And here it was the unavoidable reference to "the popular" that effected this displacement. Thus, on the one hand, "the popular" would serve as the index of all that was backward and vulgar—precisely that which needed to be changed. On the other hand, "the popular" was also that which was truly indigenous, authentic, uncontaminated—that which needed to be recovered and preserved.[67]

The attempt to relate the high culture to the popular would give rise to several strategies. In 1854, Pearychand Mitra and Radhanath Sikdar started a literary magazine entitled *Māsik patrikā*. In a short preface to its first edition, it said: "This magazine is being published for the [benefit of] ordinary people, especially women. Articles here will be written in the language in which we ordinarily converse. If scholars wish to read it, they are welcome to do so, but this magazine is really not intended for them."[68] Pearychand was clearly aware of a divide within the literate society of Calcutta and was consciously addressing those who were not part of the English-educated, elite group to which he obviously belonged. But equally significant was his motive for writing. It was not necessarily that of artistic creation; Pearychand recognized that there was a cultural distance between the intellect and sensibility of the writer and his intended audience. To reach the latter, the writer would have to make concessions to the "unsophisticated," the popular. And yet, he must also "educate." He must not concede so much as to himself become "low" and "vulgar"; he must, in other words, write for a popular readership without immersing himself in "the popular."

This division, in some ways, was recognized and reconstituted into a principle for the definition of good literature. On the one hand, there was literature that fell into the category of high art, which assumed a commonality of taste between author and reader. But this was not the only kind of "good" literature. The other kind sought to communicate with the popular without conceding to bad taste. And the imperative to communicate with what was popular was of course to raise its cultural standard and elevate its taste.

Such didacticism, in other words, was aimed not only at creating good taste but also at creating a society with good taste. Writing about *Māsik patrikā* in the 1880s, Haraprasad Sastri observed:

> Earlier [i.e., before the publication of this magazine], books were written in Bengali prose, their contents either drawn from Sanskrit texts, or law, or they were plays and novels. They were of such ugly taste that they definitely could not be given to women. This magazine was published so that women could read it; it was for their amusement; it was full of good advice, conducive to fostering happiness in their body and mind.[69]

Although Haraprasad's concerns were quite representative of the literary elite of his times, this particular form of reaching "the popular" was not approved by all. Haraprasad's wholehearted applause for Pearychand's and Radhanath's efforts was not the universal reaction. Long, for instance, wrote in 1859:

> The Editor of the Masik Patrika a monthly Magazine has adopted the colloquial style—very good for females and others who have never learned thoroughly their mother-tongue—but this is not the style of books generally acceptable. Natives consider language ought to have some elegance and not the baldness of the bazar. This latter style has not answered, though the Editor Radhanath Sikdar devoted much time and zeal to popularize it.[70]

Ramgati Nyayaratna's reactions to this project of experimenting with the colloquial were skeptical and substantiated Long's comments.[71] Ramgati felt that such a simplified language was not conducive to writing books for a general readership. He said this not only in the context of *Māsik patrikā* and Pearychand Mitra's style, but also for Kaliprasanna Sinha's colloquial *Hutom pyācār nakśā* and even Bankimchandra's novels. As it happened, in spite of Ramgati's blanket condemnation, Bankim's *sādhu bhāṣā* became commonly accepted as the standard literary prose in the late nineteenth century.

But despite the enforcement of the chaste *sādhu bhāṣā* through standardized grammars, the school system, and the entire "respectable" print media, the sources of difference remained alive and unresolved. The issue would be reopened in the middle of the twentieth century when the standard *sādhu bhāṣā* would be condemned as artificial and formal, and the colloquial would be celebrated once more as natural and popular. On the other hand, the attempt would also be made to discipline the popular by incorporating the folk as the most basic and authentic element of the national culture. From the late nineteenth century, systematic efforts were made to institutionalize the collection, editing, and preservation of the materials of folk literature, especially under the Bangiya Sahitya Parishat, which was conceived as the national literary academy of Bengal, and later under the Department of Bengali of the University of Calcutta. The formation of the folk into an academic discipline was, of course, to freeze and sanitize the unsavory and dangerous elements of a popular culture.

But each attempt to impose a disciplinary norm that was derived from a pedagogical conception of high culture encountered resistances in its performance. Reviewing Bankimchandra's first novel, *Durgeśnandinī,* in 1862, *Rahasya sandarbha* agreed that the novelist's efforts were indeed pathbreaking, even if the influence of the English novel was a bit too obvious. But it went on to allege that Bankim had not always managed to break out from the crudities of the traditional forms, especially in the description of feminine beauty and in creating humor:

> We would have liked to have quoted some of the sentences here but they contain such explicit descriptions that they would not be acceptable to our readers who include our women and our young boys. . . . Bankim has certainly taken care to evoke laughter. But it is to be regretted that he has not always kept in mind that Bengali books are now being read by cultured women. Or perhaps his book is not meant for them.[72]

We may find it ironic that Bankim, the most magisterial guardian of good taste in literature, was accused of writing a book unsuitable for cultured women. But the accusation shows precisely the limits of the project to impose an internalized discipline on literary practices as well as explaining an endless series of new strategies that writers adopted in face of these efforts. A little-known author, Nilkanta Goswami, in a fictional work entitled *Āmi tomāri* (I am yours only), published in 1874, had a short preface for his readers: "I have no hopes of winning your applause by publishing this mystery," he wrote (he called his book not a novel but a strange mystery),

> because I do not know how to vulgarize humour. That I will be regarded as among the leading authors is also beyond my expectations since Scott or Reynolds are not my companions. I do not expect that you will accept my fiction with enthusiasm as I am not one of those upstart writers who become successful. But so what? I only wish to converse with you.[73]

The dig made at those who looked up to Scott or Reynolds (Bankimchandra is the obvious target) by someone from a less privileged position was not uncommon. But, as we have seen, the possibility of such a subversive move was opened precisely because the disciplinary effort in the name of the "national" culture had to be constantly legitimized by its relation to "the popular." Writing his autobiography in the 1880s, the playwright Amritalal Bose came out strongly in support of the Baṭtalā publications: "I say, O Sir! where would your Bengali education, Bengali literature, Bengali language, Bengali religion, Bengali piety, Bengali blank verse be, if the Bengali Mahabharata and Ramayana did not sell at Baṭtalā for fourteen annas?"[74]

Notes

1. Subsidiary table V, Statistics of Factory Labour, *Census of India, 1911*, vol.VI (Calcutta: Bengal Secretariat Book Depot, 1913), pp. 73–74.
2. Febvre and Martin, *Coming of the Book*; Chartier, *Cultural Uses of Print.*

3. Hicky set up the earliest known Calcutta press sometime during 1777 and for the next three years or more enjoyed a monopoly on printing in Calcutta. In January 1780 he began publication of the weekly *Hicky's Bengal Gazette*, the first newspaper to be printed in any language anywhere in India. Because of its frequent scurrilous allusions to prominent figures in the Bengal administration, the newspaper came under fire, and in June 1781 Hicky was sentenced to imprisonment and ordered to pay exorbitant fines on three counts of libel. He continued to print his weekly from prison for a further nine months until, in March 1782, his press and types were confiscated. Busteed, *Echoes.* A recent work is Mukhopadhyay, *Hicky's Bengal Gazette.*

4. Kesavan, *History of Printing*, pp. 179-229; Nikhil Sarkar, "Printing," pp. 128-36; Chittaranjan Bandyopadhyay, ed., *Dui śataker bāṃlā mudraṇ o prakāśan;* Sripantha [Nikhil Sarkar], *Yakhan chāpākhānā elo.*

5. Kamal Chaudhuri and Parimal Chaudhuri, eds., *Kalkātā chāpākhānā*, p. 16.

6. Long, *Descriptive Catalogue,* reprinted in Dineschandra Sen, *Baṅgabhāṣā o sāhitya,* pp. 818-19.

7. *Samācārdarpāṇ*, 30 January 1830, reprinted in Brajendranath Bandyopadhyay, *Saṃbādpatre,* p. 85.

8. Long, *Descriptive Catalogue,* p. 819.

9. Cited in Brajendranath Bandyopadhyay, *Saṃbādpatre*, pp. 67, 73, 85-86; Sukumar Sen, *Baṭtalār chāpā o chabi,* p. 45. For more details on these early presses, see Barunkumar Mukhopadhyay, *Bāṃlā mudrita granther itihās*, pp. 335-46, 435-49.

10. Sukumar Sen's account has no footnotes and it is difficult to ascertain the sources of his information.

11. Reprinted in Jatindramohan Bhattacharya, *Tālikā*, pp. 1-14.

12. The classifications were history, biography, classical tales, medicine, poetry, Christian tracts, fiction, moral tales, scriptures and mythologies, journals and periodicals, natural science, Vedic and Vedantic, Vaishnav, law, geography, Musalmani, prose, dictionary and grammar, and newspapers.

13. Jatindramohan Bhattacharya, *Tālikā*, Appendix, pp. 159-60.

14. From Long to G. F. Cockburn, chief magistrate of Calcutta, 23 June 1854, ibid., p. 161.

15. Long, *Descriptive Catalogue*, Preface.

16. Long, "Returns," para 1.

17. Brajendranath Bandyopadhyay, *Saṃbādpatre*, p. 59; Long to Cockburn, 23 June 1854, in Bhattacharya, *Tālikā*, p. 161.

18. Long, "Returns," para 2.

19. In Brajendranath Bandyopadhyay, *Saṃbādpatre*, p. 60.

20. Ibid., p. 70.

21. Ibid., p. 85.

22. Long, *Descriptive Catalogue*, Preface and p. 828.

23. Ibid., pp. 823, 830-31.

24. Ibid., pp. 827-28.

25. The following names occur in the 1852 as well as the 1855 list: Adi Ras, Beshea Rahasyea, Charu Chita Rahasea, Hemlata Ratikanta, Kam Shastra 1820; Kunjari Bilas, Lakhmi Janardan Bilas, Prem Ashtak, Prem Bilas, Prem Natak, Prem Taranga, Pulakkan Dipika, Prem Rahasyea, Shringar Tilak, 1st ed. 1817; Ratibilas, Sambhog Ratnakar with sixteen filthy plates, Ramaniranjan, Ras Manjari, Ras Sagar, Rasrasamrita, Rasatarangini, Rasomanjari, Rassindu Prem Bilas, Rati Kali, 1st ed. 1820; Rati Shastra, Ras Ratnakar, Shringar Ras, Shringar Tilak, Stri Charitra, Stri Pulakhen Dipika.

26. "Correspondence relating to the Vernacular Education in the Lower Provinces of Bengal. Returns of the names and writings of 515 persons connected with Bengali literature, either as author or translator of printed works, chiefly during the last fifty years, and a catalogue

of Bengali newspapers and periodicals which have issued from the press from 1818 to 1855." *Selections from the Records of the Bengal Government*, No. XXII (Calcutta, 1855).

27. Long, "Returns," paras 2 and 3.

28. Ibid., para 25.

29. The Obscene Books and Pictures Act was passed in 1856. It contained the following clause: "Whoever, within the territories in the possession under the Government of the East India Company, of any shop, bazar, street, thoroughfare, highroad, or any places of public resort, distributes, sells or offers or exposes for sale or wilfully exposes to public view, any obscene song, ballad, or works to the annoyance of others; shall, upon conviction, . . . be liable to a fine not exceeding hundred rupees, or to imprisonment with or without hard labour, for a period not exceeding three months, or to both." See Chittaranjan Bandyopadhyay, "Aślīlatā nibāraṇ āin," pp. 75-78.

30. Long, "Returns," pp. xxv and xxiv.

31. "Correspondence relating to the Vernacular Education," p. 93.

32. Long, "Returns," p. vii, para 7.

33. Ibid., p. ix, para 11.

34. Jatindramohan Bhattacharya, *Tālikā*, Introduction. Jatindramohan thinks that the omissions occurred because Long employed agents and did not collect the information himself.

35. Long, "Returns," p. xx, para 22. Jatindramohan's lists for the period 1853-67 show the number of almanacs rising from four in 1853 to twelve in 1855 to nineteen in 1857. Jatindramohan Bhattacharya, *Mudrita bāṃlā granther pañjī.*

36. Long, "Returns," p. xxiv, para 26.

37. Long, "Returns," p. viii, para 7.

38. The four are: Chandrika Press at Kolutolla, Levendier Sahib's Press at Bowbazar, Sambad Timir Nashak Press at Mirzapur, and Mahendra Lal Press at Sankharitollah.

39. Although Chandrika and Mahendra Lal survived into the 1850s, Chandrika Press had meanwhile moved from Kolutola to Peter's Lane and Mahendra Lal Press had moved from Sankharitola to Bowbazar. The list under discussion excludes missionary presses (e.g., the Baptist Mission and the Bishop's College Press).

40. Baṭtalā appears only once as "Bartala," but in a short appendix Ahiritola and Banstala also appear as Bartala.

41. Before this, we only have the case of Iswarchandra Bose's Stanhope Press, established in 1840, which won a reputation for printing books of an improved quality; Michael Madhusudan Dutt's works and journals such as *Bāmābodhinī patrikā* were printed here. *Rahasya sandarbha*, part 1, vol. 7, Bhadra, Sambat 1920 (1863). This is one of the earliest evidences we have of the emergence of specialized hierarchies among printers of Bengali books.

42. Long, "Returns," pp. xii and xiii, para 14. A Copyright Act (XX of 1847) was passed on 18 December 1847.

43. Computed from lists given in *Samācārdarpaṇ*, 2 February 1822, in Brajendranath Bandyopadhyay, *Saṃbādpatre*, pp. 64-65.

44. Computed from lists in "Correspondence relating to the Vernacular Education," pp. 90-91.

45. Bandyopadhyay, *Saṃbādpatre*, p. 77.

46. "Correspondence relating to the Vernacular Education," pp. 90-97.

47. Long, "Returns," pp. xx-xxi, para 22.

48. Ibid.

49. Ibid., p. xv, para 17.

50. From C. W. Bolton, undersecretary, Government of Bengal, to the secretary, Government of India, Home Department, 29 April 1879. Bolton, "Reports on Publications," p. 159.

51. Wenger, "Catalogue." The compiler, Wenger, was "officiating Bengalee translator to the Government of Bengal."

52. Ibid., p. 20.

53. Jatindramohan Bhattacharya, *Pañjī*. The 1993 posthumous publication was the first time *Pañjī* had been published.

54. There is a problem in using this list in that it includes the names of all printers who published anything between 1853 and 1867. There is no way of telling how many of them operated in any particular year.

55. *Act XXV of 1867* (reprint Calcutta: Superintendent of Government Printing, 1890).

56. Computed from Blumhardt, *Catalogue*.

57. Bolton, "Reports on Publications," p. 145.

58. Ibid., p. 133.

59. *Baṅgabidyā prakāśikā*, 23 October 1865.

60. There have been several studies on nineteenth-century literary criticism in Bengal. See Srikumar Bandyopadhyay and Praphullachandra Pal, eds., *Samālocanā-sāhitya-paricay;* Arunkumar Mukhopadhyay, *Bāṅlā samālocanār itihās*; Asitkumar Bandyopadhyay, *Samālocanār kathā*.

61. Quoted in *Bāndhab*, 1, 10, Chaitra 1281 (1874).

62. *Rahasya sandarbha*, part 1, vol. 8, Bhādra, Sambat 1930 (1863).

63. *Baṅgadarśan*, *Śrāban* 1284 (1877).

64. Ramgati Nyayaratna, *Bāṅgālābhāṣā,* p. 142.

65. *Bāndhab*, vol. 1, no. 1, Āṣāḍh 1281 (1874).

66. *Baṅgadarśan*, Āṣāḍh 1279 (1872).

67. For the distinction between the "pedagogical" and the "performative" in nationalist narratives, see Homi Bhabha, "DissemiNation," pp. 291-322.

68. Quoted in Haraprasad Sastri, "Pyārīcāṅd mitra," p. 143.

69. Ibid., p. 144.

70. Long, "Returns," p. xviii, para 19.

71. Ramgati Nyayaratna, *Bāṅgālābhāṣā,* Preface.

72. *Rahasya sandarbha*, 2nd series, vol. 21, Sambat 1921 (1854), p. 142.

73. Nilkanta Goswami, *Āmi tomāri*.

74. Arunkumar Mitra, ed., *Amṛtalāl basur smṛti,* p. 117.

3 / Recovering the Nation's Art

Tapati Guha-Thakurta

> It is with a great sense of sorrow that we have finished reading this book. It is the same sense of sorrow which arises from watching the destruction of the great achievements of our ancestors. . . . We feel not only grieved, but at the same time, ashamed and reprimanded. Are we the same Aryan race, only a sample of whose glorious deeds have been described by Mr. Srimani? If so, [look at] what we have been now reduced to, from what a high status to what a lowly position we have fallen.[1]

This was a reviewer's response to a pioneering Bengali book entitled, in translation, Fine Arts of Ancient India, published in January 1874. It echoed a sentiment and conjured up an image that pervaded Bengali middle-class writing in this period. The dual themes of past glory and present decline that structured such writing, and its concerns with national regeneration and progress, were sharply etched in the emerging Bengali discourse on art and aesthetics. We confront here a recurrent motif of a fall from a prior golden age. As in European academic art theories, here too the very notion of classicism—the idea of a distant classical past, offering itself to the present as a source of renewal and inspiration—emerged from a profound feeling of decline and loss. The yawning gap between the past and the present was sought to be bridged by indigenous initiatives in "superior" forms of art practice, and in the production of new "authentic" forms of knowledge on Indian art. The past, as a symbol of the nation's autonomous history and civilizational lineage, had to prepare the way for a present in which tradition and modernized knowledge would together frame a new national self.

This chapter focuses on two Bengali texts on Indian art history in order to map out two distinct and significant phases in the unfolding of this agenda: the first, avowedly the earliest art historical venture in Bengali, Shyamacharan Srimani's *Sūkṣa śilper utpatti o āryajātir śilpacāturi* (1874); the second, a relatively little-known early tract by Abanindranath Tagore, the leading artist and ideologue of the nationalist art movement in Calcutta, entitled *Bhāratśilpa* (1909).[2] The thirty-five years that lapsed between Shyamacharan's and Abanindranath's writings were witness to major changes in aesthetic tastes, in the very definitions of *art* and *Indian-ness,* and in ideas of what constituted the essence of the Indian fine arts tradition. I explore the implications of this shift by positioning these texts as two parameters of differing opinions and aspirations. Moving from the earlier to the later text, I look at the extent to which the use of the vernacular medium involved merely local and popular dissemination of new scholarship, and the extent to which it tied up with different enunciative strategies to produce an almost novel category of knowledge.

In picking these two samples, I have also been concerned with identifying types of authoritative texts, around which accreted considerable degrees of power and influence in their own period. The authority of these writings emanated from the way they situated themselves within a dominant Western field of practice and knowledge (namely, the disciplines of art and art history), demarcating at the same time the separate space and positions from which they addressed a Bengali readership. The indigenous point of view of these texts, I argue, can be recovered in the search for locations from which this new disciplinary field could be penetrated, mediated, and transformed into an effective site of nationalist activity. In their own ways, each of the books was premised upon points of both similarity and difference vis-à-vis Western models—a similarity implicit in organizational structure, method, or modes of argument; a difference articulated in the choice of language and metaphor, in styles of enunciation, in the ascription of nationalist urges and motives, and in attempts at claiming the subject as the nation's exclusive prerogative.

The First Bengali History of Art

When Shyamacharan Srimani, a former student and teacher of the Government School of Art, Calcutta, published *Āryajātir śilpacāturi* (hereafter *AS*) in 1874, he set out to fill what he saw as a major gap in the field—the absence of an easily accessible, popular, Bengali book on the subject of Indian art. Existing books by European or Indian scholars were all expensive publications, written in English, and hence outside the reach of the common reader. It was now important to give that reader the same—indeed, a more developed—sense of the great artistic achievements of his Aryan forefathers and inculcate in him a lost racial and national pride.[3] This was what Shyamacharan marked out as the main purpose of his book. Principal H. H. Locke, of the Government School of Art (to whom Shyamacharan dedicated the book), also located the main significance of this work in its intervention within a new domain of language and readership:

> The very fact that you have attempted to engage the attention of those of your countrymen to whom the vernacular is the only vehicle for knowledge, and through their mother tongue to teach *somewhat* . . . of the admirable Art of your forefathers should to my mind secure for you the very hearty commendation of all who are interested in the spread of Art-knowledge in India.[4]

Art, with a capital *A*, defined in the new Westernized sense of "the higher arts," was seen as a matter of superior, refined knowledge imparted by the West. *AS* made Bengali a vehicle of that "higher" knowledge and artistic sensibility; but, in doing so, it also laid claims to a kind of understanding of the subject that was a prerogative of Indians or native-language-speakers. Shyamacharan's book, thus, was not just the first of a new modern genre of art histories in Bengali; it was also among the first nationalist histories, with the modern becoming part and parcel of a national self-awareness. It set out to disseminate at a local level a modernized, systematized, nationalized knowledge of India's "great art" tradition. I will analyze each of these different but integrated components of this knowledge.

First, we can take a look at the new social and professional milieu of the book's author, for this constituted an important point of location of the text and defined much of the authority and expertise with which it spoke. Shyamacharan Srimani was operating from well within the circuit of British art education in Calcutta and the professional space it had created. He exemplified the new Bengali middle-class professional in the field of art teaching and practice, as yet a small, limited group.[5] A product of the Western pedagogic discipline of art, whose academic training methods and realistic conventions of drawing, painting, sculpting, and printmaking were by then well ensconced in local practice, he had successfully imbibed the best employment opportunities thrown up by this training. Among the first batch of students of the School of Industrial Arts, set up in Calcutta in 1854, Shyamacharan Srimani was the first Indian, along with another prominent student, Annadaprasad Bagchi, to be absorbed by Principal Locke into the teaching staff of the school in the late 1860s.

The focus of art teaching in Calcutta, as in all other colonial art education centers in India begun in this period, was on the applied and industrial arts. The aim was to provide new kinds of vocational and technical training (along with training in the rudimentaries of academic art conventions) to produce skilled personnel—masters of drawing, draftsmen, surveyors, engravers, and lithographers—required by the expanding public services in India.[6] While Annada Bagchi stepped into the relatively privileged sphere of oil and portrait painting, Shyamacharan remained confined to the more mundane drill of teaching geometrical drawing. Like other art school students of the time, Shyamacharan would use his training to branch out from his art school job into other types of indigenous enterprise. Whereas many began setting up their own lithography and engraving presses, Shyamacharan, as an activist of the Hindu Mela (the early nationalist cultural movement led in particular by Nabagopal Mitra), found his main alternative forum of activity in Nabagopal's National School, set up in 1872 specially "for the cultivation of Arts, Music, and for Physical training." There, he became the organizer and chief teacher of the art curriculum. The course at the National School was overtly technical, involving academic courses in drawing, modeling, geometrical drawing, architectural drawing, engineering, and surveying, similar to those at the government school.[7] These were perceived as the "science" of art, and initiation in these scientific methods of representation was seen to be as important for Bengali youth as physical education or training in chemistry or botany.

Nevertheless, the prevailing gradations between the so-called fine arts of painting and sculpture and such "applied" and "industrial" arts generated tensions. The Bengali *bhadralok* (literally, the respectable member of the educated class) found himself caught between a recognition of the practical value of such technical education in the arts and an aspiration to enter that charmed world of fine arts that lay outside his bounds. Colonial art education in India had evolved on the assumption that the "fine arts" (or higher arts) were, by and large, a monopoly of Western artists, while the future for Indians lay in a revival of their traditional craft skills and in a new employment-oriented training in the "applied arts." A reversal of this verdict became central in the aesthetic self-awareness of the indigenous elite. Claims and aspirations in a newly construed realm of "fine arts" became a vital segment of nationalist thought, during the very years that British art education secured its grounds. Shyamacharan's venture of writing his book reflected the tensions and torn identities generated by this art education. His training and livelihood required him to teach geometrical and mechanical drawing; but his book was a distinct attempt to move beyond these confines, to recover for his people a more elevated sense of "high art" and claim it as a part of the nation's ancient heritage. And in this project, he had the full support of the Western institutional and professional forum from which he had emerged. The patronage and encouragement of his benefactor, Principal Locke, loomed large across this book, giving it its first legitimizing stamp.

Domesticating a New Discipline

As an exercise in the new genre of art history, *AS* had its lineage in an emergent group of authoritative texts on Indian art and antiquities, primarily by Western scholars. As a discipline with the status of an exact science, art history had begun to emerge in Europe in the second half of the eighteenth century. Its pioneering exponent, the German scholar Winckelmann, had structured this history as the evolution of artistic styles, the central idea being that of the continuous "progress" of European art from its classical infancy in the Hellenic civilization to its modern maturity in the Renaissance.[8] In writings dealing with art outside Europe, the ancient civilizations of Egypt, in particular, and occasionally China and India, began to feature in these eighteenth-century art histories as a part of "the debate on the origin of the arts."[9] The context was provided by the persisting European obsession with the biblical origins of history, and the resulting theory of all nations of the world springing from a single original land. For the belief was then strongly rooted among antiquarians and classical scholars, whether their preference was for the Egyptians or for the Hebrews as the oldest nation, that the arts, like the sciences, were actually "invented" by the first nation in existence. It is from this period that India began occasionally to displace Egypt and to figure in European writing as "the original nation," the "cradle of civilizations"—a center, thus, of the birth of the arts, and, thus, a perfect instance also of the early primitive stage of art, trapped in antiquity, outside the pale of history and progress. While travelers and scholars visiting India marveled at the antiquity of the cave temples of western India and sought to unravel their mysteries, Europe began to locate in India (as it did also in Medea, Babylon, Egypt, and Persia) its own distant lineage and prehistory.

Such trends took a distinct new turn over the duration of the nineteenth century, as the empire in India orchestrated its own concerns for survey, documentation, and conservation of India's arts and antiquities. By midcentury, systematic efforts were under way for a full-scale excavation and mapping of

Indian antiquities,[10] for recovering through these India's absent history, and for gleaning from this history a chronology of religions and kingdoms through which the archaeological sites and monuments could be classified and given a stylistic slot. With the beginnings of the Archaeological Survey in 1861, the extensive programs for documentation and collection of Indian art in museums in India and abroad, and the writing of the first detailed and general histories of Indian art and architecture, the project developed its main institutional and scholarly apparatus. Under pioneers like Alexander Cunningham and James Fergusson, the new disciplines of archaeology and art history began to frame themselves as the privileged repositories of knowledge on India's artistic past.[11]

It is within this new disciplinary form of scholarship on Indian art that Shyamacharan Srimani's book must be situated. When it appeared in 1874, this new field of knowledge was establishing itself, marking out its terrain, defining its main preoccupations. That same year, Henry Cole's *Catalogue of the Objects of Indian Art Exhibited in the South Kensington Museum* was published, containing what was seen as "the very first history of Indian art."[12] This book emerged out of the contemporary widespread Western fascination with Indian craftsmanship and ornamentation and the lessons it offered for the crisis in English industrial design. However, in construing a general history around the subject of Indian art, it laid out what was soon to become a dominant conceptual framework. To begin with, it established art and civilization in ancient India as a monopoly of the Aryan race. It blocked out three main chronological and stylistic phases in Indian art history (the Buddhist, the Brahmanical Hindu, and the Muhammadan phases), suggesting in it an evolutionary movement from the simple to the complex and overornate. At the same time, it created an inverse hierarchy in which Buddhist art, in its simplified "rationalized" form, naturalist iconography, and suggested affinities with Graeco-Bactrian art, was seen to mark the high point of the Indian tradition. It also privileged, in each phase, architecture above sculpture and painting as the highest form of artistic expression in India, relegating the latter to the position of the so-called ornamental arts.[13]

In all this, Cole's book anticipated the more extensive writings of this period of the pioneering scholar of Indian architecture, James Fergusson. In 1874, Fergusson's comprehensive *History of Indian and Eastern Architecture*, intended as a fourth volume to his general compendium on the history of world architecture, was still to be published.[14] However, Fergusson's other writings, beginning with his first illustrated surveys (*Ancient Architecture of Hindostan*[15] and *Rock Cut Temples of India*), and building up to his powerful manifesto (*The Study of Indian Architecture*),[16] had already established him as the first in a new field—the first to conduct thorough, organized research and the first to systematize the study of Indian architecture as a discipline in itself, converging on archaeology, ethnography, and art history. By the 1870s, because of Fergusson's "one-man architectural survey" and scholarly endeavors, a large number of Indian monuments had been placed on the map and described, and a broad pattern of chronological and stylistic development (moving through the so-called Buddhist, Jain, Hindu, and Muhammadan phases) had been established. This clearly framed the space from which Shyamacharan's book emerged and addressed a new Bengali readership.

Shyamacharan's book shared the fundamental premises of Western Orientalist approaches to Indian art. In keeping with the preoccupations of eighteenth-century European art history, it opened with a brief section delving into what were seen as the origins of the arts of architecture and sculpture in ancient societies, claiming that these ancient arts had their earliest traces in India.[17] The notion of antiquity—of a civilization originating in the mists of time—achieved an easy transition from the "primitive" to the "classical." The savagery of tribal iconography was paralleled by the growing sophistication of architectural form and intricacy and artistry of ornamentation in ancient India. The ideal of a classical past was built around twin concepts, *Aryan* and *fine arts,* each of which was both embedded within a surrounding history of reification in colonial India and highly valorized in the structure of Western Orientalist knowledge.

The idea of the Indo-Aryan races that permeated Western and Indian writing of the time had become central in the new Bengali sense of a national heritage. As the notion of the Indo-Aryan was conflated from a linguistic to a racial, cultural, and civilizational category, a heightened sense of antiquity and pedigree came to attach itself to the term, rendering it into the most powerful metonym of the nation's lost, ancient glory. Shyamacharan's use of *Aryan* as a concept was rather generalized and nonspecific. In contrast to Henry Cole's or Fergusson's employment of Aryan and non-Aryan racial categories to explain the transition from the Vedic Hindu to the Buddhist phases, or to classify different regional artistic styles of north and south India, Shyamacharan employed the term *Aryan* to broadly cover the entire pre-Muslim period of Indian art history.[18] Implicitly, the beginning of Muslim rule in India was the cutoff point that defined what was "ancient" and "Aryan" in India's art tradition, the two complementary categories encompassing the Hindu, Buddhist, and Jain traditions.

Given his central concern with establishing the antiquity of Indian art,

Shyamacharan used the age of the Vedas as a yardstick. Proved by Orientalist scholars to be more than three thousand years old, the Vedas, he argued, were composed over long periods of time, pushing the origins of Aryan civilization even further back in time. Equally important, he believed, was the antiquity of Indian architecture as manifest in cities like Hastinapur, Indraprastha, and Mathura, described in the Mahabharata, which must have been constructed shortly after the Vedic era.[19] In contending with the antiquity of the Vedas, Orientalists and antiquarians, he felt, had failed to take stock of the early history of Indian architecture, refusing to accept the "evidence" of the Mahabharata.

It was in variance with established scholarly opinion that Shyamacharan went all out to assert the status of architecture, sculpture, and painting in ancient India as a form of fine art. Like Fergusson and other contemporary writers, Shyamacharan privileged architecture as the major genre of Indian art, devoting to it maximum space and attention. However, while Cole or Fergusson were reluctant to concede to Indians any aptitude for sculpture or painting, Shyamacharan read into examples of early Indian sculpture and painting qualities that were most valued by the academic art conventions of the time—qualities like shading, lifelikeness, and soft, realistic modeling of anatomies.[20] These qualified them as fine arts and retrieved them from the positions of "monstrous iconography" or "ornate decoration" to which they had been relegated. Similarly, a right blending of the functional and the ornamental and the intricacy of decoration was seen as marks of the "fine arts" status of Indian architecture. Although, in the construction of columns and in ornamentation, ancient Indian architecture had its parallels in Egyptian or Greek styles, it was said to be distinctively individual and superior to its Egyptian or Greek counterparts.[21]

This point about the autonomy and superiority of Indian architecture had earlier been made, with specific reference to temples in south India, by the first Indian writer in the field, Ram Raz. Written fully under the aegis of Orientalist scholarship, Ram Raz's *Architecture of the Hindus* (1834) was the first textual analysis of the traditional canons of south Indian temple architecture. The specialty of the "native" contribution here was located in the linguistic skills of deciphering fragments of a Sanskrit aesthetic text (the *Mānasāra*) and in the efforts at mediating between the "high" world of knowledge of the Brahmin pundits and the "practical" knowledge of a group of working craftsmen.[22] This work had also laid open the importance of ancient texts—the aesthetic treatises of the *śilpaśāstra*—as a key to the study of Indian art. Shyamacharan's book claimed to follow directly on the lead of Ram Raz.[23]

While it highlighted the value of the aesthetic texts studied by Ram Raz, adding on others relating to the construction of statues and idols, it conveniently conflated the analysis to stand for all of the "ancient Aryan" tradition of Indian architecture. In this book, thus, *Hindu* became synonymous with *Aryan*; particular texts and a regional style became synonymous with the nation's ancient art tradition.

Drawing on the information contained in *Mānasāra*, in particular, it laid out a detailed table of measurements and conventions for the construction of the four main elements of a Hindu temple—the entablature (divided, in turn, into the cornice, frieze, and architrave), the column (consisting of capital, shaft, and base), the pedestal (consisting of cornice, body, and base), and the foundational plinth—accompanied by lithographed line drawings of each form.[24] Then, identifying three main types of Indian temple architecture—cave temples, temples with carvings both on the inner and outer mountain walls, and independent structures in brick, mortar, or stone—the book sketchily plotted out what it saw to be the prime examples of each type, drawing at will on Buddhist, Hindu, and Jain specimens. So, Elephanta, Salsette, Ellora, Ajanta, and the Udaygiri and Khandagiri cave temples came to exemplify the first type; the rock-cut temples of Chidambaram and Mahabalipuram, the second type; and the great temple of Bhubaneswar (described in great detail), the Dilwara temple of Mount Abu, and the Avantipur temple at Kashmir, the third type. This selection of temple architecture, in turn, provided the author with his examples of the best of Aryan sculpture and iconography. A selection even more haphazard and random, the examples ranged from the Buddhist sculptures of Sanchi and Amaravati to the sculpted panel of Mahishasuramardini at Mahabalipuram, the sculptures in the Kailasa temple at Ellora, and a female figure from the Kapileswari temple of Bhubaneswar.[25] The main criterion of evaluation all through was the evocation of human likeness—of realistic expression and suppleness of form—in stone, accepting the criterion as a universal aesthetic standard.

There was no attempt in *AS* at a chronological history of artistic styles and influences, nor any categorization of Indian art into historical periods. The book mainly boils down to a statement on the antiquity and the Aryan pedigree of Indian art—an assertion that seemed to stand on its own logic, requiring little argument or evidence; an assertion that, in itself, sufficed to make the work stand as a "pathbreaking" venture in Bengal. Without providing a history on a par with other contemporary writings, the book could still stand in for a new, modernized form of knowledge on India's ancient art tradition.

"Art Knowledge" Modernized and Nationalized

Moving from the sections on architecture and sculpture to the final section on painting, we confront a sudden lack of examples and descriptions. Failing to catalog much by way of ancient surviving specimens, except the fresco paintings of Ajanta and Bagh, the author was concerned more with gleaning evidences of a well-developed knowledge of painting from ancient textual sources like the Ramayana and the Mahabharata, or the dramas of Kalidasa—instances of the use of light and shade, of the skills of portraiture, and even of "history" painting, of a talent not merely in brushwork and coloring but also in the invocation of the expressions and emotions suggested in the literary narratives.[26] Such opinions were fairly widespread at the time, and similar pictorial qualities would be stressed by subsequent writers and critics, especially in the context of the creation of a new Indian art.[27] In the context of *AS*, this last section ("Citravidyā") is particularly significant for the way it ties together the past with the present, and foregrounds the motif of loss and degeneration against which the ancient achievements loom large.

The complete disappearance and decline of the art of painting over time were attributed to what was becoming the favorite bogey of Indian history—the Muslim invasions. While Hindu temple architecture and sculpture suffered the desecration of invaders, painting, as the most perishable of these arts, suffered the most, and all the more because of the Islamic injunctions against the creation of human images. In this construct of the Indian art tradition, the entire medieval and late medieval period, in its rich output of regional genres of miniature painting, remains totally obscured. Court painting traditions, which lingered in hybridized forms into the period in which Shyamacharan was writing, figured only as a sign of the "debased," in the same way as the new "bazaar" art of Kalighat and Baṭtalā. What predominates in the author's sense of things is only a remote ideal of the "classical," offset by the idea of a continuous downward slide into the present. So, as paramount images of decay, the classical heritage of Sanskrit drama stands contrasted with the present-day *jatra*, the lyrical artistic talents of ancient India with the "lifeless, monstrous" art of the village and Kalighat *paṭuā*, folk painters who were more artisans than artists.[28]

In this desolate scenario, English art education raised hopes of a revival of the art of painting. But, Shyamacharan argued, what had emerged in the name of art were mere skills of imitation, bereft of creativity and imagination. These latter qualities, he believed, were what defined the "artist" and enabled a painter to go beyond a surface imitation of appearances to invoke moods and emotions.[29] As a writer on the nation's art, Shyamacharan had ventured well beyond his professional skills of teaching geometrical drawing, locating *art* within a clearly differentiated aesthetic sphere. In privileging *bhāva* as a prime aesthetic category, he was already anticipating the main thrust and content of art criticism in Bengal.

The last pages of the book proclaim, loudly and clearly, its nationalist content. Here the art teacher and scholar stands firmly in his role as a nationalist ideologue. This is where *AS* can be placed in line with Shyamacharan's activities in the Hindu Mela—his teaching at the National School, his organization of exhibitions of Indian art ware at the Mela, and the lectures he gave at the Mela forum in 1869 on the glory of ancient Indian art, exhorting the nation's youth to revive that glory.[30] The same agenda repeated itself in the starting and closing sections of the book: to set up the Hindu past as a model for inspiration and emulation. This agenda also lay at the base of the author's other literary endeavors.

Within a year of the publication of *AS*, we find Shyamacharan writing a long "epic poem" entitled *Siṃhal-bijay-kābya* (The conquest of Ceylon by Vijaya, Prince of Bengal), with the main intention of recollecting the past valor and heroism of the "Bengali race" to rouse it out of its contemporary lethargy. All along, this past was being constructed as authentic history. Shyamacharan wrote that, since the ancient epic source of this legend, the Pali text *Mahāvaṃsa*, did not lend itself to a direct historical reconstruction of the event, he had opted for a poetic narrative mode; however, this did not detract from the historical authenticity of most of the main characters in the poem.[31] The claim to authenticity was more subtly worked into his venture into art history, *AS*, where he argued for his prerogative over his own past vis-à-vis Western scholars. Thus, in *AS* the past figured both as an inspirational motif and as a target of nationalist appropriation.

Although it emerged out of the new professional disciplinary domain established by Western scholarship, *AS* tried to wrest that domain from the West and claim it more intimately for the nation (still ambiguously defined as Indian/Hindu/Bengali). For all their efforts and expertise in Indian languages, European antiquarians, it was contended, could never penetrate the mysteries of Hindu iconography; by their own admission, they were still hovering on the peripheries of the vast subject of Indian art. The full wealth and secrets of the subject would reveal themselves only to Indians.[32] Shyamacharan used two metaphors: the *garbha-gṛha* (the sacred inner sanctum of a Hindu temple) and the chaste Hindu mother whose privacy and purity were under threat from the obtrusion of Europeans. Tradition, invested with the sanctity of such imagery, was sealed off as the ultimate preserve of the nation. The exercise of writing this book amounted to an assertion of right over a heritage that only Indians could expect fully to know and comprehend. And the book's final pages resounded with a patriotic call to all the author's fellow countrymen: rise to the service of the "motherland," he exhorted them; reclaim and recover the artistic greatness of her "Aryan" past by new, improved initiatives in art, and by indigenous ventures in art education and art histories.

In 1874—the year of the publication of *AS*—another prominent Bengali in this scholarly field was about to publish a monumental work, and he, too, was to make a strong case for the antiquity and autonomy of Indian art history. Rajendralal Mitra, a well-known antiquarian and scholar of Indology, wrote *The Antiquities of Orissa* as part of a project launched by the government and the Archaeological Survey to describe and document thoroughly the ancient temple architecture and sculpture of Orissa. In challenging Fergusson's views about the Greek origins of stone architecture in India, and arguing a countercase for an ancient, independent history of stone building and sculpture in India well before the Asokan period, Rajendralal provides us with one of the earliest specimens of a nationalized art history. It is a work cast fully in the style and method of Western publications. It employed the full authority of this format and methodology, with staunch fidelity to proofs and facts, to locate in the antiquities of Orissa the most "ancient" and "authentic" of the nation's art traditions.[33]

But marked differences separated Rajendralal Mitra's project from Shyamacharan's. The nature of Shyamacharan's book—its linguistic medium, its cheapness and easy accessibility—proclaimed its difference in stance and intention. Within the new, modern terrain of knowledge, Shyamacharan defined his own space primarily in terms of a local indigenous readership, and it is thus crucial that we situate Shyamacharan's book within its local terrain. The book fed into a spate of Bengali writing and debates on art in journals and booklets that voiced a similar concern with a recovery of the past and regeneration of the present. Bengali middle-class opinion was caught in a sharp dichotomy between the past and the present, the two separated, almost torn apart, by an overpowering sense of artistic degeneration. While India's past figured as a source of pride and autonomy, the present incited a desire for self-improvement and progress on the colonial model.

The contradiction was never resolved, for it was never confronted as such. If anything, it was sidestepped in the attempts of a middle class to carve out its own "middle" space between tradition and modernity, in the crosscurrents of Western art education and the search for Indian-ness.[34] This middle class itself was uncomfortably wedged between two worlds: on the one hand, the exclusive world of European "high art" in Calcutta, to which it sought entry but was denied full access; on the other hand, the world of popular "bazaar" pictures, from which it pointedly dissociated itself even as it shared in its bonds of an inherited indigenous culture. The new artistic codes it cultivated needed both its marks of refinement and improvement vis-à-vis popular pictures, and its marks of autonomy vis-à-vis European "high art"; in other words, these needed to be situated within a separate, intermediary space.

AS had significantly opened up such a space, negotiating the multiple pulls of the modern, the national, and the popular in its agenda of an art revival. Among the many reviews and notices the book attracted, one of the most prominent was that which appeared in Bankimchandra's *Baṅgadarśan*, a journal that had been launched in the same cause of inculcating a new "artistic" literary sense among the people. Reprinting extracts from *AS* for its readers, it lamented the lack of an aesthetic sense—a love of beauty—among the Bengalis, without which they could never qualify as a "civilized race."[35] Bankimchandra's own response to the book, in an essay entitled "Āryajātir sūkṣaśilpa," raised the same lament.[36] The problem lay in matching a Western model of "fine arts" and artistic refinement with the available repertoire of local pictures—the miniatures, *paṭacitra*, clay models, religious lithographs, and oleographs. The model, it seems, could more easily be transferred to ancient Buddhist or Hindu art of the past; where the present was concerned, it only underlined the artistic "backwardness" of Indians.

Indigenous initiatives in art history thus came to be paralleled by initiatives in extending a "modern/scientific" art instruction to the average student, outside the realm of British art schools. Charuchandra Nag's student manual, *Citrabidyā* (1874), was typical of such ventures, as it set out consciously to meet a need that neither English drawing books nor books like that of Shyamacharan could fulfill. While the former were neither easily accessible nor comprehensible to the Bengali student, the latter, dealing with ancient Indian art, was said to be far removed from the problems of practical instruction. Mediating between the two, *Citrabidyā* attempted to supplement the art school curriculum through simplified, step-by-step guidelines in outline drawing, still life and anatomy drawing, shading, and perspective.[37] In such manuals, notions of what was "scientific" and "beautiful" were fully determined by European academic methods and classical canons, with ancient Greek art seen to exemplify the ideal forms of the human face and figure.[38]

Local mediation was necessary only in the dissemination and popularization of this "art knowledge."

The first Bengali art journal, *Śilpa-puṣpāñjali*, begun in 1885-86, set out with the intention of placing before readers "the artistic achievements of their forefathers" in the hope of inspiring a present-day regeneration.[39] Yet art as discussed in its pages was associated primarily with technical and vocational skills and matters of "correct" instruction. The journal brought out similar serialized lessons on elementary outline drawing and shading, object drawing, and drawing of human anatomy or animal forms.[40]

Śilpa-puṣpāñjali was the venture of Kalidas Pal, another former student at the Government School of Art, where he had also taught wood engraving. Like Shyamacharan, he moved to the staff of Nabagopal Mitra's National School before setting up on his own. Kalidas opened an engraving press at Jorasanko and launched his art journal, the main popularity of which rested on the large lithoprints it carried—portraits, cityscapes, and illustrations of the Ramayana and Mahabharata.[41] The latter genre—the most highly acclaimed—we can place within the same "middle" domain that the art histories and art manuals were trying to negotiate. This new variety of realistic pictures of myths provided a middle-class public with its first modernized alternatives, both to the traditional "bazaar" iconography of the Kalighat and Baṭtalā pictures and to the alien iconography of Western neoclassical paintings.

The Reconstitution of an "Aesthetic" Sphere

This constructed space of a middle-class art culture in Bengal would undergo vast transformations in subsequent decades. The shifts occurred both in the reading and interpretation of tradition and in the selection of routes toward an artistic "renaissance" in modern India. Intricately linked with these changes were major breaks in the realm of art practice and in the social and aesthetic positioning of the artist. A new Orientalist and nationalist agenda concerning the recovery and regeneration of Indian art lay at the center of these changes.[42] Producing a narrowed definition of Indian-ness that in turn rested on a reification of the very notions of art and artist, the agenda lent a new edge to the discourse on tradition and progress. It reconstituted, on markedly different terms, its middle grounds between "Western" and "Indian" knowledges, between past and present, between tradition and modernity.

We now leap forward almost four decades to our next Bengali text on Indian art—Abanindranath Tagore's *Bhārat-śilpa* (1909) (hereafter *BS*)—and are thus situated at the crescendo of these changes. Abanindranath, the artist and writer who stood at the head of the nationalist art movement in Swadeshi Bengal, exemplified in his person and practice the newly privileged notions of art and artist that nationalism produced. His text, *BS,* was strategically located at the conjuncture of the Orientalist and nationalist projects of an "art revival" and its appeal rested on its ability to mediate Western knowledge, to transmit and propagate it locally, and in the process to move it in quite different directions.

In marking the shift from Shyamacharan's milieu to that of Abanindranath, let us identify some of the main layers of intervention that served radically to alter the discourse on Indian art. To begin with, we face a crucial break in the sources and forms of authoritative knowledge on Indian art. The field of scholarship and expertise that had been established since the midnineteenth century by archaeological explorations, documentation projects, and a new genre of art and architectural histories continued to thrive and expand.[43] At the same time, however, a deep schism had split the field, producing the binary of the "archaeological" and the "aesthetic." The aesthetic, or idealistic, standpoint provided a banner under which a new group of Orientalists tried to reappropriate the study of Indian art from the stranglehold of Western scholarship and to recover its authentic history.

Under their reinterpretation of Indian aesthetics and art history, much of the existing Western writing was accused of a dry, "archaeological" bias that documented, described, and classified, but fell short of, an aesthetic appraisal of the objects of study. Such an approach, it was alleged, was a fallout from another great flaw of Western scholarship: Eurocentric bias. This had led it to measure all of Indian art in terms of Western naturalistic conventions and Western classical standards, blinding itself to India's alternative, "superior" aesthetics. Constructing its oppositional stand through such polarities, the new Orientalism was premised on claims to a superior and genuine understanding of India's art tradition—an understanding that Shyamacharan Srimani had claimed as the prerogative of Indians. In articulating the uniqueness of its position, the new Orientalism thus had to underline its distance from existing Western approaches and its closeness to the Indian or nationalist viewpoint.

In the 1870s, Alexander Cunningham and James Fergusson had framed the domain of scholarship on Indian art and antiquities. By the 1900s, their position was being usurped by Ernest Binfield Havell, the reformist art teacher in Calcutta and passionate ideologue of Indian art.[44] Edging out his predecessors for being practitioners of the "archaeological," Eurocentric approach, Havell set himself up as the champion of an aesthetic and Indian point of view. In this shift of authorities, the field itself underwent a transformation: from "Indian arts and antiquities" it was now recast as "Indian art and aesthetics." Indian art was transferred from the sphere of antiquarian and archaeological expertise to that of aesthetic and spiritual empathy.

Calcutta had been the initial venue of Havell's reformist activities and assertions. In the late 1890s, he started experimenting with the Indianization of the curriculum of the Government School of Art and went on to wage a battle for the preservation of India's decorative art traditions. In Calcutta, Havell "discovered" a new hope and future for modern Indian art in Abanindranath Tagore and his "Indian-style" paintings.[45] But after 1906, Calcutta was replaced by England as the new expanding arena of Havell's fame as a crusader for Indian art. Discharged from service in India and removed from the immediate scene of policy maneuver and wrangling,[46] he made writing his main weapon against the "philistinism" of British art administrators in India and the prejudices of Western scholars.[47] The publication of his *Indian Sculpture and Painting* in 1908 saw a dramatic breakthrough in Western attitudes to Indian art, releasing a wave of new aesthetic sympathies and effecting a sweeping reversal of hierarchies—between the "materialism" of Western art and the "spirituality" of the Eastern tradition. This book, and its follow-up volume, *The Ideals of Indian Art* (1911), served as powerful manifestos of the new Orientalist discourse, attributing to Indian art a range of exclusively spiritual and transcendental attributes. In addition to attaining fine arts status and an ancient classical past, Indian art now acquired an aura of deep religiosity, a divine dispensation, and a new spirit of nationalism. These qualities were embodied in the paintings of Abanindranath Tagore and his followers.[48]

Abanindranath Tagore's booklet, *Bhārat-śilpa*, published within a year of Havell's *Indian Sculpture and Painting* and projecting the same spiritualized image of Indian art, basked in the prestige of the latter text. The alignment with the new Orientalist camp came to account for much of the power and status of Abanindranath's own nationalist cause in art. By this time, alongside the Orientalist redefinitions of the Indian art tradition, the local art scene in Calcutta had seen striking shifts in middle-class art practice and aesthetic values. These shifts had largely been initiated by Abanindranath's rejection of Western academic training and experimentation with an alternative "Indian-style" of painting. In the years of the Swadeshi movement in Bengal in the first decade of the twentieth century, these different layers of change congealed, placing Abanindranath in a unique position and authority as the true representative of Indian art.

His emergence as the archetypal nationalist artist of modern India has its well-known history. This history is seen to have its beginning in the artist's discontent with Western training and his restless search for a new creative idiom in the indigenous traditions of miniature painting and decorative arts. Havell's discovery and promotion of his art in 1902 and a prize at Curzon's Delhi Durbar exhibition that winter for his Mughal-style paintings launched Abanindranath in his role of a national artist. In 1905, he was inducted by Havell into the post of vice principal of the Government School of Art, where the first group of students gathered around the guru, inaugurating his career as leader of a "new school of Indian painting."[49] Abanindranath's special position came to rest not just on the novelty of his art style but also on the new romantic ideal of an artist that he personified.

This is where we confront the crucial difference between Shyamacharan's and Abanindranath's artistic self-definitions. This difference allowed Abanindranath to construct the separateness of his own position as a genius, free from the trammels of education and rules, and professional and commercial demands. His rejection of colonial art education entailed also a rejection of its end product: its packaging of the artist as a Western-trained professional and a successful academic oil painter. Instead, his notion of a true artist came to revolve around a new hierarchy of values in art, placing *śakh* above *śikṣā*, inspiration above training, self-expression above technical perfection, feeling above form.[50] Such a privileging of the artist and the act of artistic creation became central in the nationalist canon. The same romantic idealistic values, which the Orientalists saw as the essence of ancient Indian art, were transposed onto the modern reconstructed "Indian-style" paintings of Abanindranath and his students. In these values, in this new aestheticized aura that enveloped the ideas of art and artist, lay the legitimizing stamp of Indianness. In them lay embedded the perceived embryonic links between the old and the new.

In the 1870s, Shyamacharan Srimani had struggled to accommodate his practice of teaching geometrical and mechanical drawing with a more exalted notion of fine arts that he claimed for ancient India. Like many others around him, he had been caught in the contrary pulls of the past and the present, between the pride of a glorious autonomous past and the despair of a present that could be redeemed only through a Western model of progress. By the 1900s, such tensions seem to be resolved in Abanindranath, as he consciously placed himself outside the pale of colonial values and practices, drawing the past and present together in a new symbiosis in his art. As a teacher at the Government School of Art, he insisted on demarcating the specialty of his status vis-à-vis the standard curriculum of the institution. He had taken up the job on the understanding that he could function there in an independent capacity, as a guru. Working on his own paintings, he would be watched by a group of students who took their work to him for his viewing and corrections.[51] What he aimed to disseminate was not formal training, nor techniques and skills, but the right "Indian" sensibilities and aesthetic disposition. The idea was to break the rigors of colonial pedagogy and create a new aesthetic sphere for Indian art activity.

Abanindranath's *BS*, while it elaborated on the nature of India's art heritage, powerfully propagated this heightened self-image of the artist and his art. The didactic intent of the booklet is clear from its English subtitle: "A Treatise on the Excellence of Indian Art and Reasons for Its Revival." Writing served the same cause that Abanindranath was upholding as an "Indian-style" painter and teacher. The first of Abanindranath's many writings on Indian art, *BS*, when it appeared in 1909, was already invested with the full-blown authority of his position as the cult figure of the nationalist art movement. I will now look more closely at some of the claims to authoritative and authentic knowledge in *BS*.

New Claims to Authority and Authenticity

On the face of it, it is difficult to treat this book (as would be true of most of Abanindranath's subsequent writings on the subject) as a history or a scholarly exposition on Indian art. As in Havell's writings, the arguments in *BS* are more emotional than academic. Yet, quite distinct from Havell's writing, the book stands apart in its wit and rhetoric, its imaginative metaphors, and its vivid word pictures. The use of Bengali involves here an entirely different narrative mode, and the polemical force of the book is intricately woven into this linguistic ambience. In *BS*, we can trace elements of the same style and flourish that characterize Abanindranath's stories for children—a genre of writing in which he had already excelled.[52] But targeted for a different purpose and readership, the language of *BS* moves constantly between the picturesque and the rhetorical, between description and persuasion.

At one level, the book can be read as an indigenous supplement to the new Orientalist discourse on Indian art. It propagated an identical construct of the spiritual, metaphysical essence of ancient Indian art, feeding on the same polarities between Western and Eastern aesthetics, between Western naturalism and Eastern symbolism. At another level, the book is shot through with a strident nationalism and strong proprietary rights over the nation's art heritage. The "right" understanding and appreciation of Indian art is mobilized into a category of nationalist thought. Let us follow through the text the close overlapping of the two levels at which *BS* functioned, appropriating Orientalist knowledge within its nationalist agenda.

From Shyamacharan Srimani down to Abanindranath Tagore, the muse of Indian art was invoked in the same gendered image of purity and tradition. The figure of a chaste and demure Hindu bride was the choice motif of both books. In Shyamacharan's, she was invested with a religious sanctity, similar to that of the inner sanctum of a temple. The metaphor signified the exclusion of all foreigners and a sealing off of the nation's own exclusive terrain. With Abanindranath, the metaphor acquired a more pointed edge, as did the claims and assertions it embodied. The figure of the Hindu wife was not merely cordoned off from the Western and public gaze. Within the space of the home, she was set off against the figure of the memsahib who had usurped her place, the latter a symbol of the borrowed Westernized culture that had infiltrated the innermost reaches of Indian life.[53] The beauty, dignity, and traditional attire of the one were contrasted with the superficial glamour, glitter, and brashness of the other:

> We are no longer satisfied that our son should set up home with a plain homely wife; we are now busy searching for a *mem* [Westernized] bride to bring home. We are no longer happy that our *kalā-lakṣmī*—the innocent Hindu girl, with kajal in her eyes, vermillion on her forehead, clothed in a resplendent Benarasi sari—will, with the soft tinkle of her anklets, brighten up our lives, and as *gṛha-lakṣmī* bring to it beauty and prosperity. We want a bride we can pass off as a memsahib. We no longer care for the goddess on a lotus-seat blessing us with her protection. We desire instead that half-undressed other woman, reclining on a couch, portrayed on a gilded frame, preening with an ostrich-feather fan in hand.[54]

Thus, the ideal of Indian art was intricately woven in with the complementary ideal of *gṛha-lakṣmī*, where the Hindu woman was reified as the auspicious symbol of tradition, domestic order, harmony, and plenitude. The notion had rich resonances in nationalist discourse, where it repeatedly figured as a residual patriarchal motif suggesting all that was pure, unadulterated, and uncontaminated in tradition. In equating *bhārat-śilpa* with images of *kalā-lakṣmī* and *gṛha-lakṣmī*, Abanindranath's project of recovering Indian art situated itself within the nostalgic realm of the home and its private sphere. It associated itself with a return to what was truly one's own—with the rediscovery of true love after the infatuation with a foreign mistress.

Since it was something that was so intimately theirs, Abanindranath thought it absurd that Indian art should have to be explained to India's people. Just as art was a matter of talent and inspiration, its appreciation, too, had to be natural and instinctive; neither art nor art appreciation, could, in his view, be taught. Like his role as an art teacher and "Indian-style" painter, Abanindranath's role as an author was pitched more at the level of rhetorical persuasion and creative example than that of instruction. All through, we find him arguing against reason and logic, facts and proofs, emphasizing empathy and intuition as the key to the subject of Indian art:[55]

> To find out what a rosogolla is, you have to taste it. In the same way, to find out what Indian art means, let me give you a local painting, a sculpture, a Kashmiri shawl, a Benarasi sari; or let me conjure before you a temple, a mosque, an old palace, or some local toys, utensils or luxurious furniture; there stretched out before you are the skies, the forests, the rivers, the mountains of India; next to you are your [classical] poetry, rhetoric, drama, legends, the Vedas and the Vedanta, and millions and millions of your countrymen. Look at them, touch them, study them, just as you would taste a rosogolla. Find out for yourself what Indian art is: don't trouble me needlessly. And if that doesn't satisfy you, go to a European chemical examiner. That man has never tasted a rosogolla in his life, but he can give you a full list of its chemical ingredients.[56]

He saw it to be a reflection of the shameful, denationalized state of Indians that they needed their art explained to them and that he had to write such a tract to impress upon them the full worth of the nation's artistic heritage. Compressed into Abanindranath's tirade was the idea of Indian art and Indian traditions as the most natural of choices and inheritances. The imagery used clearly connotes a sense of the "local" and "natural," labeling the fascination for the foreign as an aberration and a blot on the "national character." It was understandable that Westerners would require initiation into the mysteries of Indian art or that Western scholars would write volumes trying to grapple with the subject. But Abanindranath placed himself and his Bengali readers on a totally different plane, where Indian art needed to be retrieved from the clutches of dry scholarship and reclaimed in terms of emotion and aesthetic sensibility. This is how he laid out a clear difference between "Western" and "Indian" knowledges, between a knowledge that had to be acquired and cultivated and one that was instinctive, natural, and deep-rooted. This is how he also demarcated the uniqueness of his own stand, even within the new sphere of Orientalist engagement with Indian art.

Abanindranath referred his readers to three main schools of Western approaches to Indian art. There was the "conservative" school, represented by scholars like Ruskin, who looked to Indian art only for definitions of the "barbaric" and "monstrous," as a point of contrast with the "beauty" of the Greek classical tradition. Then there was the school of archaeologists and antiquarians who had built up their expertise on excavating sites and in classifying styles and periods, but who had emptied the subject of all aesthetic content. This school, too, was trapped in a "Greek bias," applying the conventions of classical Greek art as a universal standard of evaluation, attributing whatever little they considered of merit in Indian art to Greek influence. Finally, there was a third, emerging, school of writing, consisting then of only one or two representatives, who had been able to break free of Eurocentric standards to appreciate Indian art in terms of its alternative "idealistic" philosophy, who responded to Indian art "not just with their brains but with their heart and soul."[57] Abanindranath traced the lineage of his book to this third line of "authentic" knowledge, even as he claimed for himself the most privileged insider's view.

BS is strewn with the evidence of close partnership between the author and his guru, Havell, in their joint crusade for Indian art. We know from Havell's correspondence that Abanindranath had supplied him with interpretations of iconography and notes from Sanskrit aesthetic texts for his books.[58] For Havell, Abanindranath embodied both a source of correct information and the true aesthetic spirit of Indian art. In turn, we find Abanindranath repeatedly invoking the authority of Havell in presenting his own formulations on Indian art.

For instance, as with the new Orientalists, so also with Abanindranath it became a central issue to dismantle the theory of Greek influence in Indian art. The primacy accorded to Graeco-Roman influences in Indian art had brought to bear a disproportionate attention on the Buddhist sculptures of Gandhara. A systematic inversion of the Gandhara bias became a major theme in the new Orientalist discourse: it provided a platform on which Indian art staked its claims to a superior aesthetics and its own independent history of evolution.[59] Dismissing the Gandhara style as not only marginal to Indian art history but also "hybrid" and "debased," Abanindranath saw Gandhara as a sign of the broader destruction and corruption that ensued from India's contacts with Western culture. The recent history of Indian art, he believed, showed the worst traces of the intrusion of the West. But the tide in the contact of cultures, he wrote, would once again turn away from the West toward its "original" source in the East. Using the allegory of the rising sun and the break of dawn, he conjured up the vision of the reawakening of Oriental art and culture.[60]

This dream of an "Oriental renaissance" revolved around a pan-Asian notion of a single unified entity of Asiatic art, combining the heritage of the three ancient civilizations of India, China, and Japan. Such a pan-Asian ideal had its most powerful spokesman then in the Japanese scholar-ideologue Kakuzo Okakura, who, in 1903, had authored a book entitled *The Ideals of the East.*[61] Okakura's credentials in the West as "the foremost living authority on Oriental archaeology and art" were reinforced by his efforts at home "in the direction of a strong renationalizing of Japanese art."[62] Breaking away from the Imperial Art School, Okakura had set up an alternative institution that would become the center of a movement toward a reinforced Japanese artistic identity. Okakura and his school of painters became major inspirational figures for Abanindranath and his nationalist art circle. *The Ideals of the East* became a central text of the new Orientalism—an Orientalism that was in search not merely of antiquity and a lost civilization in the East but of a living wave of spirituality that could resist the colonization of the West.

In Calcutta in 1902, as a guest of the Tagores, Okakura had Sister Nivedita write the introduction for his forthcoming book, *The Ideals of the East.* Mobilizing Okakura's pan-Asian aesthetic to the cause of a nationalist art revival in India, Nivedita expanded to new proportions the idea of India as the fountainhead of Asiatic thought and religion. Okakura had looked admiringly toward India as he traced in the encounter with Indian Buddhism and its "original stream of abstract idealism" the seeds of the best of Chinese and Japanese art. For Nivedita, the spread of Buddhism to China and Japan implied a wider transference of the philosophy and culture of the "mother-religion," Hinduism, and with it, the essence of Indian civilization. And she even read into Okakura's book the promise of the reunification of Asia under the aegis of a revitalized Hinduism, enabling its united force to then sweep through the West.[63]

Offset by Okakura's book and Nivedita's introduction, Abanindranath's notion of an Asiatic art indulged in the same national egoism. Once again, Indian art was identified as the master tradition of Asia, the source from which influences spread outward in the great age of Buddhism. The greatness of Indian art, Abanindranath argued, lay in that it neither lost its individuality nor destroyed the individuality of the other art traditions in the process of diffusion. From China and Japan to the deserts of Turkey, he could discern traces of the same art that adorned the Bharhut *stupa* or the Ajanta caves of India.[64] Like any form of great art, Indian art left its mark without deleting the marks of those local traditions.

The progression from an Orientalist to an Indian nationalist standpoint hinged on the notion of art as spiritual meditation. In a chapter entitled "Mānas-carcā," the very idea of art was equated with "the cult of the mind and spirit," echoing the new Orientalist ideas about the transcendental perceptions in Indian art as against the objective imitation of nature in Western art.[65] The mind was rendered into an all-privileged category of artistic creation. The main mission of the artist was to move beyond the outer illusion of optical appearances to express an idealized inner vision of the mind; in the process, he could move from the natural to the divine order of things. In another chapter, "Śilpe trimūrti," Abanindranath exalted such a meditative, transcendental vision as a universal quality of all "great art," discovering it within the three greatest art traditions of the ancient world: the Greek, the Japanese, and the Aryan Hindu.[66] Yet, within this common ancient classical heritage, Indian art (as the core of the whole entity of Asiatic art) was singled out as the highest vehicle of a spiritual aesthetic. *Dhyāna-yoga*, or spiritual contemplation of the divine, was highlighted as the most distinctive attribute of the Indian art tradition.

For Abanindranath, the nature of the national art tradition was best encapsulated in two ancient samples, one belonging to the realm of the plastic arts, the other to the realm of aesthetics: the first was the image of the *dhyānī* Buddha, the other the art treatise of Śukrācārya. The *dhyānī* Buddha had already acquired its special status in Havell's *Indian Sculpture and Painting,* where it had featured as the ultimate expression of the divine ideal in Indian art. Fighting the exaggerated importance attached to the Gandhara sculptures, the prior and parallel heritage of Buddha images from Mathura, Sarnath, and Borobudur was held up as the more authentic Indian type and the genuine exemplars of India's spiritual aesthetic. Abanindranath backed his selection of the Buddha image with a long quotation from Havell's book. Soon, the same image of the *dhyānī* Buddha gained an international charisma. As the target of George Birdwood's oft-quoted notorious declamation, in a debate sparked off by Havell's address at the Royal Society of Arts in London in 1910,[67] it became the prime symbol of the Orientalist defense and of the new wave of empathy with Indian art that swept British art circles.[68]

In his choice of the other sample of the Indian art tradition, Abanindranath was again following an Orientalist trend of privileging textual canons in the study of Indian art. Whereas Ram Raz and Shyamacharan had highlighted a text such as *Mānasāra*, a treatise on ancient Indian temple architecture, in Abanindranath's time the *Śukranītisāra*, with its prescriptions on the construction of divine idols, came to occupy a central place in the efforts of scholars to define a set of indigenous aesthetic conventions. Coomaraswamy had drawn heavily on its example in presenting the concept of *dhyāna-yoga* as the central philosophy of Indian art and in equating the role of the artist and the worshipper in the creation of divine images.[69] Abanindranath referred to selected stanzas of the *Śukranītisāra* on the construction of images to the same end and effect. In a later article entitled "Mūrti" (which in 1914 was published in English as *Some Notes on Indian Artistic Anatomy*) he once again used the prescriptive norms of *Śukranītisāra*, along with those from another text, *Pratimā-lakṣaṇā* (a chapter of the *Bṛhat saṃhitā*), to outline a set of anatomical norms for the construction of the human figure in Indian art. For Ram Raz, the text had formed the main point of entry into the subject, and the main frame for its description and analyses. For writers like Abanindranath, on the contrary, the texts served more as sources of sanction and legitimacy for the kind of metaphysical aesthetic vision they had constructed for all of Indian art. They provided an ancient and classical genealogy to the current art theories that were being applied in the defense and valorization of Indian art.

Arrogating Power and Prerogative

From Shyamacharan Srimani to Abanindranath Tagore, the idea of art and artistic excellence had been radically overhauled. In the 1870s, Western academic conventions, with the emphasis on "correct" representational skills and techniques, had prevailed as a universal standard. By the 1900s, a different neo-Platonic aesthetic had intervened to challenge the primacy of illusionist appearances and to associate the whole notion of art with the metaphysical ideal that reigned behind material realities. Emerging out of a profound European dissatisfaction in the late nineteenth century with academic and neoclassical art, the aesthetic searched out its alternative criteria in Gothic and pre-Renaissance art forms, and lodged itself at the center of the Orientalist fascination with the markedly different conventions of Indian art. Orientalist and nationalist art parlance in Bengal came under the predominant sway of this aesthetic, as it rejected the path of colonial progress and reveled in the "superior" ideals of ancient Indian civilization.

Yet, even as aesthetic standards shifted grounds, what continued from Shyamacharan to Abanindranath was a reduction of the whole idea of Indian art to an ancient Hindu core: a collapsing of its wide and diverse history into a Buddhist and Hindu essence and a "golden age" of the Maurya and Gupta period. Abanindranath, in *BS*, did not attempt to present anything like a connected or continuous history. For him, the story of Indian art was self-evidently the story only of the ancient Buddhist and Hindu art of the land he invoked as "Āryāvarta." In a reaction against what was termed as the archaeological and antiquarian mode of scholarship, he deferred from any specific definitions of styles and forms, or any classification of genres and periods, even within this selected classical canon. His was an emotional, free-wheeling discourse on the spiritual aesthetics of Indian art. That aesthetic in itself framed the definition of Indian-ness, as did the exclusion of the entire medieval and late medieval phases of Indian art history, and the whole corpus of the Islamic schools of architecture and painting.

In the three-tiered construction of Indian history into Hindu, Muslim, and British periods, only the first was of consequence in identifying a unique and autonomous art tradition for the nation. This appears surprising in an artist who was drawing so directly from Mughal, Pahari, and provincial miniature painting traditions in his experiments with a new "Indian style," an artist whose own style seemed immediately reminiscent of India's medieval miniature painting heritage. It points to a fundamental tension between pictorial form and aesthetic assertions that was deeply embedded within Calcutta's nationalist art movement. Whatever his own choices in practice, Abanindranath's entire construct of the "idealistic" character of Indian art was such that it could never make room for the "secular" court painting traditions of the Mughal and Pahari schools on the same level as the "religious" genres of Buddhist and Hindu art.

In the subsequent decade, as Mughal architecture and painting and the Rajput and Pahari miniatures began increasingly to feature in Orientalist and nationalist writing, they were accommodated within a hieratic pattern of art history that placed the religious above the secular, the Buddhist and Hindu above the Mughal, the ancient above the medieval past. And Abanindranath would establish his own artistic and Indian pedigree in relation to his pictorial sources by underlining the way he infused a missing emotional element (*bhāva*) into the intricate workmanship of Mughal miniature techniques.[70] While Mughal painting was defined in terms of a lack, Abanindranath's own position as an "Indian-style" painter and a modern master was defined in terms of what he filled in, namely, emotions and ideals. What he avowedly drew from Mughal painting was mainly an ornamental technique. The aesthetic sensibility with which he redeemed it was the gift of an ancient spiritual past that he carried over into his modern artistic self.

In the end, *BS* returns us to the issue of the uniqueness of the artist's own stand within the tradition and the subject he sought to explicate. While spirituality was upheld as the most distinctive feature of Indian art, art was interpreted as a religion in itself. The book's last chapter, "Ārṭ o ārṭisṭ," comes laden with the terminology of *dhyāna* and *sādhanā* as the sole means of artistic initiation, casting a thick aura around the image of the artist:

> Aesthetic sensibility, intense thought and emotion, a discerning taste, . . . single-minded dedication, self-control, a quest for knowledge, a deep attachment to one's country, and skills in drawing and painting—only through such an aggregation of numerous qualities is an artist made. Just as there are nine signs of the high lineage of the *kulīn*, so there are many more signs of the lineage of an artist.[71]

Abanindranath reserved for himself this hallowed status of an artist—a status that automatically endowed him with exclusive access to Indian art and exclusive powers to propagate its cause. In the process, as both artist and author, he located his impact and influence within a space quite different from that of the European Orientalists.

Havell's *Indian Sculpture and Painting* found important local publicity in Sister Nivedita's three-part review that appeared in 1909 in the *Modern Review*.[72] That same year, its ideas found a still more powerful point of local dissemination in Abanindranath's *BS*. As excerpts from the book began simultaneously to appear as articles in the journal *Bhāratī*,[73] the ideas gathered an altogether new pace and momentum. Vis-à-vis Havell, Abanindranath emerged as a new source of charismatic authority and leadership in the campaign for Indian art. *BS*, in its timing and enunciative strategy, stands as a subtle exercise in such a displacement and appropriation of power within the nationalist art movement. The booklet has been obscured in history by Abanindranath's other more prominent writings on art, particularly his later body of essays in *Bāgeśvarī śilpa-prabandhābalī*. These dominate his image as an aesthete and commentator on matters artistic, and stand as supreme examples of his evocative style of prose, but *BS*, with all its ardor and polemics, needs to be retrieved and relocated.

BS marks a moment when Orientalist knowledge gets effectively transmuted into the language of art criticism and nationalist aesthetic discourse in Bengal. It also provides, in an early concentrated form, the full flavor of the emotional and mystical ambience that came to surround the redefinition of the subject of Indian art history. What comes up in *BS* as a resistance to a dry, classificatory, documentative form of scholarship, and to the earlier "archaeological" and Eurocentric biases, was already inscribing itself within the new Orientalist writing as a counterdisciplinary mode. It became central in the constitution of Indian art as a new "spiritual" and "aesthetic" field. The staging of Indian art history as a counterdiscipline would revolve around the privileging of intuition over reason, of aesthetic sensibility over orders and systems, of spiritual empathy over acquired knowledge. We encounter the first effects of this process in Abanindranath's *BS* as it unfolded with all the force and persuasion of the dissenting nationalist voice. We see the way in which the author's strategies of retreat and reclaim effect the process: his refusal to explain Indian art to his own people slides subtly into an assertion of superior knowledge and understanding and a deliberate reification of the subject. The entire subject of "Indian art and aesthetics" was sealed off in terms of its restricted access and appeal to the initiated.

Abanindranath's singular stance found powerful replication and reinforcement in the celebrated battles waged by Havell and Coomaraswamy for Indian art on the international front. Over the next decades, the demarcation of an autonomous, esoteric sphere for the subject went hand in hand with the institutional monopolization of Indian art history by the new "transcendentalist" camp and its "aesthetic" dispensation. Shyamacharan's first Bengali history of Indian art, in seeking to disseminate modern knowledge, had attempted to throw open the doors of what he saw to be both an unknown and an exclusive terrain. Abanindranath's book, by contrast, in removing the subject from the clutches of colonial knowledge, marked a fresh bounding in of the terrain, with new codes of authority and exclusiveness. Those codes would soon become synonymous with the framing of Indian art history as a new discipline.

Notes

1. *Bhārat saṃskārak*, 16 Phālgun 1280 (1874). Extracts of reviews of Shyamacharan Srimani's *Sūkṣaśilper utpatti o āryajātir śilpacāturi* (1874) were published in the following year at the end of another book by Srimani, *Siṃhal-bijay-kābya*.

2. Shyamacharan Srimani, *Sūkṣaśilper utpatti o āryajātir śilpacāturi*; Abanindranath Thakur, *Bhārat śilpa*. A reprint of the entire text of Shyamacharan's book is available in Shobhon Shome and Anil Acharya, eds., *Baṅlā śilpasamālocanār dhārā*.

3. "Bhūmikā," *AS*, p. 6.

4. Letter from H. H. Locke, 4 February 1874, *AS*, pp. 4-5.

5. The nature of this emerging professional group of Bengali artists, the structure of their training, patronage, and livelihood, has been discussed in Guha-Thakurta, *New "Indian" Art,* pp. 45-92.

6. On the setting up and the early history of the School of Art in Calcutta, see Bagal, *History*; also see the detailed report by Principal W. H. Jobbins on the functioning of the school, incorporated in *Papers Related to the Maintenance of the Schools of Art as State Institutions* (Lahore, 1896), pp. 88-94.

7. Referred to in Jogeschandra Bagal, *Hindu melār itibṛtta,* pp. 83-85.

8. For a recent discussion of Winckelmann's notions of progress and excellence in European art and the "chain" of artistic evolution in classical antiquity, see Jenkins, *Archaeologists.*

9. Discussed at length in Mitter, *Much Maligned Monsters,* pp. 189-220.

10. Dilip K. Chakrabarti, *History of Indian Archaeology,* provides an extensive history of the Western interest and engagement with Indian antiquities in colonial India.

11. The full details of Cunningham's archaeological excavations, methods, and conclusions are compiled in Imam, *Cunningham.* More important in this context is Chandra, *Study of Indian Art,* which situates the writings of Cunningham and Fergusson within the framework of an evolving methodology of Indian art history.

12. Cole, *Catalogue.* Discussed in Mitter, *Much Maligned Monsters,* pp. 256-60.

13. Cole, *Catalogue,* pp. 6-16.

14. Already, in his *Illustrated Handbook of Architecture,* Fergusson had worked out his main structure for the history of Indian architecture, identifying ancient Buddhist, Jain, and Hindu architecture as prime examples of a "true" organic style and placing it as the starting point (topographically and chronologically) of his world architectural history. The picture and arguments therein became the core of his comprehensive *History of Indian and Eastern Architecture.*

15. *Ancient Architecture in Hindostan,* which was among Fergusson's earliest publications, grew directly out of the extensive study tours he undertook across India between 1835 and 1842, in the course of his career as an indigo merchant.

16. Fergusson delivered a lecture, "The Study of Indian Architecture," at a meeting of the Society of Arts, London, in 1866, in which he elaborated not only the aesthetic/historical/ethnographical need for the study of Indian architecture but also laid out the principles he felt to be germane to such a study. The lecture was published in 1867.

17. *AS,* pp. 7-17.

18. See Mitter, *Much Maligned Monsters,* pp. 258-68, on the varied use of the Aryan race theory in Cole's and Fergusson's analyses of Indian art history.

19. *AS,* pp. 19-21.

20. Ibid., pp. 53-55, 63-76.

21. Ibid., pp. 51-52.

22. Ram Raz, *Essay,* pp. iii-ix.

23. *AS,* p. 22.

24. Ibid., pp. 23-29.

25. Ibid., pp. 33-55.

26. Ibid., pp. 63-76.

27. In particular, they anticipate the art criticism of Balendranath Tagore, published in the journal *Sādhanā* in the early 1890s—the way he discovered a new Indian "high art" form in the mythological paintings of Ravi Varma, marking in them the "right" combination of academic realism and lyric emotions of the Sanskrit texts. See Balendranath Thakur, *Citra o kābya,* pp. 97-113.

28. *AS,* pp. 68-71.

29. Ibid., pp. 72-74.

30. Referred to in Shobhon Shome and Anil Acharya, eds., *Bāṅlā śilpasamālocanār dhārā,* pp. 5-6.

31. *Siṃhal-bijay-kābya,* "Bhūmikā."

32. *AS,* p. 76.

33. Rajendralal Mitra, *Antiquities.*

34. This process and its implications are discussed in greater detail in Guha-Thakurta, "Ideology."

35. *Baṅgadarśan,* Bhādra 1281 (1874).

36. *Baṅkim racanābalī*, vol. 2, pp. 192-94.

37. Charuchandra Nag, *Citrabidyā*, pp. 1-3.

38. This type of art manual and serialized lessons about art in journals, propagating the same visual values and the same "scientific" conventions of drawing and painting, continued to thrive in Bengal into the first decades of the twentieth century. Marginalized by Abanindranath Tagore's "new school of Indian-style painting," they nonetheless fed on a persisting local demand. We find examples in the serialized drawing and painting lessons by Manmathanath Chakravarti, "Barṇa-citraṇ," in his journal *Śilpa o sāhitya* 1312 (1905) and 1315 (1908-9), and Baradakanta Datta, "Citrabidyā o prakṛtijñān," *Bhāratbarṣa*, Māgh 1322 (1915-16).

39. "Sūcanā,", *Śilpa-puṣpāñjali* 1 (1886), pp. 2-3.

40. Ibid., "Citrabidyār upayogitā" and "Citrabidyā," pp. 30-31, 70-71, 73-76, 117, and passim.

41. For illustrations and discussions of these *Śilpa-puṣpāñjali* pictures and other similar genres of "improved" realistic Hindu mythological pictures that circulated in Calcutta from the 1870s onward, see Guha-Thakurta, *New "Indian" Art*, pp. 78-116.

42. See ibid., pp. 146-211, for an analysis of these reinterpretations and the new agenda of a "renaissance."

43. For the expanded workings of the archaeological establishment in the Curzonian era, see Chakrabarti, *History*, pp. 120-29; and Sourindranath Roy, "Indian Archaeology."

44. For details on Havell's career in Calcutta and his writings, see Guha-Thakurta, *New "Indian" Art*, pp. 149-59, 175-84.

45. Havell's first statement on this can be found in his article "Some Notes on Indian Pictorial Art," in the *Studio*, 15 October 1902, where he reproduced for the first time the new "Indian-style" paintings of Abanindranath and placed them in line with India's past "great art" traditions.

46. Havell left Calcutta in 1906, initially on sick leave, later to be discharged from further service in India.

47. The term and the accusations it entailed are well encapsulated in an earlier article, "British Philistinism."

48. E. B. Havell, *Indian Sculpture and Painting* and *Ideals of Indian Art*.

49. Abanindranath's own memoirs, *Gharoyā* (1941), *Āpankathā* (1946), and *Joḍāsāṅkor dhāre* (1944), in *Abanīndra racanābalī*, (collected works) give us a significant autobiographical reconstruction of the history of his emergence as a nationalist artist and stand as vital texts on the artist's self-image.

50. Such a case is repeatedly stated, for instance, in the memoirs *Gharoyā* and *Joḍāsāṅkor dhāre*, and in another small tract he wrote, *Priyadarśikā*.

51. *Joḍāsāṅkor dhāre* in *Abanīndra racanābalī*, pp. 307-11.

52. Abanindranath's first self-illustrated children's stories, *Śakuntalā* and *Kṣīrer putul,* came out in 1896, and his collection of Rajput tales, *Rājkāhinī*, was published in 1909, the same year as *Bhārat-śilpa*.

53. *BS*, pp. 2-3.

54. Ibid., p. 3.

55. Ibid., pp. 8-10.

56. Ibid., pp. 9-10.

57. Ibid., pp. 11-12.

58. Letters from Abanindranath to Havell, July 1907 to September 1908. Havell Papers, Rabindra Bhavan Archives, Santiniketan.

59. For an elaboration of this point of view, see, for instance, Havell, *Indian Sculpture and Painting*, pp. 83-109, or A. K. Coomaraswamy's article, "The Influence of Greek on Indian Art" (lecture delivered at the 15th International Orientalist Congress at Copenhagen in 1908) in his *Essays*.

60. *BS*, p. 19.

61. On Okakura's life and work, see Sister Nivedita's introduction to Okakura, *Ideals of the East.* Also see Surendranath Tagore, "Kakuzo Okakura."

62. Nivedita's introduction, to Okakura, *Ideals of the East*, pp. ix–x.

63. Ibid., pp. xv–xviii.

64. *BS*, p. 27.

65. Ibid., pp. 40–43.

66. Ibid., pp. 57–58.

67. Denying the very existence of "fine arts" in India, Birdwood had said of this Buddha image: "A boiled suet pudding would serve equally well as a symbol of passionless purity and serenity of soul." E. B. Havell, "Art Administration," p. 287.

68. Letter by William Rothenstein and twelve other prominent artists and critics in passionate defense of Indian art, in the *Times* (London), 28 February 1910, quoted in Mitter, *Much Maligned Monsters*, p. 270. Here the Buddha image was highlighted as the supreme embodiment of the "central religious and divine inspiration" of Indian art.

69. "The Aims and Methods of Indian Art," in Coomaraswamy, *Essays.*

70. *Joḍāsāṅkor dhāre*, pp. 308–9.

71. *BS*, p. 82.

72. *Modern Review*, October, November, December 1909.

73. *Bhāratī*, Āṣāḍh 1316 (1909), Āśvin 1318 (1911).

4 / A Modern Science of Politics for the Colonized

Partha Chatterjee

Sometime in the 1870s, a schoolteacher in a district town in eastern Bengal—a young man in his twenties—was writing a letter to a friend who was then on a trip to Europe. It was a letter in verse. What, it asked, had the friend seen in Europe? What had he seen of Britain, land of heroes, whose might was unequaled in the whole world? What had he seen of France, whose achievements in the sciences and the arts had taken that country to the very peak of civilization? What about Russia, "that barbaric land of snow?" And Germany, "blessed by the goddess of learning?" What had he seen in Italy, where the glories of ancient Rome mingled with the energies of Young Italy? In what great spiritual exercise, the young poet asked, was Europe engaged? Those who once lagged far behind were now on top: was Europe not truly advanced in learning, in religion, in industriousness, in the qualities of character?[1]

Anandachandra Mitra (1854-1903), the writer of this letter, belonged to the nineteenth-century reformist sect known as the Brahmo Samaj and came from the famous Dacca village of Bajrajogini, home of many distinguished graduates of the University of Calcutta in the late nineteenth century. Like most of them, Anandachandra came from a family of impoverished small landowners, and as a student in Calcutta probably faced considerable financial hardship. All available biographical sketches refer to the poverty that forced him to give up further education and take a job as a schoolmaster in Mymensingh.[2] His literary output was driven as much by the desire to achieve financial success as it was by the urging of the muse. His book of epic verse, *Helenākābya*, when it was first published in Mymemsingh in 1876, came out with a foreword by Srinath Chanda, headmaster of his school, who after discussing the literary features of the book added, not entirely gratuitously, that the author was "a scholar and a gifted man. Owing to his poverty, he has been denied higher education. . . . He has now made up his mind to go to Europe for further studies."[3] And two years later, when one of Anandachandra's many textbooks was published in Calcutta, Srinath Chanda made his appeal in unambiguous terms: "One of the reasons for publishing this book is the expectation of financial support for further education. It is our firm belief that the discerning and educated public will reward the labors and encourage the talents of the writer."[4]

Anandachandra wrote a lot of poetry, most of it unremarkable. "Inspired by the encouragement given by some friends,"[5] he published his first book of poems when he was only seventeen. He is chiefly noticed in the history of nineteenth-century Bengali literature as a writer of book-length epic poems somewhat in the style of Michael Madhusudan Dutt. *Helenākābya* retells the Greek story of the beautiful wife of Menelaus and her abduction by Paris, but is interesting for its repeated use of metaphors drawn from Indian mythology. Even a well-wisher such as Srinath Chanda, writing the foreword to the book, had to anticipate the obvious objection: "We realize that many will not be able to resist laughing when they hear Helen speak about Radha. It is not as though the poet too does not realize this. But it is futile to try and explain to the incredulous the reasons for his audacity."[6] Another epic, *Bhāratmaṅgal*, describing the present condition of India, was four hundred pages long and contained innumerable footnotes explaining its geographical, historical, and literary references.[7]

Most of Anandachandra's verse is suffused with patriotic sentiments. His critics, unable to find much to praise in the formal qualities of his poetry, have usually seized upon this as a significant aspect of his literary output. As a young man, Anandachandra was greatly influenced by the austerity and zeal of Sibnath Sastri, the Brahmo preacher, and along with fellow Brahmos Bipinchandra Pal and Sundarimohan Das had taken an oath to worship only the one God, not to observe caste distinctions, and never to work for the government.[8] Politically, he shared with the English-educated nationalist elite of his time a broadly liberal and progressive view of history and society, but, when he wrote his obligatory hymn to Queen Victoria, he ended with the somewhat ironic request not to be treated by her as "a son guilty of treason."[9]

A Text of Political Science

Vyavahār darśan: to most native speakers of Bengali today, the name of the book will make little sense. *Vyavahār* (or *byabahār*, if we dispense with the Sanskritized transliteration) is now most commonly used in Bengali to mean "behavior," "manner," or "to put to use."[10] *Darśan*, when it occurs in the title of a scholarly book, could only denote "philosophy." Those acquainted with sociological terminology might suppose, therefore, that the book is about "the philosophy of behavior" or "behaviorism," but coming from 1878 that hardly seems likely. If one is a little more conversant with the earlier, and somewhat more technical uses of the word, one would know, of course, that *vyavahāra* was a term employed in the *Dharmaśāstra* literature to mean "law," or more precisely "litigation," because there was nothing in that literature that would be an exact equivalent of "law" in the European sense. It was a set of practical guidelines on how judicial authorities should resolve disputes over conflicting interpretations of the dharma. By the nineteenth century, however, the word was often used to mean "law" in the Western sense. Even quite recently, a Bengali word sometimes used on formal occasions for "lawyer" was *byabahārjībī*, one whose livelihood is the law. Consequently, although the obvious term for "law" in contemporary Bengali would be *āin*, adopted from the Arabic, one might feel tempted to congratulate oneself on having solved a nineteenth-century puzzle by deciding that the title of Anandachandra's book must mean "the philosophy of law."

One would not be entirely off the mark, and yet one would not be wholly correct either. An examination of the title page of the book reveals that after the words *vyavahār darśan*, printed in bold characters, it says on the next line, *pratham khaṇḍa*, i.e., volume 1, and on the following line, in parentheses, *upakramaṇikā bhāq*, or introductory part. Next, in roman small capitals, Anandachandra supplies us with an English equivalent of the title: "Or," it says, "an Introduction to the Science of Politics." That, we can be left with no doubt, was the intended description of the disciplinary field in which Anandachandra wanted his textbook to be placed.

For a Bengali book published in 1878 and intended for schoolchildren, this description must evoke considerable surprise. There was, of course, a fairly large volume of journalistic and polemical writings on political subjects by Indians at the time, as well as a few learned ones, and in Calcutta such enterprises appeared in both English and Bengali. By 1878, there were also some textbooks in Bengali dealing with political economy,[11] and it is interesting to note that in those days the subject was called *artha-byabahār*. But as far as I can tell, Anandachandra's was the first book published in India that described itself as an introduction to the science of politics.

Indeed, if we suppose that he was following a model provided by books written in English, we would be hard put to trace it. An academic field under the name "the science of politics" or "political science" had barely emerged at the time in Britain. The holdings of the British Library in the British Museum contain only four books published before 1878 with those words in their titles.[12] Judging from Anandachandra's text, only one of these four could have "influenced" the arrangement and presentation of *Byabahār darśan* (hereafter *BD*), and that presumption also applies only to the first 25 pages or so of the book's 103 pages: this is P. E. Dove's *The Science of Politics*, which carried the subtitle "Part I: The Theory of Human Progression and Natural Probability of a Reign of Justice."[13] This book was explicitly based on "the theory of progress" and argued, on the one hand, for a political science based on "the combination of knowledge and reason" and, on the other, that there was in the history of "man's practical progression . . . a natural probability in favour of the reign of justice." Faint traces of some of those arguments may be found in the early sections of Anandachandra's book, but even there, as we will soon discover, the thrust is toward an uncompromising republicanism that is completely absent in Dove. In any case, the traces that may be noticed are by no means clear enough for us to conclude that Anandachandra had available to him the English book to serve as some sort of model.

More importantly, half of the first chapter of sixty-four pages in which the main discussion of *BD* is conducted deals with the possibilities and implications of a "science of politics" for India. Needless to say, the arguments here are Anandachandra's; they are not taken over from any British text on political science. Indeed, considering the evidence available to us from both within and outside the text of *BD*, we can only endorse the disclaimer that Anandachandra makes toward the end of his introductory chapter:

> There are no books in the Bengali language for the study of the science of politics. They do, of course, exist in other languages, but I have not been able to consult them. The question might arise in the minds of some as to why in carrying out this onerous task I have neglected such an easy option. My answer is that it is in my nature as far as possible not to depend on others in accomplishing my tasks. I will certainly admit that had I studied those books before beginning my work, I would have probably done a better job. But I would have also fallen into a trap, because I would have had to remain content with merely translating books written by others. Searching for the truth by one's own efforts does involve a high probability of error; yet without it there is the

> great disadvantage that one's mind does not develop the desire for truth or the capacity for fine judgment. . . . Besides there is still another reason [for rushing into print] which I cannot disclose; for this I must beg the reader's indulgence. (pp. 61-62)

This last reason, however, is not unknown to us. Anandachandra had got it into his head that by becoming a successful author he might earn enough money to enable him to go to Britain for his education. His wishes never materialized. In any case, *BD* does not seem to have been adopted by many schools as a text suitable for their students, and it did not run to a second printing. Indeed, if this was meant to be only "the introductory part" of a multivolume work, the subsequent volumes were never published.

Science and Law

Anandachandra's political convictions were those of late-nineteenth-century liberalism. Whereas his patriotic fervor was fierce, he was very much a liberal constitutionalist and a modernist reformer.

The modernism and liberalism are evident in *BD*, as is a commitment to the "scientific" method that shows itself in the rigorously deductive form of presentation. It may be relevant to point out here that one of the striking features of the serious discursive prose employed in the new print-literature of nineteenth-century Bengal was its analytical and argumentative character. Although some of this may have been influenced by the Comtean positivist sociology much in fashion in Calcutta's high-intellectual circles of the mid-nineteenth century,[14] and some more of it may have derived from the forms of argument used in English legal literature, a more formative influence seems to have been the precolonial intellectual tradition of logic. *Navya nyāya,* or the new logic, was the most well developed and prestigious scholarly discipline in Bengal until the introduction of Western education in the early nineteenth century. Although the formal language of nyaya was Sanskrit, it is clear that arguments were conducted among Bengali logicians in the vernacular, and there exist some specimens from the early nineteenth century of introductory nyaya texts with translation and commentary in Bengali. Much of the new literati of the nineteenth century came from an intellectual background in which nyaya was still in vogue, and among the early writers of printed books and periodicals in Bengali were many who were formally trained in that discipline. If one thinks, therefore, of the linguistic preparedness of particular precolonial cultures to "receive" the discursive forms of modern science, then Bengali must be considered rather well prepared, not only because it could draw upon the vast resources of Sanskrit, but also because there was this living tradition of analytical prose.

BD begins, in the fashion customary in European social philosophy, with a general proposition about human nature: "All human beings prefer to act according to their own desires (*prabṛtti*). But desire is blind; it does not have the capacity to distinguish between good and bad. . . . Desires need to be guided. . . . That which disciplines and guides the desires along the proper path is called knowledge (*jñān*)" (p. 1). Some of the observations offered in support of this proposition are meant to be empirically valid, such as: "Even when one is ill, one's tongue craves precisely for the wrong kind of food" (p. 1). Others are analogical; thus, desire and knowledge are said to be like the feet and the eyes. The kitten, when its eyes have not opened, must feel around in the dark searching for its mother, but only a foolish kitten will choose, even after its eyes had opened, to keep them shut and fall prey to the fox (p. 2). Humans too, in the early stages of evolution, are driven mainly by desire, but in time desire has to be brought under the control of knowledge. As we will see, evolution here is meant to apply both to individual lives and to the stages of advancement of society.

At any given stage, however, it is unlikely that all people living in society will acquire and act according to knowledge. The majority of people in all societies are ignorant. Besides, even among those who have knowledge, it is likely that judgments will vary. In all societies, therefore, there are certain rules that everyone has to follow. Just as there are self-evident axioms in geometry that must be accepted as true if the science is to be developed step by step, so also there are certain fundamental rules to which obedience must be obligatory if society is to be constructed. In time, these rules are amended and refined in the light of knowledge (p. 4). "That whose study produces knowledge is called *darśan*. And the set of rules by which knowledge is translated into action is called *śāstra*" (pp. 4-5). Here Anandachandra adds that in English *darśan* is called "science," and *śāstra,* "law." All fields of knowledge, whether religion or politics, or literature, have their science as well as law. Thus, for instance, the *darśan* of religion says that it is necessary for the improvement of the human character regularly to devote some time to prayer and worship. That Sundays should be reserved for this is a dictum not of the *darśan* but of the *śāstra*. All of the detailed rules and regulations of the *śāstra* are summarized in the form of a few general principles in the *darśan* (p. 5).

Although every implication of science is not necessarily actualized in law, the latter must nevertheless always be in conformity with science. A law that is not in conformity with *darśan* is a bad law (*kuśāstra*). Thus, the science of *byabahār* tells us that the imposition of tariffs on trade between two countries acts as a barrier to free trade and is harmful to both countries. Yet many countries impose such tariffs. Tax regulations of this kind come from bad *śāstra* (pp. 6–7).

The Evolution of Society and the Emergence of Politics

In very ancient times, explains Anandachandra, when human beings were uncivilized, their actions were motivated solely by desire. People did not have the leisure to think about reason and logic. Desires belong to the realm of the heart (*hṛday*), where they take the form of faith, hope, devotion, affection, and so forth. Reason and the faculties of thought and judgment reside in the mind (*man*). In individual lives as well as in the history of human society, the faculties of the heart develop earlier than the faculties of the mind. Thus, in every country we find that the growth of religion and poetry occurred long before the advent of science. In India, for instance, the Vedas and the epics come long before the treatises of Sāṃkhya philosophy; in Greece, too, the mythologies and epic poetry such as the *Iliad* were composed several centuries before the birth of philosophers such as Plato and Aristotle (pp. 9–10).

We will soon see that this evolutionary view of social development will be employed in many different ways. Indeed, evolutionism provided perhaps the most powerful "scientific" justification in the nineteenth century (and its uses have not ended even today) for hierarchizing and normalizing human groups. In colonial ideology, its use was pervasive. But within the colonized, it was also used by the aspiring nationalist elite, as we see here in *BD*, to establish and justify in the terms of a modern civilizational agenda its own superiority over the rest of indigenous society and to speak on its behalf. An evolutionist ethnology, anticipating in the nineteenth century many of the twentieth-century arguments about postcolonial modernization and development, provided the means by which a nationalist elite, itself subjugated by colonial science, managed to make its own the post-Enlightenment language of autonomy and representation.

"There does not exist," says Anandachandra, "a history of the foundation of human society" (p. 13). All that can be said is that human beings have always had the desire to live close to other human beings. Besides, they were also motivated by self-interest (*svārtha*), because by living together it was possible to obtain the cooperation of others in the gathering of subsistence and protection from danger. At this stage of evolution, there was only a minimal level of sociability (*sāmājikatā*) among human groups living together, such as still exists among uncivilized hill people, and there was no possibility of the emergence of a science of politics (pp. 14–15).

In the next stage, one or a few among such minimally socialized people are able, by force of arms or some other form of superiority, to dominate others. Here is the emergence in human society of the phenomenon of lordship (*prabhutva*). Those who are dominated accept the superiority of the lord because of the fear produced by their own lack of power. A very inferior social organization can be created through such forms of domination, as can be seen, once again, among some uncivilized, hill-dwelling people (*jāti*). In every country, it is at this stage that the first lordships and kingdoms were set up (pp. 15–16).

Soon fear turned to devotion (*bhakti*). The lord or king came to be invested with divine powers and was often imagined as a prophet or incarnation of divine beings. The narratives of antiquity in every country illustrate this tendency. In India, the mythical genealogies of the Candra, the Sūrya, and the Nāga dynasties were created precisely in this way.

The kind of social life that was created at this stage in every country was much superior to what existed before; indeed, some of its elements are worthy of great respect. Yet even this is not the best form of social organization. No one in those days was aware of the fundamental principle of the true science of politics: that of a mutual equality in the share of happiness and pain. This was not the principle of social life in those societies; on the contrary, the principle was that of devotion, on the one side, and benevolence (*sneha*), or right conduct (*sadbyabahār*), on the other (p. 17).

But at this stage of social evolution, the coming together of devotion and benevolence produced a body of law called the laws of politics (*rājnīti-śāstra*). These laws laid down the ways in which the subjects could express their devotion to their ruler and the ruler his benevolence toward his subjects. Indeed, the relation was often such that the subjects regarded their obedience to the ruler as the service of god, while the ruler was prepared to sacrifice his life in the protection of his subjects. The relation was not, properly speaking, that of ruler and subject; rather, it was that of father and son (p. 17).

In time, with further improvements in the state of human society, such devotion to rulers gradually decreased. Earlier, people had regarded the oppression or misrule of kings as divine ordinance and could do little except blame their fate; now, when the ruler was no longer seen as the singular source of earthly happiness, who could the people turn to for their welfare? Before, the ruler held society together and administered it authoritatively, if not always satisfactorily; now, when the king was no longer invested with divine authority, how was society to be administered? Soon people realized that the only way this could be done was by promoting the general welfare, and this meant the organization of society according to the principle of a mutual equality of happiness and pain (*sama-sukhduhkha-bhāgītā*).

The Politics of Self-Discipline

Of course, the question might arise: Why should people bother about the good of all? They were not concerned about this when they gave unquestioned obedience to the ruler; now, when the ruler did not have the same authority, why should not each person look only to his own good? Eminent thinkers, however, soon saw that this would only lead to chaos and oppression. That which promotes the good of one might mean disaster for another. The welfare of each member of society was so intricately tied to the welfare of others that any true social organization had to recognize this as its first principle. Thus, it became evident that a collective force needed to be mobilized, one that would legislate for the good of all and that all would obey. This force is called the general will (*sādhāraṇ mat*) (p. 21).

Of course, it is not possible that there will be unanimity on all matters at all times. When there are disagreements, the best principle, says *BD*, is for all to accept the decision of the majority of the people. This ensures that each has the same right of opinion; those who are in a minority on one occasion always retain the chance of becoming a majority on the next occasion. Thus, the will of the majority is the general will, and acts that are in accordance with it are in the general welfare (p. 22).

As soon as the general will was born, it came into conflict with the established monarchies. In many countries, this led to serious clashes between the ruler and his subjects. Some of these bloody conflicts even led to the execution of kings, as in ancient times in the Roman Empire and more recently in Germany, France, and England. In some countries, it is the general will that rules, and in many others, although the monarchy still continues, it is under the control of the general will. "Given the pace at which the general will is establishing itself in recent times, it can be hoped that all existing monarchies will soon be abolished" (p. 23).

A state (*rājya*) constituted on the basis of popular sovereignty (*prajāśakti*; i.e., the general will) and ensuring the rights of the people (*prajāsvatva*; i.e., the general welfare) is the best state and is in accordance with the science of politics. When human beings were uncivilized, there was a need for a sovereign monarch, for otherwise society would have been destroyed. "But in a society where most, if not all, people are aware of their rights and of their mutual dependence and are capable of expressing their opinion on matters of general welfare, it is not desirable that the system of rule should be in accordance with the wishes of only one or just a few persons" (p. 24). In countries where the government is run according to a despotic constitution, the subjects have no secure rights over their wealth, reputation, or property, and every arbitrary wish of the ruler becomes an act of government. A single criticism and the critic is put to death. "You could ask: 'If there is a good ruler, why should the subjects be oppressed?' Even this is not a valid objection, because what the ruler thinks to be beneficial might be regarded as oppressive by his subjects. And if the ruler is wilfully arbitrary and unjust, who is there to protest or to seek redress?" (p. 25).

Although these remarks occur in the context of a discussion of the general principles of political representation, Anandachandra's allusion to the theoretical illegitimacy of British rule in India is unmistakable. Except for the single qualification about "most, if not all, people" being "aware of their rights . . . and capable of expressing their opinion on matters of general welfare," his arguments point decisively toward making a claim for an end to the "despotic constitution" and for greater representation of the people of the country in the organs of government.

Nevertheless, an interesting point that needs to be noted is that although Anandachandra is expounding a theory of popular sovereignty based on the general will, and although his republicanism is far more explicit than would be usual in any contemporary British text of political theory, he does not coin a term for *citizen* but uses the word *subject* to mean "the people." *Prajā* in Bengali stands unequivocally for "subject"; a *prajā* is one who is under the authority of a ruler, and in colonial Bengal the most familiar meaning of *prajā* would have been the tenant in a landlord's estate. Yet when Anandachandra talks of popular rights and popular sovereignty, he says "rights of the *prajā*," "sovereignty of the *prajā*." In these early dreams of democratic self-government, the leaders among the colonized have still not mastered the means to think of themselves as "citizens." Notwithstanding the principles of their newly learned "science of politics," it remained the case that others were in fact the rulers and they only subjects. (In the twentieth century, the word *nāgarik* would be used to mean "citizen," but, curiously, "republic" is still designated by *prajātantra*, "rule of the *prajā*," indicating the origin of the concept in the overturning of the relation between monarch and subject.)

Absence of a Science of Politics in India

"Among Indians, the heart is more powerful than the mind." This is the proposition with which Anandachandra opens his discussion on the applicability of the science of politics to India. "From their birth, Indians are naturally more prone to the dictates of the heart and the tendency is further strengthened by the natural conditions of the country" (pp. 27-28). This is shown by the power of religion in India, the feelings of devotion among its people, and the emotional appeal of its literature. In particular, emotions such as faith, devotion, sympathy, bravery, and the love of beauty are especially strong among the people of this country. It is for this emotionalism that there has been so little attention paid in India to the sciences.

In the first place, among the vast body of literature in India, including the Vedas, the Upanishads, and the *śāstra*, only a small amount goes by the name of *darśana,* and not all of it actually deserves to be regarded as science. Second, the highly developed philosophy of Sāṃkhya, which, according to Anandachandra, once influenced the development of religion and social practices in many countries and is still a model (*ādarśa*) for many sciences, has virtually disappeared in the country of its birth. (Anandachandra seems to be referring here to the influence of Sāṃkhya on Buddhist philosophy.) This shows that although great thinkers in India, with their superhuman powers of intellect, have created major systems of *darśan*, those systems have subsequently vanished because of a lack of interest among the people. Third, since the development of the sciences directly influences the development of religion, the continuous decline in the state of religion in India from Vedic times is directly attributable to the absence of discussion on *darśan* (p. 29).

As we have noticed earlier, an evolutionary view of civilization is accepted here, even to the extent of admitting the inferiority of Indians. Emotional rather than intellectual, Indians are closer to the state of natural society than modern Europeans. Nevertheless, other distinctions are immediately built into this evolutionary scheme so as to make ambiguous the oppositions emotional/intellectual, natural/civilized, religious/scientific. It is not as though all Indians at all times were incapable of philosophical or scientific thought; some, by virtue of their individual genius, had even managed to construct entire philosophical systems that are still admired by advanced peoples. These individual efforts did not, however, meet with a climate of intellectual activity and appreciation. Even if there was (and, by implication, still is) in India a small intellectual elite that is capable of scientific thinking, the general conditions of the country and its people cannot be described as being conducive to science.

This strategy opens up the space where a new intellectual elite among Indians can define its project of modernism. This elite, in spite of belonging to a society that has fallen behind in the scale of civilization, does not consider itself intrinsically inferior in intellectual ability to the most advanced in the world. On the contrary, it gives to itself its own "national" intellectual heritage: it is the successor of the great philosophical geniuses of the ancient past, whom the people had forgotten. At the same time, it is part of the modern enlightenment, whose sources lie in another part of the world but access to which is universal and restricted only by appropriate institutions of education. By imagining the history of the nation as one of a decline from ancient greatness, and by embracing the emancipatory claims of science and modernity, the nationalist elite is able to overcome the disabling implications of the evolutionary theory that identifies Indian society as inferior.

There is no science in India, says Anandachandra, called *vyavahāradarśana*. Some of the *śāstra* contain good advice on the duties of rulers and subjects, and there are some *saṃhitā* that have detailed instructions on administration and statecraft, but there is no text that discusses the principles of *byabahār* as a science.[15] It should be remembered that the celebrated text on the principles of state administration entitled the *Kauṭilya arthaśāstra* was discovered by modern scholarship only in the first decade of the twentieth century. Although other *arthaśāstra* texts had been in circulation, they were usually considered relatively minor parts of the immense corpus of the *dharmaśāstra* literature on rules of ritual and social behavior. It was only after the discovery of Kauṭilya's *Arthaśāstra* that the field of state administration and finance came to be recognized as a distinct part of traditional Indian scholarship and that parallels were explicitly drawn between Kauṭilya and Machiavelli. Unlike Anandachandra here, twentieth-century nationalists would not say that there were no ancient Indian texts on the science of *byabahār*.

According to Anandachandra, the reason for the absence in India of a scientific discussion of politics is obvious. The science of politics is based on three elements: the sense of individuality, the sense of the collective, and the sense of fellow feeling (p. 30). The first is an awareness of the existence of certain self-evident rights of the individual that cannot be taken away from him or her. (Since most common nouns in Bengali are not gendered, "individual" here could be male or female. Nowhere in *BD* does Anandachandra specifically exclude women from the body of citizens, although he does not explicitly mention them either. From other evidences, it would not be wrong to surmise that Anandachandra would have theoretically subscribed to various progressive views circulating at the time in British intellectual circles on the question of the emancipation of women, such as those, for instance, of John Stuart Mill.) The second is the sense that each is a member of society as a whole and that society is in truth the collective of individuals. The third sense involves the awareness that no one can live independently of others and that an injury to one is an injury to all. All of these three elements, he continues, are absent in Indian social life.

Evidence of this, says Anandachandra, is to be found in the Indian caste system. A society that acknowledges the rights of individuals could never allow the cruel and discriminatory treatment that is meted out to the Sudra. The Sudra is denied the right to education, the right to participate in warfare, and the right to engage in trade; he is thus denied all opportunity for self-improvement. Society, too, deprives itself of the chance of benefiting from the Sudra's efforts.

Second, by restricting the army to the Kshatriya castes only and denying military training to the populous Vaisya and Sudra castes, society makes itself more vulnerable to sudden attacks from outside (p. 31). This shows that the sense of the collective is insufficiently developed in India.

Third, the absence of a sense of fellow feeling is evident from the denial of education to the lower *varṇa* (caste), by which not only are they not given the opportunity of self-improvement but society as a whole is deprived of the benefits of the improvement of all of its members.

Anandachandra here is of course considering only the theoretical scheme of the *varṇa* system, according to which Kshatriyas are supposed to be the warrior caste, Vaisyas engaged in production and trade, and Sudras in lowly, menial occupations. Obviously, in fact, armies in India have never been confined to only the Kshatriya castes, nor was it the case that the lower *varṇa* were always denied education. This is yet another instance of the Orientalist preference for a "scriptural" description of tradition.

Possibility of a Science of Politics in India

Having thus outlined the ill-effects of the lack of a science of politics in India, Anandachandra then raises the crucial question: What are the possibilities of such a science emerging in India? Interestingly, the answer to this question is prefaced by a discussion of the state of political ethics in India.

"In spite of the absence of a science of politics in India, there were surprising advances in political ethics" (p. 32). Of course, since there was no *darśan*, all questions of political ethics were discussed within the framework of the *dharmaśāstra*. The king was regarded as an incarnation of *dharma*, appearing in human form in order to preserve the natural order in the human world. In his human aspect, he was paid taxes and other dues; as a divine being he enjoyed the devotion and complete obedience of his subjects. If there were famines, epidemic, floods, or drought, people did not seek remedies from the ruler, but explained them as signs of divine displeasure. Even the rulers sought to propitiate the gods and atone for their sins by performing sacrifices and penances.

In fact, the relation between *rājā* and *prajā* in India was always mediated by *dharma*. It was a relation that involved worship on the one hand and protection on the other. This is why Indians called their king *dharmāvatāra* and the court *dharmādhikaraṇa*. (It is interesting to note that these were precisely the terms by which the magistrate and the court were formally addressed in British Bengal. It is difficult to decide if Anandachandra's observation here was meant to be ironic.) In order to specify the mutual duties of rulers and subjects, there came into existence a body of moral tales or fables (*nītikathā*), which could be said to represent political ethics in India. Although these are not consistent with the science of politics, they contain many ideas that are serious, elevating, and reflective of a keen intellect. There were also in circulation several codes of law (*āin*), of which the Manusaṃhitā is the best known. These were designed in accordance with the principles of political ethics and were not based on the science of politics. They should therefore be regarded as a collection of edicts, rather than as codes of law, because by completely ignoring the opinions of the *prajā*, advocating worship of the ruler as god, and declaring the unquestioned superiority of the Brahmans, they struck at the roots of a true system of law (pp. 34-35).

But now that a system of university education had been instituted in India, what were the prospects for the cultivation of a science of politics? Anandachandra is not very enthusiastic about the prevailing quality of education in general and of law education in particular. Echoing the familiar sentiments of the new intelligentsia, he says that as long as the object of education remains only the acquisition of certain moneymaking skills, there is no possibility of serious discussion on the philosophical principles of science. Precisely for this reason, those trained in law might be knowledgeable about specific provisions of ancient or modern law, but are completely ignorant of the principles on which the provisions are based. Thus, lawyers will tell you that according to the Dāyabhāga system (the system of "traditional Hindu" law of property codified and administered in colonial Bengal) the sons inherit the property of a deceased Hindu, but they will fail to tell you whether the principle on which the daughters are excluded is a defensible one, or whether the English system of primogeniture is based on a better or worse principle (pp. 36-37). Those who are known in this country as politicians or legislators (*byabahārbid*) are equally ignorant of the scientific principles of legislation. Thus, some legislators congratulate themselves on having enacted the law of civil marriage, but do not realize that without an appropriate law of divorce the principle of self-chosen (*svayambar*) marriage remains incomplete. Even newspaper editors have wondered why, when the penalty for severe assault is only thirty rupees, the illegal use of a postage stamp should incur a punishment of two months in jail (p. 40).

Yet another qualification is being introduced here into the depiction of Indian society as backward and in need of improvement. It is not merely formal university education that will create a class of public-spirited citizens with adequate understanding of the modern science of politics. Even the introduction of modern judicial institutions, of formal training for professional lawyers, and of modern legislative bodies will not necessarily promote a general interest in the scientific principles of legislation. Implied here is a criticism of the colonial institutions of law and education: although they adhere to the forms of advanced institutions, they do not, only for that reason, produce an understanding of the principles of their functioning even among those who are professionally connected with them. Also implied is a distinction within the class of Indians with a modern, Western education. Despite their involvement with the new institutions of the state, most members of this class are incapable of that true understanding of the scientific principles of politics that would enable them to lead and guide civil society: only a few have this ability. Notwithstanding its celebration of the general will and majority rule, the nationalist intelligentsia, we find, is defining its claim to represent the nation, not by any formal electoral criterion, but by its superior command over the principles of modern knowledge.

Benefits of a Science of Politics in India

BD declares that if the science of politics is properly appreciated in India, there will be three benefits: unity, self-discipline, and toleration. Unity (*ekatā*) will be the consequence of a heightened sense of both individuality and the collective. A few wise men, acting separately, cannot run society: their efforts must join up with the general will; they must respond to that general will (p. 41). But this general will can only be the result of a general acceptance by the members of society of the need to subordinate their personal desires to the general interest of society. This unity is very different from the contingent and accidental agreement among those subjected to the same oppression: the negative unity of oppressed subjects against a bad ruler is not true unity.

Anandachandra is particularly exercised by this question of unity—for understandable reasons, since this was a major subject of discussion in Indian nationalist circles at the time. He expends much rhetoric on the need for unity:

> India is being ruined by disunity. Once a land of gold, India is now a wilderness. Notice how five little streams come together to form a huge river. Notice again how the river separates into five narrow courses—its force, its current, vanished. India has no unity, Indian society has no vigor, there is no hope for its future. (p. 46)

Even the clamor about unity that is heard in political circles is misplaced:

> The ruler is oppressing you, he is oppressing me, he is oppressing others. All of us are angry with him; all of us are shouting in the same voice. This is no unity (*ekatā*). When this oppressive condition will be removed, none of us will recognize one another. . . . What appears now as unity is merely the result of being in the same condition (*ekābasthā*). (p. 47)

The science of politics teaches us that true unity must exist in society regardless of circumstance; it cannot be merely accidental or contingent. Society cannot last without unity. True unity comes from the shared feeling that I cannot live without your help, you cannot live without my help. Here, swimming with the tide of his rhetoric and forgetting for the moment that there could never have been true unity in Indian society as he has described it, Anandachandra adds:

> This unity has vanished from India. . . . Otherwise why should the Māgadh [Bihari] do nothing else but till the land, the Oriya only carry the palanquin, and I, the Bengali, feel gratified by serving my master? Twenty blades of grass can come together to become a strong rope; we, twenty crore Indians, have no feeling for one another. (pp. 47–48)

The second benefit of practicing the science of politics would be self-discipline (*ātmaśāsan*). The idea of pursuing one's private interest even by harming the general interest of society might seem immediately attractive to the private individual, but on proper reflection it turns out that ultimately this is harmful even to one's private interest:

> If you do harm to your neighbors today, you will deprive yourself of their cooperation for all time. Perhaps tomorrow, it is they who will harm you. What you did to them alone, they might combine to do twice as much to you. Perhaps all of society will turn against you. If you obstruct the lower classes from seeking education or improving their condition, thinking that this would keep them under your domination or that you would enrich yourself by exploiting them, . . . then those people might one day rob you of all your possessions. (p. 43)

Curiously, nowhere does Anandachandra make the classic argument (à la Rousseau) about self-discipline as the essence of modern political obligation: that the citizen must obey the general will because he himself has made it. As we have noticed before, Anandachandra is still unable to conceive of Indians as citizens making the laws of a self-governing society. For him, the general interest of society stands apart from and opposed to the private interests of individuals; it is the task of a superior moral sense, a virtue that can only be inculcated by "true" education, to uphold the general interest. Until then, his method of persuading people to subordinate their private interests to the general interest is to warn of the possibility of private retaliation. In fact, Anandachandra is quite pessimistic about the incidence of such virtue among Indians:

> Self-discipline implies the formation of character (*caritra*). It means getting rid of selfishness and pettiness in order to become a person of such good character (*saccaritra*) that true good will come both to oneself and to society. But in its present degraded condition, India is full of people who are so indisciplined and selfish that it would be hard to find even a few who can be relied upon to look after the welfare of society and the country. (p. 48)

Owing to the lack of knowledge of the true principles of both religion and the science of politics, Indians are now entirely absorbed in the pursuit of their selfish interests. The virtue that comes from a sense of responsibility toward society does not exist among them.

The third benefit of practicing the science of politics is toleration (*udāratā*). There are bound to be differences in ability, intelligence, and taste among people living in society. True toleration teaches that each must have the individual liberty to pursue his own tastes and to hold her own opinions without endangering the general interest of society. "It is for reasons of toleration that the entire science of politics is never implemented as law" (p. 45). Anandachandra seems to be echoing here the liberal objections to a radical Jacobin program of legislating de novo a uniform rational code of law.

But he is particularly critical of the lack of toleration in Indian social life.

There is no tradition of toleration in India, he says, either in religious or in secular matters. This is so in relations within domestic society as well as in relations with outsiders. Domestic intolerance is shown in the treatment of untouchables: for a supposed offense committed in some ancient time, the untouchable *caṇḍāla* is relegated for generations to the bottom of society with no hope of redemption. And intolerance of foreigners is the reason why Indians never ventured beyond the river Indus (pp. 50–51).

Although the criticisms of caste discrimination and of the supposed lack of interest of Indians in the outside world have always been important parts of the reformist agenda of nationalism, Anandachandra's attribution of all this to a fundamental lack of toleration antedates the other nationalist idea of the immense absorptive power of Indian society, of its ability to accommodate diverse beliefs and practices, and to create, as the overused phrase goes, "unity in diversity." *BD* is rather more thoroughgoing here in its rejection of "traditional" social practices, and more consistently modernist in its reform project. Anandachandra also adds a paragraph here (pp. 51-53) to say that the undoubted achievements of ancient Indian civilization were nevertheless limited by the fact of its intolerance, and the period of Muslim rule did not help matters. Like ancient China and ancient Egypt, ancient India failed to sustain its civilizational achievements. Had it not been for this absence of toleration,

> given the degree of development of its art and literature, India should certainly have been the first country to invent the printing press, and given the military skills of its soldiers, Ayodhya or Indraprastha [the legendary capitals of the *Rāmāyaṇa* and the *Mahābhārata*, respectively] should have been, like Rome, capitals of the world. (p. 53)

Religion and Politics in India

What is the object of propounding the science of politics? "To organize national life in degraded India." No national life is possible without two elements: religion and politics. Religion is the vital force, but excess of religion leads to fanaticism and bigotry, and has to be controlled by the scientific practice of politics. It is true, of course, that some nations, such as those of the Muslims, have achieved power and glory by their religious zeal alone. But this is not true national life; it is a perversion of national life. Because of their lack of understanding of the scientific principles of organizing political life, Muslims have gradually lost control of their conquered territories, and where they continue to rule, there is little hope of social progress (pp. 55-56).

On the other hand, it is not possible to organize national life on the basis of the science of politics alone. A great political agitation can awaken or regenerate a nation, but without religion it cannot secure the support of the common people and the agitation cannot last. The French Revolution is a good example, says Anandachandra, of the failure of scientific politics. The motive force of that revolution was not religion but self-interest; it did not get the support of all and did not last for long (pp. 56-57). The historical example that Anandachandra cites of the right combination of religion and politics is, curiously enough, that of the Roman Empire. What he describes as the "true sociability" found among the leaders of Rome is what European philosophers would have called "virtue."

For a book that is intended to propagate the science of politics in a country that does not know this science, *BD* strangely closes with this statement on the limits of scientific politics: A strictly secular politics concerns itself with issues of *svārtha*, self-interest. Notwithstanding its search for a harmonious balance between individual and collective interests, scientific politics left to itself can produce only a knowledge that will be confined to a few. Far more general in its appeal and long-lasting in its influence will be a sense of virtue produced by the combination of religion with politics.

Perhaps it will be useful to point out that there is in operation here a certain construction of the meaning of *artha* as "interest" and *svārtha* as "self-interest" that was very much the work of the nineteenth-century intellectual representation of "Indian tradition." *Artha* was always recognized in the *Dharmaśāstra* literature as a legitimate object of human life, although its worth was universally declared to be inferior to that of *dharma*. The principles governing the pursuit of *artha* were usually discussed in the *smṛti* literature in the context of the duties of rulers, and the science of *artha* was often taken to be synonymous with the principles of *daṇḍa* (punishment). The *Kāmasūtra* of Vātsāyana listed the components of *artha* as: "education, lands, gold, cattle, corn, domestic utensils and friends and the augmenting of what is acquired."[16]

However, notwithstanding the doctrinal subordination of *artha* to *dharma*, there did exist considerable textual material that independently dealt with the pursuit of *artha*. In these discussions, there were many points, especially in the *Mahābhārata* (which was of course widely known) and in the *Kauṭilya arthaśāstra* (of whose existence, as we have mentioned before, Anandachandra was not aware), where the choice between a single-minded pursuit of *artha* and the dictates of morality and fairness was at best ambiguous. But in the nineteenth-century, nationalist construction of "tradition," *artha* would be unambiguously relegated to a lowly materialism, and, hence, *svārtha* to the pursuit of narrow self-interest; and both would be considered unworthy of being talked of within the elevating discourse of *dharma*. Needless to add, it was the latter that was declared to be the essential characteristic of Indian tradition.

Significantly, there was no place in this nationalist reconstruction of an Indian tradition of law and statecraft for the centuries-old experience of the people of Bengal and of most of northern India with legal and administrative practices informed by Islamic doctrines. The Orientalist distinction between "Hindu law" and "Muhammadan law," as representations of two distinct civilizational (and, hence, textual) traditions was adopted without qualification by the nineteenth-century nationalist writers. Anandachandra is entirely typical when he locates the intellectual tradition of Indian law and politics exclusively in the *smṛti* and *itihāsa* literature.

It may also be relevant to point out that, in the 1870s, Anandachandra could not have formed any judgment at all of the possibilities of modern political organization involving large sections of the Indian population. The early political associations, which would lead a decade later to the first meetings of the Indian National Congress and which were then only beginning to appear in Bombay and Calcutta, were confined to a handful of notables.[17] A conception of the polity involving the whole of the people could not be credibly represented by Anandachandra as "the organization of common interests." It is, as we have seen, "unity" that seems to him to be the crucial missing element that explains the absence of scientific politics in India. Not surprisingly, notions such as kinship and the rightful conduct of ruler toward subjects become the bonds that hold the polity together. Translated into the language of modern politics, and then immediately caught between the polarities of the supposed differences between West and East, these bonds come to be described as "religion."

Before Virtue

In 1876, two years before he wrote *BD*, Anandachandra had brought out a small pamphlet entitled "Two Faces of Civilization: Ancient India and Modern Europe."[18] It consisted of four essays that discussed the contrasting principles of the methods of warfare, art, literature, and politics in ancient India and modern Europe. Read alongside *BD*, the essays are striking because of the sharp contrast they set up between *dharma* in ancient India and *nīti* in modern Europe. If *BD* appears merely to register a note of caution about excessive enthusiasm over scientific politics, "Two Faces of Civilization" raises fundamental doubts about the merits of a secularization of politics, art, and literature.

The driving force of civilization in ancient India was *dharma* (here, in Anandachandra's sense, the word can be easily translated as *religion*) and the object was liberation, release from the world (*mukti*) (p. 2). In modern Europe, civilization is guided by policy (*nīti*), and the object is utility (*maṅgal*). Modern historians from Europe criticize ancient Indians for a lack of competence in military tactics. But the criticism, says Anandachandra, is misplaced. The object of war in ancient India was not the defeat of the opponent, but victory of *dharma*. It is possible, by superior tactics, for five boys to defeat a great warrior, but ancient Aryans looked upon such tactics as unfair and cowardly. War was a great celebration of *dharma*: the object of a *digvijaya* was not the annexation of territory but the holding of a great ritual of sacrifice; to die in a battle against invaders was to go to heaven. "Such blind faith in *dharma* was the reason why Arya liberty was lost to the Yavanas" (p. 6). Aryans could not imagine that a great warrior like Muhammad Ghuri would, for the sake of self-interest, resort to the perfidious tactics (*kucakra*) with which he won the battle at Thanesar.

In modern Europe, the object of war is not *dharma*; it is utility. Go to war to improve trade; go to war to increase the wealth of the nation; go to war to free people from slavery. Such reasons, while not being inconsistent with *dharma*, could well be pursued independently of it, as indeed they are in Europe. Witness the European methods of warfare.

> There is no distinction there between the strong and the weak, the trained and the untrained, the guilty and the innocent. Following the principle of promoting the general utility, strong men fire cannons at young boys, those who have taken to flight are beheaded, the entire population of a city is thrown to starvation because the commander refuses to open the city gates. All means are permitted to strike a blow at the enemy forces. . . . The Aryas despised such warfare as unjust and regarded such warriors as cowards. (pp. 7–8)

In art, too, the guiding principles in the two civilizations are opposed to each other. In ancient India, the greatest achievements of architecture are to be found in temples and of sculpture and painting in the making of idols and in scenes of divine play. In modern Europe, architecture reaches its peak in public offices; painting and sculpture attain their heights in the portrayal of love and heroism in human life and history. If anyone objects that religion might still be an important source of inspiration for modern European art, Anandachandra is ready with his reply. Look, he says, at how modern Europe presents itself in its own colonial capital. The High Court in Calcutta is a far more impressive building than any of the churches in the city, and portraits of the family of Prince Albert far more spectacular than those of Christ on the cross. When the inventive spirit of Europe confronted a range of mountains in India, it did not, like Indians in Ellora, build temples within its caves; it laid a railway line across it. When it crossed a desert, it did not think of bringing in the waters of the Gaṅgā as Indians would have wanted to; it expanded the network of internal trade (p. 10).

In modern European art, there is a celebration of the natural and the real. Inspired by *dharma*, the Arya imagination turns the unreal into the real, the unnatural into the natural, the false into the true. The idol of the goddess with ten hands is unnatural; indeed, by the standard of realism, it is false. But in its beauty, it is unsurpassable. Even in respect of articles of daily use, European aesthetics concentrates on items of dress and furniture. Beauty is sought to be combined with comfort and happiness. In Arya civilization, beauty must lie in religion, which is why the most beautiful articles are those that are used in worship and ritual. "In short, on the one side we find religion, other-worldliness, liberation; on the other side, welfare, progress, utility" (p. 14).

The posing of opposites here is as sharp as in any text of pristine Orientalism. The argument is carried on into the field of literature: whether in philosophy, poetry, or grammar, religion is said to be the mainstay of Sanskrit literature, whereas modern European literature thrives on history and science. "In modern European poetry, one does not come across eroticism in the same way that one does in Sanskrit poetry. . . . It is regrettable that the love which Arya poets celebrated as an aspect of the divine is condemned as animal love by Western poets" (p. 23).

In politics, the contrast is between the notion of the king as a divine incarnation in ancient India and the complete separation of state and religion in modern Europe. In ancient India, if the king did any wrong, only the gods could punish him; his subjects had nothing to say in the matter. In modern Europe, a despotic ruler will be forced to mend his ways by the combined pressure of his subjects (*prajāśakti*), and if he still proves recalcitrant "his blood will wash away the sins of his kingdom" (p. 27).

As we have seen before, Anandachandra would use the same contrast between the religious and the secular views of politics in *BD*. But there the argument would occur within an evolutionary theory of civilization in which the religious conception of kingship, for instance, would be clearly identified as an example of backwardness. And even when he would talk about the limits of scientific politics—the failure of the French Revolution, for example—his preferred solution would be a judicious balance between religion and politics, in which one would temper the excesses of the other. Why, in these earlier essays, does he seem to reject altogether, and with such passion, the very idea of secularization?

I do not think that the question can be dismissed as an inconsistency in the writings of an individual author. Nor is it a matter of a shift from one set of views to another. What appears as an inconsistency here belongs in fact to nationalist discourse itself. It needs to be investigated as to what purpose, and with what effects, these ambiguities are introduced into the modernist project of nationalism.

One interpretation would be to see this as a conservative tendency within liberal political theory. We could attribute this conservatism to the reluctance of the nationalist elite to accept the radical democratic consequences of the concepts of rationalism and popular sovereignty. To some extent this is true, as is shown in Anandachandra's remarks on the French Revolution, which echo the familiar sentiments of nineteenth-century English liberal politics.

But it would be incorrect to equate the nineteenth-century political situation of the Indian nationalist leadership with that of the English ruling class. The appeal to religion in the nationalist agenda had to have a specific value that was very different. One of the arguments here was that modern science was elitist; any attempt to enforce "scientific" principles of social interaction would be resisted by the people. This was particularly so because "science and modernity" were also associated with the foreign ruling power. What is often at stake here is the violence involved in the institution and enforcement of modern disciplinary regimes.

The objection that is made, therefore, is that it is futile to try to be thoroughgoing with science and rationalism, because Indian society is fundamentally different from European society. Any attempt to do so would only alienate the nationalist project from its sources of popular support. The argument is bolstered by the familiar orientalist-nationalist play on civilizational difference. An enumeration of the limits of rational science and a celebration of the spiritual nobility of indigenous tradition are the usual forms of this rhetoric, as we found here in Anandachandra's essays. These, as I have argued elsewhere, are the marks of a failed hegemony.[19]

But modern projects of power are unrelenting in their persistence. The ambiguity about secular politics in the nationalist ideology opens up new avenues for the pursuit of secular politics. It is not just a matter of going slow on modernist reform—a gradualist form of the "passive revolution." The criticism of Western secularization and the celebration of indigenous religion can also enable the organization, within the framework of modern politics, of religion itself as an "interest." Paradoxical as it may seem in terms of the familiar counterposition of *dharma* and *svārtha*, religion and self-interest, *dharma* itself can become a matter of *svārtha*. This, as we have seen in recent years, can also mobilize for its purpose all of the modern disciplinary institutions—law, education, scientific research, the public media, democratic forms of representation, and the rest. The ideological means for this is contained in the nationalist project of modernity. Strange as it may seem in the case of a nineteenth-century Brahmo liberal, Anandachandra Mitra can be shown to have anticipated several of the crucial strategies of the recent, thoroughly secular, politics of "communalism."

But of course he could not have been aware of this implication of his position. The strategic situation in which he attempted, as a modern intellectual belonging to a colonized people, to make sense of the new science of politics was one in which he was all too conscious of the tenuousness and fragility of his claims as an equal participant in that discourse. In the same letter in which he had asked his friend about what he had seen in Europe, Anandachandra also made the following inquiries:

> Should I ask you—in the midst of all their happiness
> And festivity, and all their accomplishments,
> Do they, even for a moment, think of India?
> Do they know at all about our forefathers?
>
> Should I ask you—there in the land beyond the seas,
> Surrounded by peaks of civilization and science,
> Do you sometimes, perhaps, forget the present?
> Do you then, perhaps, remember the past, and weep?

Notes

(I have discussed this paper at a Social Science Research Council meeting in Cairo. I am grateful to Dipesh Chakrabarty and Gyan Prakash for detailed comments on an earlier version.)

1. Anandachandra Mitra, "Yurop-prabāsi bandhur prati," in *Mitrakābya,* pp. 75-79.
2. For instance, Brajendranath Bandyopadhyay and Sajanikanta Das, *Sāhitya-sādhak-caritmālā*, pp. 19-46.
3. "Bhūmikā," in Anandachandra Mitra, *Helenākābya*, pp. i-iv.
4. "Bijñapan," in Anandachandra Mitra, *Byabahār darśan.*
5. "Bijñapan," in Anandachandra Mitra, *Kabitākusum.*
6. "Bhūmikā," in *Helenākābya*, pp. i-iv.
7. Anandachandra Mitra, *Bhāratmaṅgal.*
8. Sibnath Sastri, *Ātmacarit,* p. 110.
9. "Kalir rājsūya" in Anandachandra Mitra, *Mitrakābya*, pp. 30-31.

10. Bengali dictionaries of the early twentieth century give the first two meanings of *byabahār*. Jnanendramohan Das adds that *byabahār* is equivalent to the English "behaviour." *Baṅgālā bhāṣār abhidhān*, p. 1650. More recent dictionaries have the third meaning: *byabahār karā* ("to put to use"). Rajsekhar Basu, *Calantikā*, p. 539. Interestingly, a nineteenth-century encyclopedia has an entry under *byabahārdarśan* in which it is described as "knowledge of the procedures of litigation; adjudication." Ramkamal Vidyalankar, *Sacitra prakṛtibād abhidhān,* p. 1631. I am grateful to Keya Dasgupta for this reference.

11. The 1875 catalog of Bengali schoolbooks prepared by the School Book Society lists six books on economics. Of these, four were in the form of questions and answers and were less than thirty-six pages in length. Only two books seem to have had substantial discussions on political economy: Ramkrishna Ray Chaudhuri, *Artha-byabahār* and Nrisinghachandra Mukherjee, *Arthanīti o artha-byabahār.* Both were apparently based on contemporary English textbooks. See Durgaprasad Bhattacharya and Rama Deb Ray, eds., *Bāṃlā bhāṣāy arthanīti carcā,* pp. 1-34.

12. Of these, the earliest is Craig, *Elements,* 1814. This is virtually a "Scottish Enlightenment" tract whose first volume, heavily influenced by Adam Smith's theory of moral sentiments, deals with the "principles of moral approbation" and the "rights of government." The second volume deals with the "duties of government" (containing chapters on civil and criminal law, national defense, "superintendence and direction of capital and industry," and so forth), and the third volume with taxation. Three books were published in the 1850s: Dove, *Science of Politics* (1850); Alison, *The Future, or the Science of Politics* (1852); and Humphreys, *Manual of Political Science* (1855), the last being an elementary textbook of political economy. The next set of books came in the 1880s and resemble more closely what would come to be known by the turn of the century as "political science": Amos, *Science of Politics* (1883) and Mills, *Science of Politics* (1888). The *London Bibliography of the Social Sciences* brought out by the London School of Economics in 1931 has nothing to add to this list.

13. Dove, *Politics,* 1850.

14. On this subject, see Forbes, *Positivism.*

15. Taking the term literally, Anandachandra is wrong: *vyavahāradarśana* in the sense of "administration of justice" is frequently discussed in the *smṛti* literature—for example, Mitākṣara on the Yājñavalkyasmṛti cited in Kane, *History of Dharmaśāstra,* p. 242. In general, the texts of Bṛhaspati, Nārada, and Kātyāyana, "the leading triumvirate of law," may be said to deal primarily with the science of *vyavahāra.* Of course, Anandachandra would deny that these texts represent a "science of politics" in his sense.

16. Kane, *History of Dharmaśāstra,* pp. 6-7.

17. For a history, see Seal, *Emergence.*

18. Anandachandra Mitra, *Prācīn bhārat o ādhunik iyorope sabhyatār bhinna mūrtti.* The pamphlet was a reprint of an article Anandachandra wrote in his short-lived journal *Bāṅgālī,* published in Mymensingh.

19. Chatterjee, "Urban Domesticity," pp. 40-68.

5 / Sons of the Nation: Child Rearing in the New Family

Pradip Kumar Bose

A New Discourse on the Family

Santāner caritra gaṭhan is a pedagogy on the formation of the "character" of children.[1] This was an important part of the new normative discourse on the family that was produced in nineteenth- and early-twentieth-century Bengal.[2] This discourse conceived the "isolation" of the family not only from the kinship system but also from the world of work. The conception of the family as an "isolated" private domain, as a refuge from a competitive and brutal outside world, was one that was shared by most writers. The family, with its hierarchy, spatial arrangement, and disciplinary mechanism, constituted in this discourse one way of distributing powers and pleasures. The discourse generated a radical separation between work and leisure, public life and private life, childhood and adulthood.

In this private world, husband and wife were to find solace and spiritual renewal in each other's company. The woman in particular would serve, in the favorite phrase of our authors, as one who would provide comfort, succor, and support. The child occupied center stage in this discourse; indeed, a new idea of childhood helped precipitate the new discourse on the family. The child came to be regarded as a person with distinctive attributes—impressionability, vulnerability, innocence—that required a "correct," protected, and prolonged period of nurture. It was only through a certain practice and strategy that the child's character-building exercise was to be pursued. In this process, the child was required to be segregated from premature contact with various corrupting influences and subjugated to a regime of love, affection, discipline, and punishment. Only this, it was asserted, would help the gradual and gentle unfolding of his nature (the *his* is used advisedly, because, as we will see below, this is a discourse almost exclusively about the male child). In a sense, this discourse implied more intense emotional ties between parents and children within the family and a weakening of ties with relatives outside the immediate family.

That the child should be subjugated to various disciplinary regimes within the family was due to the fact that the family was conceived as a domain that played the most effective role in shaping the individual's life. As Satischandra Chakrabarti, the author of the text we are examining, writes in a different essay:

> The word "life" has given a new turn to the family system. In earlier times, the principal question before the family was how juniors would behave toward elders and superiors and how elders would behave toward juniors. Now the main subject of discussion is how every life in the family, especially the life of children, can be developed. The family is now a center for the development of life.[3]

The traditional notion prevailing in a Bengali household was that seniority was to be respected, elders were to be given the respect (*sammān*) due to their age, and that children would receive *ādar, sneha* (affection, love) from elders. The father was a disciplinarian, a figure of authority, and the children in return offered *bhakti* (devotional love) to their parents, a kind of love that a deity is supposed to receive.[4] The new normative discourse on the family accorded children the right to a life of a special kind, different from that of adults and with different expectations placed upon them. It could be argued that the basic transformation in the discourse on the family was the rise of children to the position of central importance in the home. The family in this discourse becomes primarily an affective and sentimental unit, and social prestige is accorded for being a good parent.

Of course, there were disagreements about the rearing of children, about their place in society and the roles they should perform. But most agreed that children should be molded in accordance with the future needs of the nation so that they could bring glory to it. An obsessive love toward children and the increasing interest that parents were advised to take in them greatly increased the demands made on children. Parents were advised to force discipline and reason on them with a new severity, which also burdened the parents and the child with a sense of guilt.

In addition to the notion of privacy, then, the discourse on social and moral education of children was also shaped by a new notion of the family in which it was characterized by a restricted source of identification for children, internalized authority, and intense but ambivalent parent-child relations. Through the medium of the family, a system of control was prescribed over children, so that they would emerge as "men of character." *Santāner caritra gaṭhan* (hereafter *SCG*), first published in 1912, was written with this avowed purpose. The book was highly praised by many celebrities, among them Prafulla Chandra Ray, Ramananda Chattopadhyay, and Gurudas Banerjee, and recommended as a must for each household. It was reprinted several times, the most recent printing being in 1989 on the occasion of the International Children's Year.

This increased emphasis on a "proper" model of childhood also indicated an increasing importance of the themes of adulthood, maturity, development, and progress in the culture of this society. When these concepts acquired value and became linked to the physical and mental state of being, the child was negatively evaluated as an inferior version of the adult—as a sweet, endearing, tender, impulsive being who was at the same time dependent, vulnerable, unreliable, and willful, and thus a being that needed constant guidance, supervision, care, and surveillance. The proper model of childhood commended certain aspects of childhood while disapproving of other aspects. As Ashis Nandy writes:

> To the extent adulthood itself is valued as a symbol of the completeness and as an end-product of growth or development, childhood is seen as an imperfect transitional state on the way to adulthood, normality, full socialization and humanness. This is the theory of progress as applied to the individual life-cycle.[5]

The needs of the nation and the model of national cultural improvement were thus projected and tried out on children. In a sense, the conceptualization of modern adulthood was impossible without the conceptualization of modern childhood. The child became the source that could be used to satisfy the grandest of national aspirations. Childhood became an arena of adult experiments in colonial India. Needless to say, we are dealing here with a normative discourse whose principal function was pedagogical; its relation to actual practices was, of course, mediated by other institutions and discourses.

Private Life and National Life

The discourse on the new family can be situated in the background of various contradictory crosscurrents in colonial Bengal that afflicted the institution known as the joint family.[6] Most of the writers on the new family took it for granted that the joint family system was soon going to collapse because of the many irreconcilable forces working on it. Contributing to the discourse on the new family, Sibnath Sastri wrote:

> The joint family system is followed in this country. If people have enough generosity and tolerance, then it is possible to have much love and amity between brothers. But that kind of generosity and tolerance is not often found; that is why the joint family has become an abode of all troubles.[7]

A more comprehensive discussion on the joint family can be found in *Baṅgadarśan,* which pointed out the various causes behind the decline of the joint family.[8] Among these were discord over property rights, conflict due to financial indigence, disorder arising out of varying sizes of nuclear units within the joint family. ("If a person has more children than others, then it becomes difficult to allocate expenditures proportionally.") Besides, the author felt that women of the household were in the habit of constantly quarreling over trivial things. "Absence of tolerance, living on the income of others, etc., are the causes that give rise to discord in the joint family. . . . Everyone is eager to give advice, but whether old or young, none is willing to accept any." The breakup of the joint family was felt to be inevitable. "Every Bengali is aware of the quarrels in the joint family. On this issue we would just like to say that they are inevitable. To expect that there would be no quarrels is a fantasy."

The essay mentioned a large number of issues contributing toward the disintegration of the joint family:

> In many joint families, the guardians are unable to fulfill their duties. It is true that affinity between members of a joint family can develop quickly, but it can disappear equally fast. A son's devotion toward his parents is of course not so easily destroyed, but in relation to other members of the family what he often displays is not love but extreme animosity and acrimony. In earlier times, younger brothers used to look upon the eldest brother like a father; they would obey him in every matter. But now, with new kinds of desires, the elders are unable to gauge the wishes of the family members or act accordingly. Moreover, if younger members express those wishes, then they incur the elders' displeasure. Earlier, to treat the wife with contempt was considered a sign of the husband's moral character; now love between husband and wife is not disapproved of, although they are often ridiculed for this by ordinary people, causing much distress to the householder. . . . In the joint family, authority among brothers is determined by seniority, but for offspring the father should be the master. The head of the household should not interfere in this particular matter with the authority of the younger members, for this would cause se-

rious damage. When children are disciplined by one elder, they seek the protection of another; if both the father and the head of the household act as guardians, neither will be able to fulfill his duties and the children will behave as if they were under no one's authority.

A significant point in this discussion is the feeling, increasingly prominent, that in practice the joint family was unable to fulfill the demands being made by new desires and sentiments, the new value set on the family, and the new sense of the significance of ordinary life. There was also a teleology attached to the notion of the new family: that it would eventually rejuvenate society and the nation. That the family should be an abode of peace and tranquillity was emphasized repeatedly, and perpetual discord and disorder could be avoided only by discarding altogether the institution of the joint family. The author of the *Baṅgadarśan* article concluded his discussion by recommending:

> Two rules to be followed without fail: 1. The constituents [of the joint family] should separate before conflicts take place. 2. After separation they should settle so far apart that they can come together only when they actually wish to. Avoidance of conflict is impossible when so many members live together; hence, it should be so arranged that one could live in isolation if one wanted to.

This already indicates the breakdown of the idea of a larger order and the assertion of individual independence and of the new value given to intimate personal relations, all of which suggest a gradual withdrawal of the family from the control of the wider society.

A family based on affection had to be formed by affinity and not merely as the result of the property arrangements and social norms that were so important in traditional society. It could flourish only within the private intimacy of family life. In the new discourse on the family, therefore, sentiments took on a greater importance; thus, sentiments of love, concern, and affection for one's spouse came to be cherished and articulated. Something similar occurred with the affection of parents for children. And, partly as a result, childhood took on an identity as a separate phase of the life cycle, with its own peculiar feelings and needs. As a further consequence, child rearing became a subject of absorbing interest to the literate public.

The procedures of transformation of the family employed those techniques that implanted the forms of integration into other domains. The attempt to transform the family from inside, as it were, called for the dissemination within it of medical, educative, and relational norms that would protect children from those old practices and corrupting influences that were considered harmful.[9] Such influences were said to have caused the spiritual impoverishment of the nation. The nation could advance only if the family could be regulated to keeping a regime of proper home management, child rearing, dietary habits, hygiene, and so on.[10] The family thus became the site for national regeneration and mothers were accorded a crucial role in it.[11] As Pratapchandra Majumdar, one of the early authors on the new role of women, remarked: "Because of the flaws of the mother, the child is ruined; when the child is ruined, the family is ruined; when family life crumbles, society decays; and when society is polluted, no nation can advance."[12] It was argued that women who were ignorant of the rules of the body would not only harm themselves, but by producing weak and deficient children would also destroy the nation.[13] "Food soaked in ghee or oil, sweets and unripe fruit are like poison to the child," complained one author of domestic science; yet "uneducated housewives" continue to ruin the nation's children with such a diet.[14] Atulchandra Datta, an early writer on domestic science, wrote: "Well-trained children are the pride of the country; with bad training and corrupt morals, they only bring disgrace to the family and become the scum of the nation."[15] Nationalism was thus at work in restructuring and redefining childhood. By augmenting the authority of the mother, she was furnished with a social status, and by promoting the woman as mother, educator, and medical auxiliary, the family was insulated against the negative influences of the traditional educative milieu, so that ultimately the nation could be enriched.

While the world outside remained beyond control, the family was the site where the nation's future was to be structured. The family was a space viewed as inviolate and autonomous, where initiatives could be taken, and the desired results manipulated. Sibnath Sastri, writing on the family, remarked: "The qualities for which a nation attains brilliance and remains well preserved have to be achieved within the family."[16] By its isolation and distance from the outside world, where the political arrangements fostered only deprivation and oppression, the nationalist image of the family shed a critical light on the degraded and loveless external world that offered no scope for self-fulfillment. Those "absences" of the outside world became the organizing principle of the new family.

The origin of the family was seen as "naturally" given. Thus, the domain of private life appeared in consciousness as an island in the midst of social turbulence, a residue of the state of nature. The new notion of family in this discourse emerged as isolated and hermetic because of social, not asocial, concerns. It expressed its social concerns through its pure, unspoiled image; the more purely this quality was revealed, the more it pointed out the ills of society.

The new family of desire and myth was based on order, rule, discipline, love, and affection, where the child's character formation required a firm but gentle style that would not only be good for him but for the nation as well. Thus central to the creation of the new private life was the idea of the nation conceived as an ideological force, where the male child was to play a crucial role in the construction of the future national culture and identity. The family was conceived as the repository of civilizational values and the spiritual essence of the national culture, and the child became a part of what was desired or asserted.

The private life of the family thus became fundamental to the national construct. In a sense, both family and nation signify eternal and sacred ties whose origins are unknown and mythical. Both denote something to which one is naturally tied. They have about them "a halo of disinterestedness,"[17] which is precisely why they can ask for sacrifices. The family asks for sacrifices from the parents so that the children remain unspoiled and upright; the child, as we shall see, has to make sacrifices because he is not in this world to enjoy its luxuries but to be guided by the ideals of renunciation and sacrifice. In protecting and preserving all that is meaningful, the child should learn to sacrifice his own pleasures. Parents who are careless or negligent about their children, or those who disown their roles, betray not only their families but also the nation. On the other hand, children unable to attain the desired maturity and integrity "bring disgrace to the family and become the scum of the nation."

For Satischandra, the idea of the child-in-the-family is crucial for the nation. There is no other space for the child outside the family that Satischandra recognizes as even remotely significant for the construction of the nation.[18]

Character

At a very general level, one can describe the process engendered by the new discourse on the family as a change from the government *of families* to government *through the family*. Earlier, the head of the household wielded power over his family precisely insofar as this power was in keeping with the requirements of public order. In the changed circumstances, the family became a relay, an obligatory or voluntary support for social imperatives. Instead of being a complex web of relations of dependence and allegiance, the family became linked with a machinery that was exterior to it. From the moment the idea of the family as a private domain made its appearance, the same forces that gave rise to the new privacy began to consume it. The so-called privatization of experience went in concert with an unparalleled invasion of privacy. The family was exposed to various kinds of expertise—on medical matters, child rearing, character building, hygiene, cooking—and parents, especially mothers, became the experts' allies, the supposed educators of the family and executors of the experts' orders. Parents were advised to follow the dictates of the experts and to prepare themselves by reading appropriate books and journals. Instructions like the following, for instance, were quite common:

> For the proper rearing of children, for proper knowledge about the child's nutrition and health, you should read appropriate books, you should take advice from expert physicians. . . . Every mother should learn the new teaching methods for children called kindergarten.[19]

And about *SCG,* Ramananda Chattopadhyay wrote, "It is necessary that every educated mother should possess a copy of this book." Aswinikumar Datta said to Satischandra, "If all parents in Bengal have your book and if they form the character of their children accordingly, the country will progress."

This, in other words, was a new style of domesticity. Children were supposed to grow up under "supervised freedom." The strategy rested on the proper instruction of women, who were given the weapon of domestic management and told how to use it: Keep out strangers in order to bring in the husband and especially the children. In this way, the independent authority of families gave way to social management through families and increased intervention and supervision of the family. The "social" problems caused by inadequate families were to be resolved by a technology of expert supervision of family relations.

Satischandra Chakrabarti writes *Santāner caritra gaṭhan* as an expert:

> Who does not know that the moral development or degradation of children depends upon the behavior they receive [from parents]? Still, future parents do not learn a word about the child's upbringing: what could be more surprising and distressing than this? If someone starts a grocery business without learning elementary arithmetic, we have doubts about his prospects. If someone who has never studied physiology claims to be a surgeon, we are amazed at this quack's unauthorized activity and refuse to be treated by him; if a patient dies at his hands we even try him under criminal laws. But we are not amazed when we see so many people totally ignorant about character formation of children taking on the heavy responsibility of parenthood on their shoulders.[20]

The need for specialized training and expert education, following definite moral and ethical norms, was projected as the essential condition for a proper family order. An article in a magazine meant for women expressed the need as follows:

> In these times, if a new family and social organization are not laid on the foundation of a pure ethical system, then the old stability of Hinduism will not remain. The need for family order is even greater than the need for social order, because the foundation of the lives of men and women are laid in the family, and these patterns continue throughout their lives.[21]

It is in this context that the education of children was given greater importance, education meaning all-around comprehensive training that would help children become persons of righteous and virtuous character. *Caritra*, in the sense used in this discourse, is invested with special meanings. Traditionally, *caritra* was understood in the sense of nature or behavior (*svabhāb*), conduct (*ācaraṇ*, *strī-caritra*, *mānab-caritra*), or effort (*ceṣṭā-caritra*). But in this discourse, *caritra* acquired the special meaning of having proper moral qualities, following the right conduct, self-discipline, and self-restraint, and a *caritrabān* person was one who could subjugate or was able to control his worldly passions. It is in this sense that caritra was conceived as essential to social and moral being. Having no character meant being a lecher, an antisocial, unfit for society. A typical essay entitled "Caritra" (Character) in a recent textbook meant for small children says it all:

> Character is superior to a king's crown. A characterless person is like a beast. A proper human being is a person with character. To form one's character, one has to try from childhood. The foundation of character formation is the readiness and determination to build one's life on the basis of truth, not to waver from truth in the face of obstacles. These are the first steps of character formation. In childhood, parents influence their children; thus, the parents' character influences the children's character. Attitudes cultivated in the family influence the mind of the child. Hence children must be kept under close observation.[22]

The way this essay describes caritra is not much different from the way Satischandra understood it at the beginning of this century.

The Obedient Subject

The attributes of proper character were not strictly universal but gender-specific and age-specific. A woman of good character should ideally possess qualities different from those of a good man or a good child. This was in consonance with the dominant image of the family that relied heavily on the combination of the natural and moral. The characteristics of motherhood, inferred from the category of the "natural," for instance, were particularly heavily invested with connotations of maternal instinct, of self-sacrifice for the propagation of the species, of values superior to mundane self-interest. The category of the natural was constantly invoked, and invoked precisely to sanction and strengthen role specification and social arrangement within the family. As we will see, the analogy of the natural was also used on the question of disciplining the child.

The attempt to formulate the origin of the family in a language of presocial nature rests on a blindness—in some sense, a necessary blindness—to problems of its own formulation. All such myths of origin must simultaneously inaugurate the moment of authoritarian appeal and take recourse to an ultimate legitimizing power.

Character is an omnibus term signifying a large number of things. Similarly, character formation is a process that needs knowledge and expertise in various subjects. The text by Satischandra discusses topics such as self-organization, obedience, offense, light punishment, physical punishment, reproach and censure, care and affection, free will, cruelty, the habit of breaking things, crying, lying, complaining, competitiveness, praise, reward, deprivation, fear, curiosity, self-reliance, respect, love, company, celibacy, and love of the motherland. Obviously, there could have been many more topics, but what is crucial in such a training strategy is the question of power over the child's body and soul. The character, translated in terms of the body and the soul, thus becomes the issue of conflict between parents and children, between the child and the instances of control. The body and the soul, taken as principles of behavior that signify character or the lack of it, form the elements that are now proposed for disciplinary intervention. This intervention rests on a studied manipulation of the child's individuality; what is constructed out of this intervention is the obedient subject, who is subjected to habits, rules, and orders. The obedient subject follows an authority that is exercised continually around him and upon him and that he must allow to function automatically in him:

> To form the child's character, family discipline is necessary. Obedience is the principal factor in this discipline. When, after a lot of threats from parents, a child grudgingly obeys their commands, it cannot be called obedience. To obey commands immediately and gladly is the sign of real obedience. It is not sufficient that your children should submit to your reasoning or flattery. It is desirable that his head should always be lowered before your authority. Of course, sometimes parents should, by giving reasons, convince children of the

> justifiability and necessity of what they were being asked to do, but parents should have so much authority that even if the children do not understand the justification, they nevertheless are compelled to act immediately. How parents can establish such authority over their children and obtain their complete obedience will be discussed now.[23]

The shaping of the obedient subject is detailed according to the general form of power. This power, however, remains concealed, and what is effected in this relationship is the automatic and immediate relation between the authority and the subject. This requires a special relationship between the agents of power and its recipient, in this case the parents and the child. The training of behavior, acquisition of habits, regular activities, application, respect, imply a special relationship in which the parents must exercise a total power that no third party can disturb. The family is the site for this disciplinary exercise. Discipline sometimes requires enclosure.

The family lies at the heart of society:

> Between family, society, and religious institutions, the family influences man's life most deeply and profoundly. Hence, for the preservation and development of life, the family should be considered as more important than society and religious institutions, and primary attention should be given to the development and enrichment of the family.[24]

The family is the foundation of society, and if the quality of domestic life is improved, the quality of society is also improved. On the one hand, the family is thus theoretically linked with the social; at the same time, the family is also considered a private domain, secluded from the outside world. That is why Satischandra reminds his readers:

> Readers, listen carefully! Until proper efforts are made in every home to form the child's character, until parents knowledgeable in such subjects are able to build the child's moral and physical nature, until children are able to drink from infancy, along with their mother's milk, the nectar of good education, until that time no political movement, no social reform, no school or college can do any good for the country.[25]

Children in the family must be entirely enveloped in the power that is exercised over them. The relations are expressed in terms of representation, sign, mark, and obstacle signs. The relationship must start with the representation of parents, who through self-discipline and self-organization should project an image that can be followed automatically:

> Parents can surely expect to see their own little images in their children. To see a beautiful image, the better method is to beautify oneself rather than to get the

> mirror polished. Who can say whether this is not the intention of the all-powerful God who, by reflecting through heredity the blemishes of the parents in their children and presenting them before the parents, is perhaps, for the good of mankind, wishing to eliminate the blemishes of both?[26]

The representations are often based on pairs of opposing values: against a bad passion a good habit is opposed; against one force, another force. The examples that the parents project should be based on the lesson, on the decipherable sign, the representation of right morality. The disciplinary mechanism should be as nonarbitrary as possible; the obstacle signs should be such that deviations should immediately bring to mind the corrective chastisement. There must be an inevitable and analogical link between the two. This should resemble natural laws—uniform, nonarbitrary, and inevitable:

> Thus if children realize that there is no escape from obeying their mother's commands, if they understand that like the rule of nature their mother's rule is also inescapable, if they understand that just as the hand that touches the fire gets burned, the needle that pierces the finger produces pain, in the same way whenever the mother's commands are disregarded they must face punishment, then, just as one who has burned his fingers keeps away from fire, in exactly the same way no child will dare violate his mother's commands. What a beauty is this rule of nature! But parents often punish their children heavily, while at other times the children are allowed to go scot free. Thus, for the same offense they are sometimes punished twice, while at other times they get away. Given such inconsistent behavior of the parents and given the possibility of acquittal, the children will not stop being disobedient.[27]

The analogy of the natural is thus extended to the disciplinary mechanism within the family; indeed, it is applied to the very idea of the family.

One of the distinctive features of the new discourse on the family is, as we have seen, expressed in viewing the family as a "natural," biological phenomenon. The family, at one and the same time, is seen as both naturally given and as socially and morally desirable. The realms of the "natural" and the sociomoral are nowhere so constantly merged and confused as in the feelings and thoughts about the family: on many other questions, the two would be rigidly separated. Hunger, disease, cruelty, and killing appear with great regularity in the natural world, but to try to eradicate them is seen as distinctively human—a mark of the progress of civilization. With the family, it is quite the reverse, for the moral and hence sociopolitical claims of the family rest in large part precisely on its being seen as a natural biological unit rather than as a social arrangement. In the same vein, the appeal to the natural is resorted to when the question of discipline within the family arises.

In the natural world, it is argued, any violation of its laws brings punishment, which in fact follows with certainty. "Ordinary parents often let their children go without punishment, but Mother Nature is not that kind of mother to us."[28] In the realm of nature, punishment is analogical to the offense; they are a pair of equal and opposite forces. "For a serious offense punishment is also heavier, for a light offense punishment is lighter. Unlike ordinary parents, Mother Nature does not punish lightly a serious offense and seriously a light offense, and thereby destroy the whole purpose behind the punishment."[29] What is important is the purpose behind the punishment, which is to discipline the child by leaving no space for any uncertainty. The idea of each offense and its attraction must be associated with the idea of a specific punishment and the precise inconveniences that result from it. The link between the two must be represented as necessary and unbreakable. This obviously implies the working out of precise measures so that the system of punishment becomes effective and the principle of certainty is not violated.

In such circumstances, the question of any appeal to a third party is completely ruled out, because if the child is allowed to get away with virtually no punishment for a serious offense, and gets the impression that punishment is not a necessary consequence of the offense committed, he may commit them again in future. The system must be inexorable, and those who execute it must be inflexible:

> There is no appeal against the punishment meted out by nature. When the mother punishes the child, the father in the presence of the child often reproaches her for this; or the father wants to punish the child and the mother protects the culprit. In the court of nature, there is no such undue intervention.[30]

For the system to work smoothly, there must be constant surveillance over the children, because no offense committed must escape the gaze of the parents. Nothing will weaken the system more than instances of the offender going unpunished. How could the parents establish in the minds of their children a strict link between offense and penalty if it were fraught with uncertainty? Ideally, the punishment should not be accompanied by threats or show of power, but should be executed without hesitation. "This punishment is not preceded by any threat; it is administered slowly but surely. Whenever rules are violated, punishment follows. Mother Nature does not admit of any excuses."[31]

Once given the form of a natural sequence, power is concealed from the act of punishment. Punishment does not appear to be the arbitrary effect of human power, but a necessity of things, and power acts while concealing itself beneath the gentle force of nature. There are punishments that are natural and there are punishments that are analogical:

> The boy has intentionally broken his doll. The next day, he is crying and asking for a new doll. In this case, the pain caused by his longing is nature's punishment. The duty of the parents is to make the boy suffer for a few more days. But instead of following this course, if you buy him a new doll, then that will be a violation of nature's rule. On the other hand, if you beat him because of his crying for the doll, then that will be an unjustified enhancement of punishment.[32]

In the case of natural punishment, then, parents are advised not to intervene because the content and intensity of the punishment are taken care of by the "naturalness" of the punishment itself. In the last analysis, "nature's punishment may be harsh but is ultimately beneficial."[33] And the child should view the punishment not only as natural but also in his own interest; he should be able to read in it his own advantage.

In analogical punishment, again the corrective strategy is based on the principle of naturalness and is represented in its form by the content of the offense. If the child steals food, he should be deprived of food; if he abuses liberty, he should be deprived of liberty and confined; if he breaks his brother's or sister's toys, his own toys will be confiscated. "The boy has broken his sister's toy. Here the boy should be compelled to give his toy to his sister. Of course, instead of calling this nature's rule, it is better described as analogical punishment."[34] In analogical punishment, the power that punishes is not transparent but is concealed. What is transparent is the relation of the sign to that which it signifies—the relation between offense and punishment. This should be immediately intelligible to the senses. It is this particular sign that is sought to be established in the form of analogical punishment.

The superiority of natural and analogical punishments, it is argued, is derived as follows (here the children learn the causal relation between offense and punishment, and they are able to comprehend the good and evil effects of their actions): First, an immediate link is established in the mind between the offense and the punishment, a link of resemblance, analogy, and proximity. Second, it is argued, the natural justice of such forms of punishment is immediately intelligible to the child, and hence he has no reason for any resentment against his parents. This also prevents both the child and the parents from acquiring characteristics that are rough and cruel. Finally, no ill-feeling or misunderstanding develops between child and parents; on the contrary, "the parents' power and dominance over their children are firmly established."[35]

What is significant here is the idea of establishing dominance over the child but at the same time escaping the child's resentment and anger by shifting the responsibility of disciplining and character formation to "natural" sources. When it is argued that every action is the product of a long causal chain, and that the child should himself immediately perceive the causal relation, it is implied that moral judgments have no place in child rearing. What is still more important is that the argument absolves the child from moral responsibility, yet does not diminish the responsibility of the parents. This ambivalence is reflected in the dependence on expert advice (of which this text is an example): the proliferation of such advice undermines parental confidence at the same time as it encourages an exaggerated idea of the importance of character-formation techniques and of the parents' responsibility for their failure.

At the very beginning, the text gives to parents a warning, reminding them of the incalculable consequences of their actions:

> When the mother admiring her little daughter dressed in pretty clothes calls her a "queen," does she think even once what terrible harm this simple word has done to the girl? Does she ever think that this has given birth to an unnecessary pride in the child's mind? . . . The child stumbles on the floor and starts to cry; the mother tries to console him by asking him to kick the floor. She does not realize what a vile attitude of vindictiveness is inflamed in his heart.[36]

Given such a forbidding set of instructions, it seems more than likely that the appeal for parents of a text like *SCG* would fade. Ironically, expert advice weakens the parents' faltering confidence in their own judgment, such advice leaving no room for parents to act on their intuitions. In their uncertainty, parents redouble their dependence on experts, who confuse them with a plethora of conflicting advice that is subject to change with changing notions of childhood. As a consequence, parents increasingly act not on their own feelings or judgment but according to the image of what good parents ought to be like.

Satischandra proposes that children's offenses be placed in a hierarchy. Parents, he says, should grade the offenses according to their long-term consequences, in terms of effects on the child's character. For instance, telling lies while playing should not be considered a minor or pardonable offense, as this habit can ultimately destroy one's character, but laughing, shouting, or the habit of breaking things are pardonable offenses because there is no threat of disgracing one's character by committing such offenses.[37]

Parents are advised to establish their dominance by a proper mixture of terror and love, but, once successful, they should utilize this dominance with restraint. The dominance must not be exercised perpetually because then it would lose its utility. But at all times it should remain hidden behind the act of punishment. The idea, based on the causal chain behind offenses, is to go to the source of the offense. If laziness is the source that produces a particular offense, that is the source to be eliminated. The desire that produces the offense has to be countered with the representation of punishment and its disadvantages in such a fashion that the latter makes a permanent imprint on the mind of the child. Since the penalty is aimed at transforming and molding the character of the child, and also at establishing signs and arranging obstacles, punishment can "function only if it comes to an end." A penalty without end is contradictory, because it leaves no scope for the reformed child to taste the benefit of his newly acquired virtues. In a similar way, a continuous display of dominance is contradictory and unproductive.

Punishing the Body

In recent social theory, the issue of the body is associated in particular with the name of Michel Foucault. Foucault has analyzed the body in relation to mechanisms of power, concentrating particularly on the emergence of "disciplinary power" in circumstances of modernity. The body becomes the focus of a power that, instead of trying to "mark" the body externally, as in premodern times, subjects it to the internal discipline of self-control. As portrayed by Foucault, disciplinary mechanisms produce "docile bodies." A docile body may be subjected, used, transformed, and improved. The methods that make possible the control of the operations of the body, that assure the constant subjection of its forces, and that impose upon them a relation of docility-utility, are called "disciplines":

> In short, it dissociates power from the body; on the one hand, it turns it into an "aptitude," a "capacity," which it seeks to increase; on the other hand, it reverses the course of the energy, the power that might result from it, and turns it into a relation of strict subjection. If economic exploitation separates the force and the product of labor, let us say that disciplinary coercion establishes in the body the constricting link between an increased aptitude and an increased domination.[38]

In *SCG,* the body occupies a crucial space in the disciplinary strategies of character formation. In the section titled "Necessity for Physical Punishment," Satischandra points out, contrary to a Foucauldian notion of modern disciplinary power, that disobedience against the parent's dominance should necessarily be met with physical punishment. "When children revolt against their parents, then that has to be suppressed by every means possible. Like revolt against the state, revolt in the family should be suppressed by taking recourse to all possible harshness."[39]

The family is here viewed as a ministate in operation. Within the confines of the family, children are segregated in a professionally supervised environment, as in the prison or the asylum, and the child's character is molded by means of dominance and punishment. The method assumes effective control over the child's body; indeed, the body becomes the site of the disciplinary exercise. For instance, disobedience can be dealt with by the control of the body:

> The father asks the son, "Naren, tell me, what is this letter?" Naren remains silent.
> The father tells him, "Say *ka*."
> Naren: "I won't say it."
> Father: "You must say it."
> Naren does not speak. The father first scolds him. But being unsuccessful, he then canes him and orders, "Say it now." Naren is still silent. The father beats him even more severely, but Naren is stubborn. Naren's mother stands nearby, but she does not say a word in favor of her son. The father, to give his son time to think, goes to another room leaving him with his mother. The mother tells him, "Say it, my son, otherwise he won't let you go. You will be beaten once more."
> Naren: "I will die, but I won't say it."
> The father comes back and tells Naren, "Say it now." But the child is still stubborn. The father then beats him so severely that Naren is unable to bear it any more. Weeping, he says to his father, "Father, I beg you, I fall at your feet, please stop, I am going to say it."
> Father: "What do you mean you are going to say it? Say it now," and continues to beat Naren. The child accepts defeat and says "*ka*."

If the father had not been so firm in performing his duties, the child would have thought himself more powerful than the father. Then the father's dominance over him would have vanished forever.[40]

Physical pain here is an essential element in punishment. In the disciplinary exercises described in the previous section, the body was touched as little as possible and then only to reach something other than the body, what might be called the soul. In the earlier exercises, the expiation was not inflicted on the body, but acted in depth on the heart, the mind, the will. Or, more often, power was operated through the "soul" on the body. It was advised that, in ordinary circumstances, power is best left concealed. However, stubborn disobedience was like waging war against the dominant power. Hence, this had to be subjected to a different system of punishment, because proper character would emerge only out of a subjected body. Against the allegation of cruelty, the answer was that bitter medicine might cause suffering, but without it the patient would die. At this limit, the disciplinary techniques of the Foucauldian kind are seen to be ineffective: power here is once more the exercise of sovereignty and its effect therapeutic.

This therapeutic conception of the child's deviance, which has become much more elaborate and sophisticated in contemporary times, also repudiates in the Indian context the traditional assumption of inevitability and *karma* and inadvertently relieves the patient of the responsibility for his actions, insisting that he is neither possessed nor willfully sinning, but sick. The new conception of the family as an enclosed domain repudiates fatalism by insisting on the child's innocence and plasticity. The child's character is the effect of such a therapeutic and disciplinary exercise. The character is the prison of the body.

However, what also worries the *SCG* text is the strong, lasting, crude, and negative effect of physical punishment. The dilemma is that giving freedom to the child suggests a laxity about rules, whereas punishment tends to create an attitude of fear, anxiety, resentment, and rejection. *SCG* could hardly recommend a defeated mind and tame, low spirits. The advice that parents should neither tyrannize their children nor burden them with oversolicitous attention is hard to maintain because a precise balance between the two always remains illusory. Quite regularly, we find in the text such cautionary statements as "severe punishment is not effective," it arouses resentment, and often induces harshness in both parents and child; it could turn the child into a weak and timid person.

This confusion is not particular to this text, but is inherent in modern family practice and reflects the more demanding nature of child rearing and consequently the more intense emotional ties between parents and children. At the same time, ties with relatives outside the immediate family weaken. This remains a source of persistent tension because of the emotional overloading of the parent-child connection. It is noteworthy that the principal characters in the text are father, mother, and children; outsiders so far have no role in this character-building exercise.

The tension is reflected in *SCG* when we find that Satischandra oscillates between the use of power over the body and the opposite notion that the remodeling of character needs warmth and affection. The text points out that, if parents are loving, the child is likely to reciprocate that love and to care about their wishes or feelings. Affectionate parents are more likely than others to be alert to the needs of the child, and to offer rewards that will reinforce what they consider good behavior. If the parent is affectionate, he or she can more effectively arouse guilt or concern in the child by withdrawing love; the hostile or abusive parent cannot use that threat as easily. The child who frequently experiences coldness or anger has much less to lose by disobedience. On the other hand, punishment is somewhat less precise than rewards, for the child does not easily learn what is right.

The guiding principle in character building remains the rule of consistency. In the section called "Love and Affection," Satischandra reminds parents that violation of this principle can cause immense harm to the child. Love and affection should never be shown by violating this principle:

> In this country, when a father disciplines the child, the loving mother's heart is flooded with pity. This strange wave of affection sometimes produces a deluge of tears, and at other times is transformed into a barrage of abuses for the father in the son's presence. Such mothers are their children's enemies.[41]

Suspicions that maternal love could, in certain circumstances, have disastrous results take an increasingly positive form. Besides maintaining consistency in disciplining the child, the parents should, in the privacy of the family, exercise it in a cool and detached manner, without any show of anger or irritation. Coldness and detachment are also necessary because excessive familiarity can jeopardize the parental authority. Otherwise, "the rough behavior of parents would cause a feeling of aversion in children toward their parents . . . if they are scolded in public, they will lose their natural shyness and, thinking they have lost their reputation anyway, will not endeavor to preserve it."[42]

That parents should present an image that can be reflected on the child is an essential aspect of *SCG*. Whereas, at first, the character-formation exercise was problematized—the relationship between children and parents being established in the form of advice, moral education, keeping the child under observation, and warnings of future dangers—later, by a strange reversal, the character of the parents is called into question. This is because of the notion, then widely prevalent and also accepted by Satischandra, that the child acquires strength or weakness of character through heredity—that is, through the parents.

We have already mentioned that, according to Satischandra, parents are bound to see their blemishes reflected in their children. This inevitably raises the question of self-discipline and *caritra gaṭhan* of the parents. Satischandra suggests that this task should be completed before the child is born. "The task is not so easy that parents can complete it even after the child is born and then start to build the child's character. If the child has to be of good character, then long before he is born, the parents' character should be well formed, because it has already been said that the child inherits the blemishes from his parents."[43] The parents can acquire the qualities of good character through self-discipline (*ātma-śāsan*), self-regulation (*ātma-śṛṅkhalā*), self-control (*ātma-saṃyam*), and self-reflection (*ātma-paryālocanā*).

Just as the argument about the causal chain absolves the child of moral responsibility without in any way diminishing the responsibility of his parents, the argument about heredity also enhances parental responsibility for their failure and heightens their anxiety. Such anxieties and faltering confidence create greater space for the proliferation of pedagogy. The character formation of the child becomes an important arena of contention, demands more and more such pedagogy, and becomes a theme around which a large number of discursive strategies are employed. Through pedagogy, schooling, and medicine (for example, what kinds of food to take and what to avoid), character formation becomes the concern of the social body as a whole. All individuals are placed under scrutiny. In appearance, we are dealing with a barrier system, but in fact all around the child, indefinite lines of penetration are dispersed.

Sexuality

The child's sexuality also receives Satischandra's attention. Here Satischandra avoids entering into detail to the degree he does, for instance, on the subject of physical punishment. But he warns parents that neglect of this aspect can lead to evil and corruption in society: "Parents by their improper exhibition of indifference toward such serious duties open up the passage for disease, sin and corruption in the social body."[44]

In the new discourse on the family, while sexuality of the legitimate couple is tolerated, the sexuality of children is looked upon with suspicion. Sexual desire is made the root of all evil, though it is very difficult to detect and guard against, because it affects the whole social body in devious ways. That is why the sexual conduct of the child is taken as a target of intervention.

Children's sexuality is characterized in terms of an interplay between what is visible and the eventual effects, which are hidden; between what is "natural" and what is "contrary to nature"; and also in terms of the idea that all children are prone to indulge in sexual activity. This tendency is said to pose dangers that are both moral and physical, individual and collective.

The argument about the "natural" again comes into play here, because untimely and unnatural use of sexual organs is fraught with danger. Satischandra believes that, in civilized societies, unlike in the realm of nature, the imagination plays an important role in arousing sexual desires. Hence, children should be warned of the untimely arrival of such dangerous tendencies. On the other hand, "to those who deny the necessity of such education, we have nothing to say. Let them suffer along with their sons and grandsons from various diseases. Driven to agony by the animal instincts of their children, let them pay the price of their foolishness."[45]

Parents who are not aware of these problems should be taught about the need for such education; those who feel shy about giving such education to their children should entrust the job to people who are competent. Satischandra, in effect, mobilizes the entire adult world around the matter of sex and children, reminds parents that all children are potentially guilty, and burdens them with the fear of being themselves at fault if they do not share this suspicion of their children's guilt. We find in Satischandra's account the combination of father, mother, educator, and doctor forming a circle around the child and sex. Satischandra points out that prevention is better than cure, but in case prevention is not possible, parents should not rely on a child's statement, nor on their own judgment, but should have the child examined by a "competent and reliable" doctor. Only on that basis should they make an evaluation. Thus, through the need for advice, keeping the child under observation, and warnings about future dangers, Satischandra problematizes the child's sexuality within the relationship established between experts (in this case, the doctor) and parents. According to Satischandra, doctors can give better treatment to the sick than families can provide and, by implication, better care for the young. The family is thus put in an indecisive position in choosing the right balance between the supportive and disciplinary aspects of cure.

One of the greatest dangers for the child, Satischandra reminds parents, is the temptation of the pleasures of the body, the useless discharge of semen, and violations of sexual austerity. These dangers hinder the development of the soul as well as the body, cause physical, mental, moral, and spiritual degeneration, and premature death. Although the family is the domain within which the child is supposed to be protected from such dangers, sexuality permeates almost everywhere, in the presence of servants, in corrupting influences in the neighborhood, and so on: "In this country, although there is a total absence of good teachers, bad teachers are available in plenty. All these bad teachers are not idle either; on the contrary, they are disagreeably ardent."[46] Even in children's storybooks, Satischandra writes, there is "in every story . . . a radiantly beautiful girl. . . . What beauty on her face! What a pretty expression she makes with her nose! What feeling in her eyes! It is really astounding! And what moral education these stories provide!"[47]

Sexuality, in other words, is viewed as a multiplying mechanism, operating in a complex network, and even when a boundary is drawn around the child, a boy remains susceptible to its dangers. Satischandra reminds the parents:

> I repeat that parents should convince their children at the proper time the necessity for conserving their semen. The parents should especially explain to them that wastage of semen causes immediate death, that misuse of semen is responsible for physical, mental, moral and spiritual degeneration, that conservation of semen is the principal component of *brahmacarya* and that by conserving their semen the Brahmins of India reached the pinnacle of glory. Parents should also remind them that this body is the temple of God, no one has the right to pollute it. No one can escape from untimely annihilation and dreadful hell if he treats his body in an unrestrained manner.[48]

It can be argued that, in this discourse, families act as relays; through the medium of families, a system of control of sexuality is sought to be established over the bodies of children. Satischandra's argument for surveillance of children, treating their sexuality as an object of analysis, is based on the mistrust of bodily pleasures and on the harmful consequences of abuse of the body. However, if one is successful in checking and controlling such desires, one can attain the status of ancient Brahmins, which is possible only through *brahmacarya*. In this context, it is useful to remember that Satischandra believes that all children are essentially religious, but the inherent religiosity of children is not encouraged by parents. The child's religiosity in combination with *brahmacarya* can really do wonders.[49] By enhancing religious feeling among children, they can be prevented from future temptations when they become young adults.

Son of the Nation

What would the child be like if he were properly trained? In the West, a new style of domestic life argued for the creation of psychological conditions that would favor the emergence of a new type of inner-directed, self-reliant, achievement-oriented personality, one with rational foresight and capable of accumulating worldly goods. But Satischandra's child when grown would be a strange mixture.[50] He would be self-reliant and hardworking, but self-denying, ascetic, obedient, truthful, austere, and unselfish, satisfied with the few things necessary for his physical upkeep. He would be a person able to engage his mind in more worthy pursuits than mere acquisition of worldly goods; one who knows well that the material side of life is less important than its spiritual counterpart.

Bhudeb Mukhopadhyay, in his *Pāribārik prabandha,* mentions that since a child's character formation depends on the needs of the society in which the child grows up, the primary concern for all parents should therefore be to educate their children in such a fashion that they can remove those deficiencies in their society. Echoing this sentiment, Satischandra points out that citizens of a poor nation like India cannot afford the luxuries that the English enjoy; hence, children should not be extravagant. Even the rich should desist from encouraging extravagant tendencies in their children. Bengalis have to endure a lot of hardships, overcome innumerable hurdles; hence, the education of Bengali children should be severe. Every head of the family should become a Lycurgus because no kingly Lycurgus will arrive to make Spartans out of Bengalis. That is why "no parent should invite annihilation by inflaming luxurious desires in the descendants of this great nation. We do not want luxury, we want self-restraint; we do not want annihilation, we want life."[51] Satischandra's demand for unquestioning obedience from children arises because the child should accept that he is not in this world to enjoy himself, particularly if he is born in India. Therefore, from an early age, he should be taught that he must be guided by the ideals of sacrifice and resignation, that life is a trial and not a pleasure. For such reasons, pride, sensuality, and cupidity are seen as the worst faults of children.

The reason that the family, working like a machine, with invariable rules and regulations, with consistent behavior from the parents invoking uniform rewards and punishments, must produce people of such ascetic qualities is that today's children will determine the future shape of the nation. They are like soft clay; the way they are molded gives shape to the nation: "If you want to see the fiery sunshine on your mother's face, if you want to see her eyes brighten with heavenly light, then mold your child in the divine image."[52]

Satischandra reminds parents of their heavy responsibility: the future hopes and aspirations of the nation are entrusted to them in the form of their children. Significantly, Satischandra completely rejects the school or any other educative institution as the proper site of character formation. The only reference in the whole text to the school appears where he says that "irresponsible cane-and-wage-dependent teachers" cannot fulfill this task nor should parents be content by sending their children to schools."[53] In fact, the text shows deep suspicion of outside influences; they are thought to be mostly corrupting. Only the family is considered to be the proper place to undertake such an important and difficult task. The family remains the sole domain within which the child can acquire a proper character. Because for Satischandra, the family is the hidden nation, where the cultural and moral essences of the nation can be defended against outside intervention. The production and regulation of private life is thus crucial to the construction of the national identity.

The other significant feature of the text that should have become obvious by now is that it is about the male child. When Satischandra talks of the *santān*, he actually means the male child who will one day go out and act upon society. The girl child needs a different kind of training so that she can manage the household and rear her children properly after her marriage.[54] The character formation of the girl child therefore requires other disciplinary mechanisms, drawn from different sources of knowledge, in order to maintain the differences between socially approved male and female conduct. The model of the male child in the family seems to resemble that of the student in the *brahmacaryāśrama* of the past. The child learns to restrain his senses mainly by control of the sex instinct. The life of the child is thus regulated in such a way that his mind and body are properly disciplined. He should be accustomed to put his body under severe strain and engage his mind in more worthy pursuits than mere comforts, bodily pleasures, and display. A life that is dedicated to the unrestrained satisfaction of acquisitive urges (*artha*) is undesirable and even dangerous. It is consequently necessary that it should be regulated by the ideal of the future glory of the nation, which is the path to spiritual realization enjoined by *dharma*. As was pointed out by one author on domestic practices: "In modern times all persons have to depend on the family, because the ashram of the guru is not obligatory any more while *vānaprasthā* and *sannyāsa* have become defunct. Domestic life is now the sole refuge of *dharma*, which is why householders have very serious responsibilities."[55] Since man learns his proper *dharma* in the first *āśrama*, the character formation of the child requires much specialized knowledge on the part of the parents. In a similar vein, the joint family was not found suitable for the proper growth and development of the child, since the heterogeneous interests and influences at play within the joint family could only distract the child from his arduous task.[56]

Satischandra advises parents that they should tell their children about their motherland, its past and present condition, and what it should be in the future. The story of how fallen nations have risen should be told to them. "Awake in their mind the desire to tirelessly serve the nation and society. Teach them to abhor laziness from the bottom of their heart."[57] They should be made to understand that "all are indebted to society and that those who do not pay back their debts are sinners . . . it is not enough simply to renounce laziness; acts born out of selfishness do not repay one's debt to society."[58] The child modeled in the "divine mold" through discipline and education would ultimately protect the cultural identity and distinctiveness of the national culture. In writing this text, Satischandra acknowledges his debt to Mill, Bentham, Locke, and Rousseau for certain notions of discipline, natural punishment, childhood, and so on, but the child envisaged in his text is quite different. For Satischandra, the family is the domain where these differences have to be regulated and produced.

Satischandra's book shows how, with the revalorization of educative and disciplinary tasks within the family, the image of childhood was redefined and transformed. The discourse of remodeling childhood opened up a multitude of areas to be contested: children's stories, love stories, ghost stories, and so forth; entertainment and games, with idle games like cards being denounced and educational games—those that strengthen moral and physical qualities—being celebrated; the daily routine; the conception of surveillance and observation, with a discreet but ubiquitous parental gaze being advocated; sexuality, with favor reserved for abstinence and celibacy; and the question of the preparation and self-discipline of parents. All these encounters, occurring at a multitude of points, were conducted around a single strategic objective: to protect the child from physical dangers and, more important, from the moral dangers ranging from romantic stories about beautiful girls to sexual deviation that could divert a boy from the path chalked out for his development and mission in life—the chosen path that would also mark him with *differences*. The methods, limits, and themes inaugurated by this notion of childhood continue to define the contemporary pedagogical discourse on family and childhood in Bengal, as a casual glance at the contemporary literature on the subject will show.[59] That is perhaps the reason why it was thought fit to reissue Satischandra's volume in 1989, almost eight decades after it was first published.

Notes

1. Satischandra Chakravarti, *Santāner caritra gaṭhan* (hereafter *SCG*). All translations from Bengali sources are mine.

2. I will cite only a few sources from a large volume of literature on the subject: Sibnath Sastri, *Gṛhadharma*; Prasannatara Gupta, *Pāribārik jīban*; Pratapchandra Majumdar, *Strīcaritra*; Bhudeb Mukhopadhayay, "Pāribārik prabandha." A large number of journals also (e.g., *Antahpur, Gārhasthya, Gṛhastha, Baṅgamahilā,* and *Svāsthya*) regularly discussed issues of family and domestic management.

3. Satischandra Chakravarti, *Nabayuger āhvān,* p. 2.

4. See Fruzzetti, Östör, and Barnett, "Cultural Construction," pp. 8-30.

5. Nandy, "Reconstructing Childhood," p. 57.

6. The issue of the joint family in India is confused by definitional problems, and the data are equivocal. The institution of the joint family has been a civilizational ideal in India and was assumed to be the social reality of traditional Indian society. There have been at least two different understandings of the notion of joint family. One, which A. M. Shah calls the Indological conception based on Hindu legal texts, viewed the joint family in terms of coparcenary property relations and regulatory control over ritual, marriage, and inheritance. The other was the sociological conception, which defined the joint family in terms of the coresidence of two or more married couples. Most of the writings on the joint family in Bengal written in the last century followed the Indological conception. See Shah, "Changes," pp. 127-34; Shah, *Household Dimension*; Madan, "The Hindu Family," pp. 211-31; Uberoi, "Family," pp. 383-92.

7. Sibnath Sastri, *Gṛhadharma*, p. 69.

8. "Ekānnabartī paribār," *Baṅgadarśan* 1, 6, Āśvin 1279 (1872). The next several quotations are from this article.

9. On the medical aspect, see Annadacharan Khastagir, *Pāribārik susthatā*; Indubhusan Sen, *Pāribārik cikitsā.*

10. On health and hygiene of the child, see, for instance, Nripendranath Seth, "Āmāder śiśu"; "Śiśu pālan," 8-9; "Cheler asukh," 3; "Mātṛstanyapāyī, 6.

11. On the construction of women under the influence of colonialism and nationalism, see Chatterjee, *Nation,* pp. 116-57; Sarkar, "Nationalist Iconography," pp. 2011-15; Sarkar, "The Hindu Wife," pp. 213-35; Karlekar, "Kadambini," pp. WS25-WS31; Jasodhara Bagchi, "Representing Nationalism," pp. WS65-WS71.

12. Pratapchandra Majumdar, *Strīcaritra*, p. 14.

13. Prasannatara Gupta, *Pāribārik jīban*, p. 82.

14. Rangalal Bandyopadhyay, *Śarīrsādhanī bidyār guṇakīrtan* (1869), cited in Dipesh Chakrabarty, "Deference-Deferral," pp. 1-34.

15. Atulchandra Datta, *Gṛhadharma* (1906), cited in Chakrabarty, "Deference-Deferral."

16. Sibnath Sastri, *Gṛhadharma*, p. 101.

17. This is a term used by Benedict Anderson in *Imagined Communities,* p. 131.

18. Sibaji Bandyopadhyay discusses *SCG,* albeit briefly, in his *Gopāl-rākhāl dvandvasamās,* pp. 194-97. His discussion is in the context of the emergence of patriarchy, the masculine ethos, and the downgrading of the affective role of women in child rearing. This he relates to notions of repression, colonialism, and underdevelopment, which, according to him, produced a "distorted" version of childhood. In this context, see also Ariel Dorfman, "Childhood." Bandyopadhyay examines Satischandra's text along with several others in order to understand the nature of children's literature within the framework of a colonial political economy. The framework of my discussion is entirely different. I consider this text within the discourse of the family, since I feel that the discursive formation of the family can be better understood if it is seen to be constituted by such texts.

19. Pratapchandra Majumdar, *Strīcaritra*, pp. 122-29.

20. *SCG*, pp. 1-2.

21. *Bāmābodhinī patrikā* 8, 108 (August 1872).

22. Pankaj Datta, *Racanā bicitrā,* p. 39. This is a book of model essays meant for schoolchildren. See also Manmathanath Bandyopadhyay, *Caritra gaṭhan.*

23. *SCG,* pp. 11-12.

24. Satischandra Chakrabarti, *Nabayuger āhvān,* p. 4.

25. *SCG,* p. 8.

26. *SCG,* p. 11.

27. *SCG,* p. 15.

28. *SGC,* p. 29.

29. *SCG,* p. 29.

30. *SCG,* pp. 29-30.

31. *SCG,* p. 29.

32. *SGC,* p. 36.

33. *SCG,* p. 30.

34. *SCG,* p. 32.

35. *SGC,* p. 33.

36. *SCG,* pp. 4-5.

37. *SCG,* p. 17.

38. Foucault, *Discipline and Punish,* p. 138.

39. *SCG,* p. 22.

40. *SCG,* pp. 22-23.

41. *SCG,* p. 23. The same sentiments appear in many moral tales: for instance, Madhusudhan Mukhopadhyay, *Suśīlār upākhyān.* See also Sibaji Bandyopadhyay, *Gopāl-rākhāl dvandvasamās,* p. 210.

42. *SCG,* pp. 20-21.

43. *SCG,* p. 11.

44. *SCG,* p. 69.

45. *SCG,* p. 69.

46. *SCG,* p. 70.

47. *SCG,* p. 68.

48. *SCG,* p. 71.

49. On the *brahmacarya* of the male child, see also "Manuṣya ki paśur adham?" *Gṛhastha* 1 (1316), 3 (1909); Saratchandra Deb, *Gārhasthya prasaṅga.*

50. For Western notions of childhood and family, see Donzelot, *Policing;* Ariès, *Centuries of Childhood*; deMause, ed., *History of Childhood*; Lasch, *Haven*; Lewis, *Pursuit of Happiness.*

51. *SCG,* p. 72.

52. *SCG,* p. 74.

53. *SCG,* p. 74.

54. For the regime of socialization for the girl child, see Jasodhara Bagchi, "Socialising the Girl Child," pp. 2214-19; Saratchandra Dhar, *Abalā bāndhab*; Sarojini Debi, *Āryasatī*; Nagendrabala Dasi, *Nārīdharma.*

55. Saradaprasad Hajra Chaudhuri, *Saṃsār-dharma o biṣaykarma,* p. 4. See also, "Gṛhadharma: saṃsār āśram," *Sacitra gārhasthyakoṣ,* Āṣāḍh 1307 (1902).

56. For a succinct argument, see "Ekānnabartī paribār," *Baṅgadarśan* 1, 6 (Āśvin 1279) (1872).

57. *SCG,* p. 73.

58. *SCG,* p. 73.

59. See, for instance, Asim Bardhan, *Śiśu kena "śiśu"*; Asim Bardhan, *Kiśor-kiśorīder youna samasyā*; Amarendranath Basu, *Śiśumaner bikāś-o-bikār.*

6 / A City Away from Home: The Mapping of Calcutta

Keya Dasgupta

Colonial Maps

Cartography has been an instrument of colonial policy at least since the sixteenth century. Indeed, it is one of the earliest "disciplines" of colonial knowledge, preceding most other modern technologies of power.

In India, surveys were made by the British of territories conquered and annexed by the East India Company from the middle of the eighteenth century. These surveys were conducted for several purposes: to plan military campaigns, to measure the extent of cultivated or cultivable lands, to detail routes of communication, and so on. In Bengal, "systematic surveying was first undertaken for civil and financial purposes"[1] in 1767 under the supervision of James Rennell, who became the first surveyor-general.

The majority of surveyors in this phase were military officers. "Though there was no training school for surveyors," it was observed, "officers with some elementary knowledge of survey were generally to be found when wanted," since "every engineer officer was presumed to be capable of surveying."[2] This was justified in an official correspondence: "We have made no provision for such surveyors as are not in the Company's Civil or Military services because we are of opinion no person should be entrusted with Inland Survey except those who are actually in the service."[3]

Towns became the objects of detailed survey as soon as the British established themselves in the three presidencies of Bengal, Bombay, and Madras.

Necessitated by its growing importance as a center of administrative and commercial activity, Calcutta was soon to become one of the most frequently mapped cities of colonial India.

Looking at the history of the cartography of Calcutta, one finds that since its beginning in the mid-eighteenth century, the items of survey have changed in keeping with the changing requirements of the colonial power. From the declared objectives of the Survey of India, it is found that the earliest plans of Calcutta were made by engineers for purposes of defense and the laying out of fortifications.[4] The objectives of map making then shifted to the naming of streets and preparing a "Registry of Lands, Houses and Estates," and for other matters connected with the administration of the city. The preservation of the health of the inhabitants was also among the objectives, because maps were necessary to plan for proper drainage and sewerage facilities.[5] Surveys were also undertaken for purposes of revenue collection. Significant emphasis was put on the social and functional uses of land. Racial segregation between the European inhabitants and the local Indian population was always given prominence when such maps were drawn. Areas of European habitation were highlighted by either shading individual plots or by naming the residents (Fig. 6.1). With the exception of the residences of a very few prominent Indians, this was never done for areas inhabited by the local people. The series of maps prepared in the nineteenth century testify to this (Fig. 6.2).

The city of Calcutta, developed on a marshy terrain between the River Hooghly on the west and the saltwater lakes on the east, had to be made habitable for Europeans. The maps illustrate how the best lands, at higher levels, were appropriated for building the fort, settling the British inhabitants, housing the East India Company's offices, and so forth. These objectives are evident from the way the surveys were conducted and the maps and plans prepared. The exaggerated emphasis on the European quarters to the neglect of the Indian even became a subject of discussion among survey officials. A chief engineer observed on a map of Calcutta of the eighteenth century: "The Chowringhee and [European] Quarter has been executed in the manner that the whole of the plan ought to have been."[6]

Most of the official surveys and mapping published between the mid-eighteenth and the late nineteenth century were carried out within the organizational structure of the Survey of India, with instruments and methods imported from Europe and using a wide network of staff and stations spread throughout the subcontinent. Even in the early years of the nineteenth century, there was no school for surveyors. "The Surveyor-General

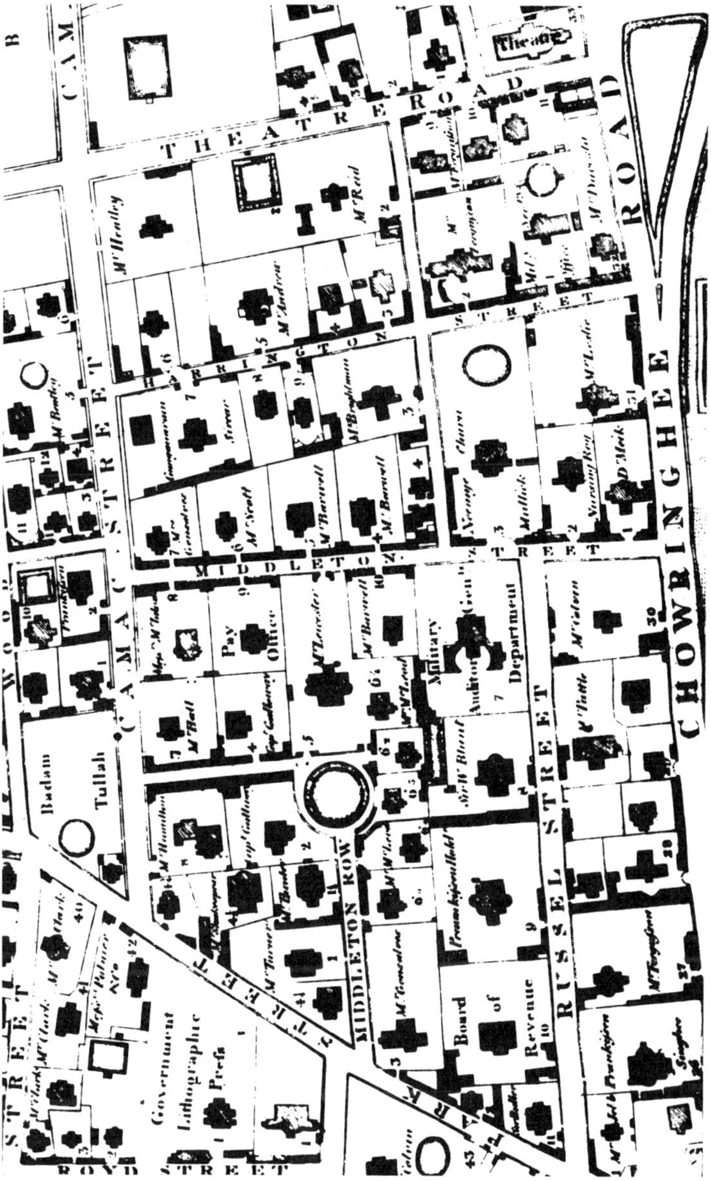

Fig. 6.1. An area of European habitation in south Calcutta, 1825, from a map prepared by J. A. Schalch

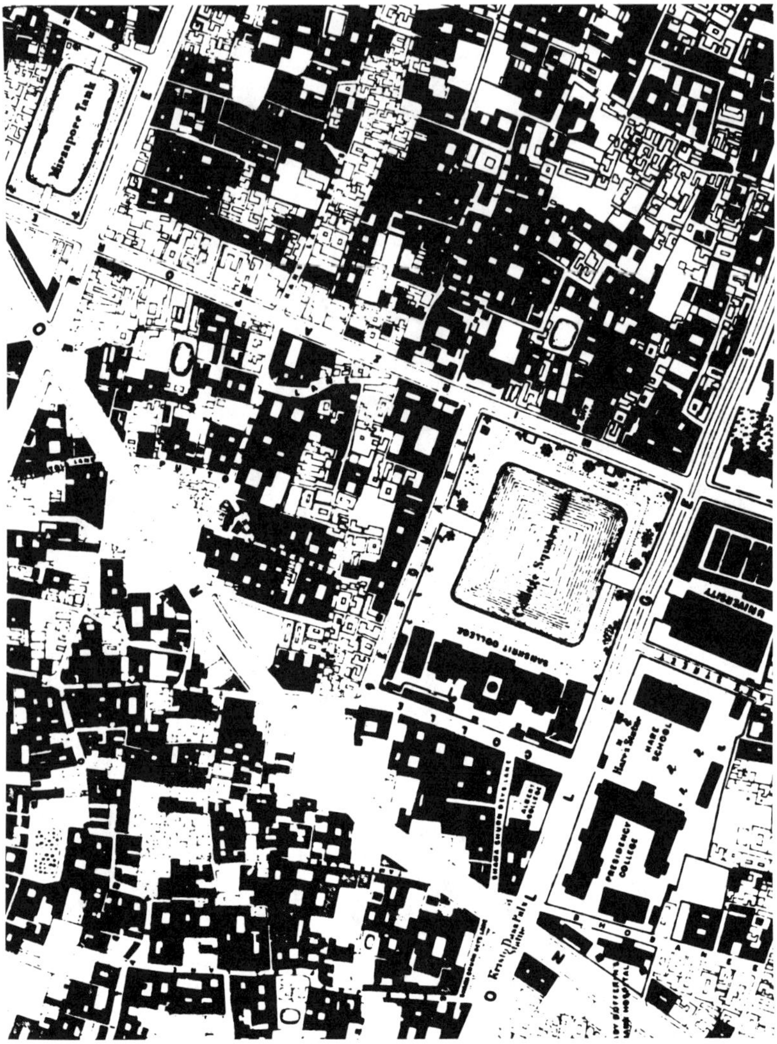

Fig. 6.2. A section of north Calcutta inhabited by Indians, from a map prepared by the Survey of India, 1887-94

had to send out lengthy elementary instructions to each new surveyor," wrote Phillmore, historian of the Survey of India.[7] Neither was much progress made in India in the matter of printing reproductions of the maps. Maps were either sent to England for engraving or the machines and stones were imported. As late as the 1830s, the surveyor-general's office in Calcutta did not have its own lithographic press. In 1823 a Government Lithographic

Press was established on Park Street under the superintendence of Dr. James N. Rind, and this became available for printing maps. A private establishment set up by J. B. Tassin was also used to lithograph Survey of India maps. Classes in engraving, etching, and lithography were started at the Government School of Art in 1855 and around the 1890s it was noted that these classes had satisfactorily served several government departments and outside parties.[8] Students from the school "won reputation as very skilled general lithographers, wood engravers."[9] Artists from Bengal were thus seen to have gained competence in a field that, for a substantial part of the nineteenth century, had been reserved for Europeans.[10]

The nineteenth and early twentieth centuries in Calcutta also saw a spate of publication of directories, registers, and almanacs, some accompanied by maps. The better known of these were published by Samuel Smith & Co., Sanders, Cones & Co., Thacker, Spink & Co. and Scott & Co. Most covered Bengal, but some were exclusively about Calcutta. Primarily they contained official information: civil, military, and commercial regulations and directories, marine directories, ecclesiastical directories, lists of societies and institutions, street directories, lists of European inhabitants, and so forth. The directories, acknowledged as "well known sources on the names and status of Englishmen who had held important positions during those days," were rather arbitrary in their selection of information. However, the New Calcutta Directory, published annually since 1855, was meant to be an exception. The directory for 1856, in addition to listing official information about administrative institutions, contained a detailed street directory with the names, addresses, and occupations of the inhabitants of various premises. Put together by the municipal commissioners, it provided information on land use at that time in the city of Calcutta.[11] Nevertheless, the directory's "List of inhabitants of the city" included only the names of European residents. The directory, accompanied by a street map, was prepared for the municipal commissioners by Samuel & Co.

Indigenous Cartography and Directories

Under colonial domination, India was "one of the best surveyed areas outside Europe." But little cartographic material prepared by Indians is known to have survived. Susan Gole writes:

> While it is true that so far no continuous line of development in the depiction of the earth, or of their own country has been found in India, there are yet several distinct types of maps using the term in the European meaning that were in use, either before the coming of the foreigners from overseas, or at the time

> that the Europeans were attempting to set down the correct positions of the various towns, roads, rivers and mountains on maps made according to travellers' tales, or later from Survey.[12]

Indigenous maps of India date back several centuries. Early "maps" have been engraved on stone, painted on cloth, and drawn on paper. In her study of two hundred indigenous maps and plans prepared over the last three or four centuries (and a few from even earlier), in different regions of the subcontinent, Gole argues that it is debatable whether any of these maps might truly be called geographical maps. More examples must be found and dates established before a clear picture will emerge. The early maps did not have what we call a scale, but those who made them must have had their own idea of scale, "based not on distance, but on importance." They can be categorized broadly into groups: religious, topographical, cosmological, and military. Since no list of symbols is given, possibly the information contained in these maps has not been properly understood.

Certainly, in the case of town plans it is hard to trace a pattern of development among the documents made in the indigenous styles. They "vary in every respect, in size, in material, in symbolization, in scale, and in the purpose for which it is presumed they were made." Most of the indigenous maps illustrated in Gole's *Indian Maps and Plans* were known to have been "drawn by Indians without any training in Survey by the British or French, though many of them are from a period when measured surveys were already being made."[13] The majority of these maps and plans are from western India, especially Rajasthan, south India, and the northwest.

Gleaning the documentary evidence on indigenous maps in India, I have been unable to trace any detailed indigenous maps of Calcutta done locally. However, found recently among the records of the Sawai Man Singh II Museum in Jaipur, Rajasthan, and compiled in an interesting collection, are two maps of Calcutta. The first, a "map of Bengal," beautifully painted in the late-seventeenth-century Mughal style, has place-names written in Nagari and Arabic characters. The other, a "map of the southern sea [Bay of Bengal]," also painted on paper in the seventeenth century, has the place-names Baghbazar, Chitpur, and Khidirpur marked in the Bengali script.[14]

As far as is known, cartography in Bengal, in the Bengali language, made its beginning in the midnineteenth century. The pioneer in the field was Rajendralal Mitra, who under the aegis of the School Book Society and the Vernacular Literature Society published "physical charts" to accompany his geography primer, *Prākṛta bhūgol*, in 1854; his work is known to have influenced cartographic efforts in Bengal. Noteworthy was Rajendralal's publication in 1871 of a series of district maps of Bengal, Bihar, and Orissa.[15] The significance lies in the quality of the contents, which give minutely detailed place-names, even down to the level of the smallest villages. Rajendralal carefully followed a correct system of orthography, identifying local people who could provide accurate information. This marks a fundamental difference between foreign and local cartography. On the English practice, Phillimore has observed that "the spelling of place names on English maps of India has remained a vexed question even to the present day," and in the eighteenth century it was "largely regarded as a matter of personal taste, and the precise form even of personal names was not regarded as at all important."[16] Obviously, for maps made by foreigners for the use of foreigners ignorant of the local languages, getting the name right was not crucial. This was not the case with indigenous maps meant for local use, and Rajendralal Mitra's atlas can still be regarded as a masterpiece.

Directories of Calcutta published in the English language have already been mentioned: their contents emphasized European elements. A parallel set of directories, mostly accompanying almanacs, began to be published in Bengali from the last quarter of the nineteenth century. These publications differed in quality and approach, but they shared a common urge to satisfy needs that the English directories could not meet. Not only in language but also in content, they clearly addressed a different clientele.

One such book was Durgacharan Ray's *Debgaṇer martye āgaman*, published in 1886. Written in the form of a fictional narrative of travels on earth by deities from heaven, this was a tourist guide with religious overtones. Noteworthy among the places described are the pilgrimage centers of north India—Hardwar, Mathura, Vrindavan, Kashi, Allahabad—and, nearer home, Tribeni, Tarakeswar, and Kalighat. Also mentioned were centers of historical importance—Delhi, Agra, and Lucknow. In the section on Calcutta, Durgacharan describes places of religious and historical importance, and bazars, along with the names of the commodities sold.

More in the nature of a directory than a guidebook was Upendranath Mukhopadhyay's *Kalikāta darśak,* published in 1890.[17] The introduction to this little book says it was meant as a guide for "young boys from rural areas" on a visit to the city of Calcutta. Containing a list of "well known Indians" residing in the city, with their addresses, and of important buildings, transport, fairs, hotels, bazars, midwives, and so forth, it also listed the items sold in the main commercial centers.

The *Directory and Pañjikā,* published by P. M. Bagchi & Co. since the

1880s, is an important landmark in the tradition of Bengali directories because of its sustained popularity. It is extremely difficult now to procure any of the nineteenth-century P. M. Bagchi directories, but copies of early-twentieth-century editions add up to a massive compilation of information on the city of Calcutta.

A Bengali Map of Calcutta

Ramanath Das's *Kalikātār māncitra* (hereafter *KM*), published in 1884, is a distinctive, pioneering effort—a map-cum-guidebook in the Bengali language. Compared with the English maps and directories of the city, it stands out because of its attempt to develop a different cartography and a different classification and listing of information. In this, it faced a fundamental problem with the role of cartography in the new, urban culture of Bengal.

Published by "Romanauth Dass of Beniapukur, Calcutta," and accompanied by a map lithographed by Ramanath, the first edition was printed by B. M. Chakravarti, at the B. P. M's Press, No. 22 Jhamapooker Lane, Calcutta, in 1884. Although the map as well as the directory is in Bengali, the title is first given in English; the Bengali follows (Fig. 6.3). The aim of the publication is stated by Ramanath in an introductory note:

> For the use of the "common people" a book entitled *Kalikatar Manachitra* (Bengali Hand Map), along with a map of the city, has been written in the Bengali language. The names and signs provided in the book, along with the signs given in the map will enable one to locate all places, roads, lanes, *galis*, offices of the company, banks, courts, work places, European and Indian medical stores, schools, doctors, *kabiraj*, midwives who have passed out from the Medical College, main concentration of things sold, traders, lawyers of the high and lower courts, residences of "affluent people," European and Indian shops, hotels, presses, police stations, bazars, *hats*, ponds, as well as location of several other places.[18]

The map was lithographed at the Calcutta Art Studio in 1884. This studio, established in 1878 by former students of the Government School of Art, did lithographic and copperplate printing. In the absence of other evidence, we can surmise (considering the year of the publication of his map) that Ramanath learned the techniques of lithographic printing at the Government School of Art; or he might have been trained at the private lithographic presses mentioned earlier and later have become associated with the art studio in some capacity. A stray piece of evidence, collected from the New Calcutta Directory of 1856, could be a pointer. In the street directory, we find two names: Roopchaund Doss, lithographer and copperplate

BENGALI HAND MAP.

OF

CALCUTTA:

EOR GENERAL USE

BY

ROMANAUTH DASS·

First Edition

কলিকাতার মান চিত্র।

কলিকাতার এবং ইহার নিকটবর্ত্তি ২৪ পরগনার, হাবড়ার, শিবপুরের, এবং
সালকিয়ার, সর্ব্ব স্থানের নাম এবং ঠিকানা অনুসন্ধান করিতে হইলে এই
পুস্তকে অনায়াসে পাওয়া যাইবে, প্রধান ২ স্থান, রাস্তা, গলি, কোম্পানির
আপিস, ব্যাঙ্ক, আদালত, খাবার স্থান, কোম্পানির ইউরোপিও এবং
এতদ্দেশীয় ডাক্তারখানা ইস্কুল, পুস্তকালয়, ডাক্তার, কবিরাজ, মেডি-
কেল কলেজের পরীক্ষোত্তীর্ণ ধাত্রী, কোথায় কোন দ্রব্য অধিক
বিক্রয় হয়, সওদাগর, হাইকোর্টের এবং ছোট আদালতের
উকিল, প্রাচীন ভাগ্যবন্ত লোক দিগের বাটী, ইউরো
পিও এবং এতদ্দেশীও দোকানদার হোটেল
ছাপাখানা, থানা, বাজার, হাট, পুষ্করিণী,
এতদ্ভিন্ন আরং অনেক স্থানের নাম
এবং ঠিকানা আছে।

টীকা পাঠ করিলে স্থানসকল নকশাতে সহজে বাহির
করিবার উপায় পাইবেন।

সর্ব্বসাধারনের সুবিধার্থে

শ্রীরমানাথ দাস প্রণীত

বেনেপুকুর।

কলিকাতা

PRINTED BY B. M. CHAKRAVARTI, AT THE B. P. M'S PRESS.
No. 22, Jhamapooker Lane, Calcutta.

1884.

Fig. 6.3. Title page of *Kalikātār māncitra*

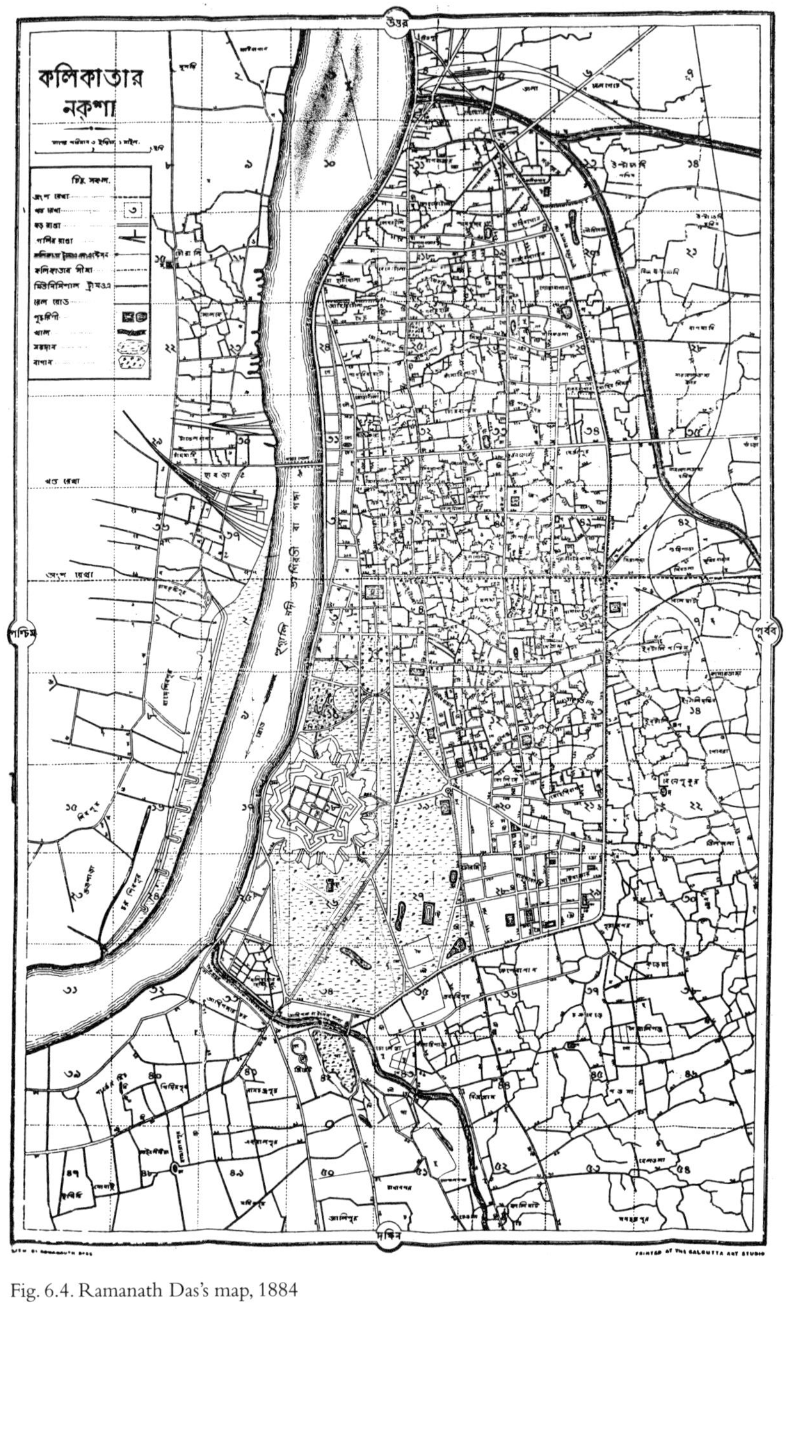

Fig. 6.4. Ramanath Das's map, 1884

printer; and Radacaunt Doss & Co., lithographers and engravers. Possibly Ramanath Das was related to one of these persons.

Drawn perfectly to a scale of three inches to a mile, the map (Fig. 6.4) extends beyond the limits of the town as defined for purposes of municipal administration.[19] The territory covered includes, in addition to the city of Calcutta, parts of Howrah and Sibpur, west of the River Hooghly, and the suburbs on the east, Ultadengi, Narkeldanga, Beleghata, Entally, Tiljala, and Kareya; Ballygunge in the southeast; and Chakrabere, Bhawanipur, Kalighat, and Khidirpur in the south. Information on this whole area is provided in the directory.

Technically comparable to any cartographic production of the period, Ramanath's map is distinguished by its way of presenting spatial information. The whole area is divided into two sections, the northern and the southern, by means of a thick, dotted line along almost the center of the map, i.e., Bowbazar Street, and across the River Hooghly and the eastern suburbs. Thin dotted lines divide the entire area into grids. The grids form squares for the most part, but toward the margins they cover larger areas and become rectangles. The northern section is divided (from northwest to southeast) into forty-two grids, whereas the southern section has fifty-four. Each grid is marked by a Bengali numeral, and readers have to refer to each number by its northern or southern location. Streets and lanes are marked by smaller numerals, whereas all other places of importance are marked by Bengali alphabets. The index given in the map shows the grid lines, the main roads, lanes, Calcutta tramways and their extensions, the boundaries of the city, the municipal tramway, the railroad, ponds, creeks, parks, and gardens. All other information relating to the residences of well-known Bengali inhabitants, professionals, bazars, offices, educational institutions, roads, lanes, ponds, ghats, and so on are given in the accompanying directory with corresponding letters and numerals, whose locations have to be traced on the map (Fig. 6.5).

Ramanath's use of the grid system is remarkable: there is no evidence of this method having been used in the maps accompanying English-language directories of Calcutta in the nineteenth century. Possibly, the method was used in contemporary maps of British or European cities that Ramanath had seen. A modern example of such a grid, much more detailed and exhaustive, of course, is to be found in the *London A to Z*. We will return to the question of why Ramanath chose this method.

We have mentioned earlier the importance placed on orthography in Rajendralal Mitra's atlas dated 1871. Ramanath Das's map shows an equal care for the correct naming of localities, roads, and so on. Ramanath clearly favored the locally used name rather than classicized or anglicized variants: Mechobazar, Ultadengi, Belgeche, and Intally are examples.

The localities shown in the map (redrawn in Fig. 6.5 and noted in Table 6.1) are far more numerous than those found in other cartographic sources of the period. Also, the information base of roads, lanes, and ghats is far more detailed than any available elsewhere. Of course, the English maps of the city did not go into detail about areas of native habitation, but Ramanath, branching out as he did, was catering to a wide range of interests.

The diverse elements in the contents of *KM* include both functional and social categories. We could list these as follows: administrative institutions (government offices, courts, police stations, jails, the mint, consulates, banks, hospitals); religious institutions (temples, mosques, churches, synagogues, Brahmo Samaj, and also burial grounds and burning ghats); places of entertainment and culture (museums, theaters, clubs, buildings for other societies, and other halls); educational institutions (schools, colleges, and libraries); markets (retail and wholesale) and other commercial establishments, including European mercantile houses and Indian and Eurasian traders; presses and art and photographic studios; and hotels. A few of these are shown on a redrawn map in Fig. 6.6. Of course, the map and directory also showed the roads and lanes, the ghats along the river, bridges, and the departure points of ships and boats. In addition, they showed places of interest, such as monuments and statues, and more interestingly, and in some detail, the residences of prominent Indians—zamindars, traders, and cultural and political leaders. Thirty-eight such residences were listed in north Calcutta and eight in the areas of the Twenty-four Parganas bordering the city. Users of the map were also provided with address information for doctors, midwives, and lawyers of the High Court and the lower courts.

The most detailed information in the directory is on wholesale markets. Ramanath listed every kind of consumer item used in daily life and in religious ritual; he even thought of uncommon items such as materials for decorating horses. We have listed in Tables 6.2 and 6.3 the bazars and the commodities in which they specialized (see also Fig. 6.7). There are clear spatial concentrations and these have been highlighted; for instance, wooden furniture in Baithakkhana and Bowbazar, books and stationery in Radhabazar and Battala, musical instruments in Tiretta Bazar, spices in Raja Sukhomoyer Posta and Bardhaman Rajar Posta, foreign and Indian cotton goods in Barabazar and China Bazar.

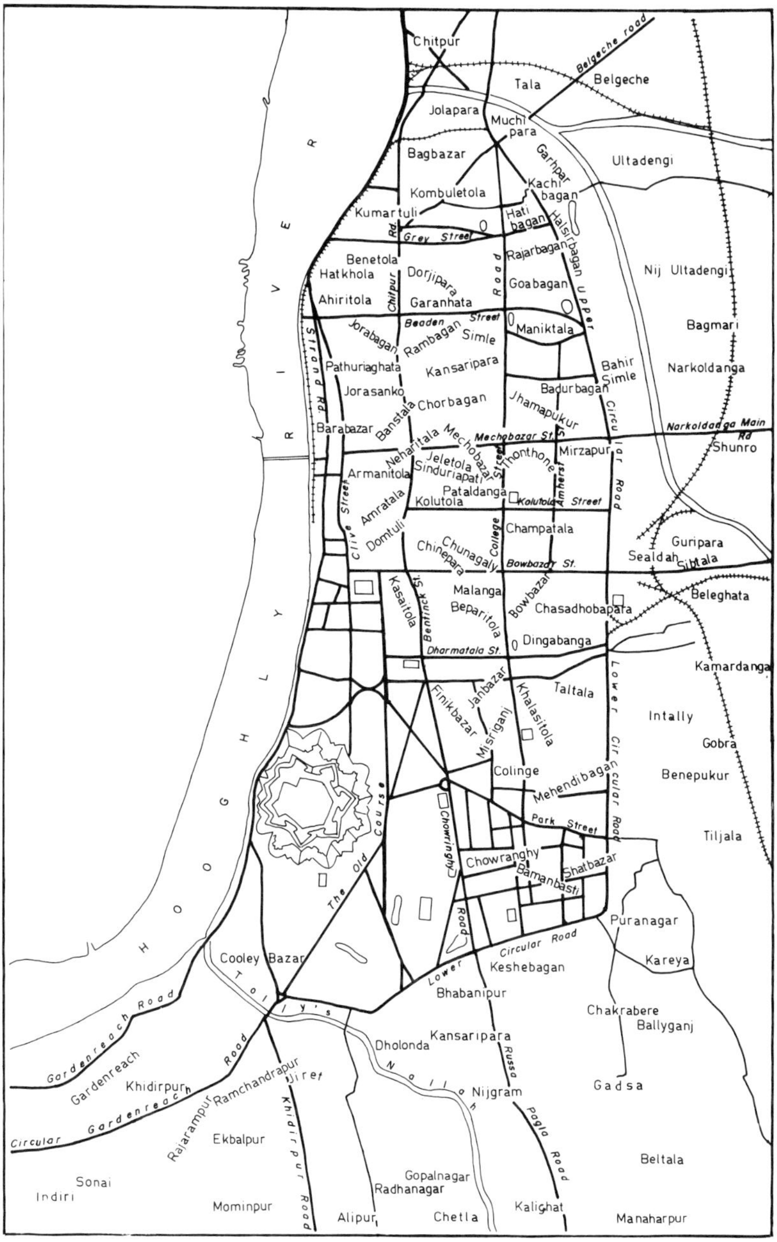

Fig. 6.5. Localities of Calcutta, 1884

Table 6.1. Localities of Calcutta

North Calcutta (north of Bowbazar Street)			
Muchipara	Ahiritola	Barabazar	Domtuli
Badurbagan	Dorjipara	Bagbazar	Chunagali
Jhamapukur	Garanhata	Mechobazar	Chinepara
Garhpar	Rajarbagan	Thonthone	Champatala
Kombuletola	Goabagan	Mirzapur	Neharitala
Kachibagan	Jorabagan	Armanitala	Simle
Kumartuli	Rambagan	Jeletala	Pathuriaghata
Hatibagan	Maniktala	Sinduriapatti	Banstala
Halsirbagan	Jorasanko	Pataldanga	
Benetola	Chorbagan	Amratala	
Hatkhola	Kansaripara	Kolutala	
South Calcutta			
Kasaitala	Chasadhobapara	Misriganj	Mehendibagan
Malanga	Dingabhanga	Khalasitola	Chowrangi
Beparitala	Shatbazar	Taltala	Bamanbasti
Bowbazar	Janbazar	Kolinge	
Suburbs of Calcutta			
Ultadengi	Beleghata	Chakrabere	Ekbalpur
Bagmari	Kamardanga	Ballyganj	Jiret
Bahir Simle	Intally	Garfa	Bhabanipur
Narkoldanga	Gobra	Keshebagan	Kansaripara
Shunro	Benepukur	Kuli Bazar	Dholonda
Guripara	Tiljala	Khidirpur	Nijgram
Sealdah	Puranagar	Rajarampur	Beltala
Sibtala	Kareya	Ramchandrapur	

Source: Ramanath Das, *KM.*

Cartography and the Culture of Spatial Representation

As noted earlier, Ramanath Das's map is unique in its use of a grid method and the presentation of information by interpolation. Why did he use this method?

Whereas other maps of the period, prepared mostly under the aegis of the Survey of India, show the built-up area and major land-use categories, *KM* takes a different approach. Its emphasis is almost entirely on the social and functional categories of the daily life of the Bengali-dominated segment of the city. Although streets and lanes are numbered on the map, and identified by name in the index, it is not, properly speaking, a street map of Calcutta. The details are provided in the naming of localities and neighborhoods—the longest such listing we have for any map of the city.

Two considerations appear to have operated on Ramanath Das as he executed the map. In both, he needed to depart from the models provided by

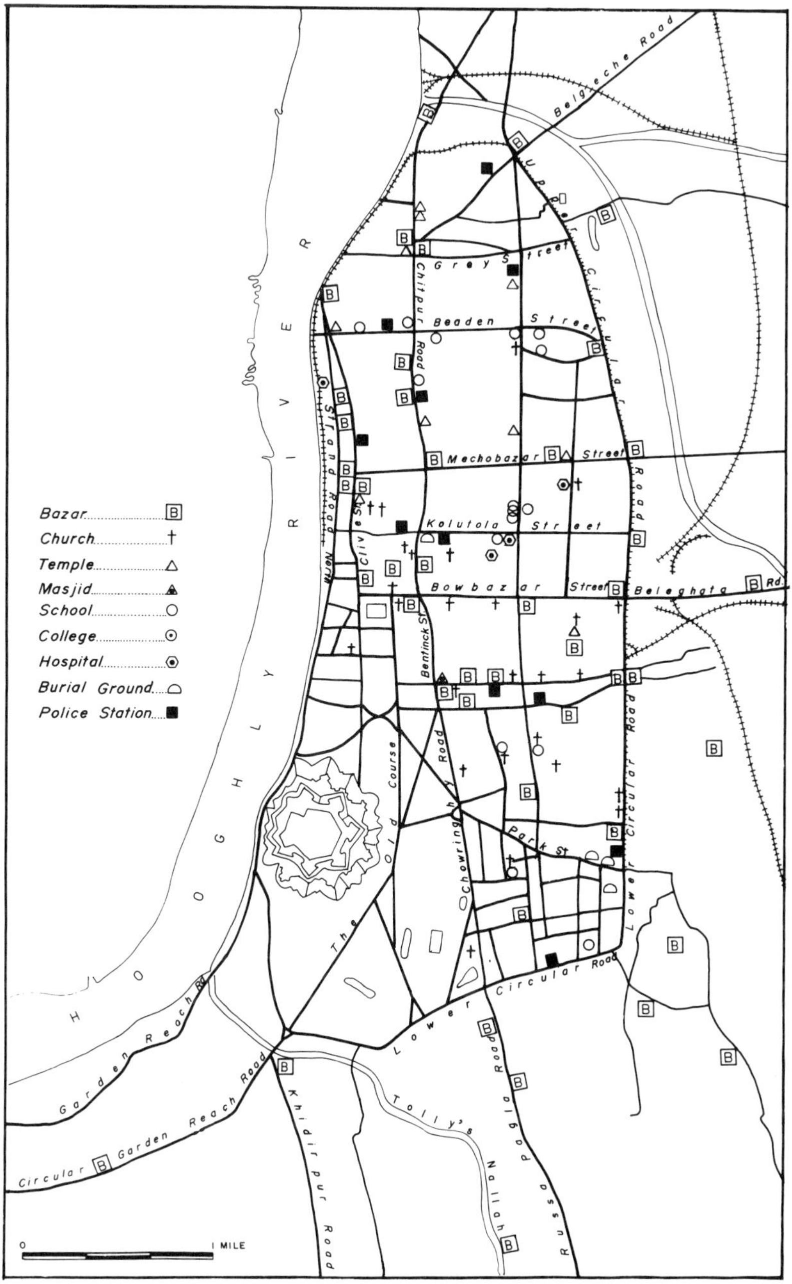

Fig. 6.6. Calcutta, 1884

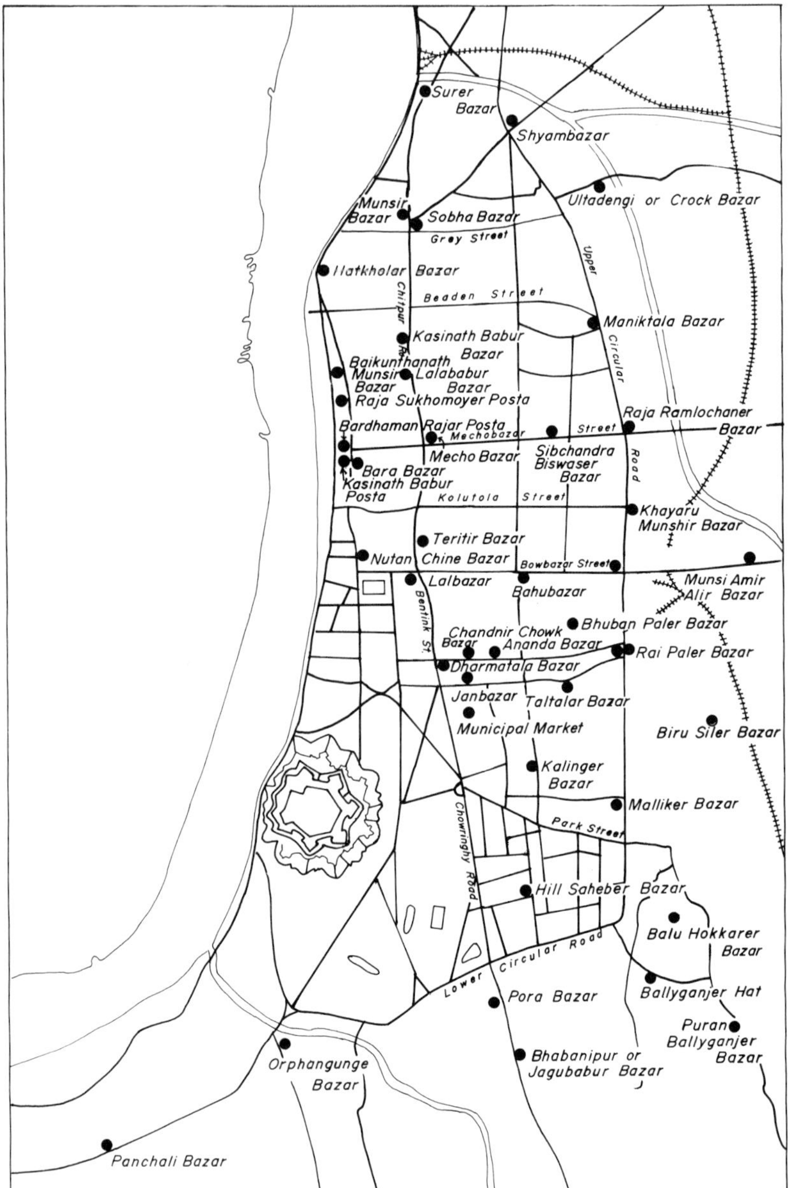

Fig. 6.7. Bazars of Calcutta

Table 6.2. Bazars of Calcutta

North Calcutta

1. Baithakkhana Bazar
2. Harimohan Daser Bazar
3. Madhab Babur Bazar
4. Teritir Bazar
5. Nutan Chine Bazar
6. Sibchandra Biswaser Bazar or Tiktikir Bazar
7. Mecho Bazar
8. Bara Bazar
9. Kasinath Babur Posta
10. Bardhaman Rajar Posta
11. Raja Sukhomoyer Posta
12. Maniktala Bazar
13. Hedor Bazar
14. Lalababur Bazar
15. Baikunthanath Munsir Bazar
16. Sobhabazar
17. Kasinath Babur Bazar or Nutan Bazar (presently Rajendranath Malliker Bazar)
18. Munsir Bazar
19. Hatkholar Bazar
20. Kagla Bagan Bazar
21. Shyambazar
22. Radhabazar
23. Bagbazar
24. Puran Chine Bazar

South Calcutta

1. Dharmatala Bazar
2. Chandnir Chowk Bazar
3. Bahubazar
4. Ananda Bazar
5. Bhuban Paler Bazar
6. Kalinger Bazar
7. Malliker Bazar
8. Hill Saheber Bazar
9. Napiter Bazar (now nonexistent)
10. Lalbazar
11. Janbazar
12. Taltalar Bazar
13. Kuli Bazar (Hastings)
14. Finik Bazar
15. Shot Bazar
16. Municipal Bazar

Twenty-four Parganas (North)

1. Surer Bazar
2. Khayaru Munsir Bazar
3. Munsi Amir Alir Bazar
4. Ultadengi or Crock Bazar

Twenty-four Parganas (South)

1. Rai Paler Bazar
2. Balu Hokkarer Bazar
3. Pora Bazar
4. Ballyganjer Hat
5. Puran Ballyganjer Bazar
6. Orphanganj Bazar
7. Panchali Bazar
8. Kalighat Bazar
9. Biru Siler Bazar
10. Bhabanipur or Jagubabur Bazar
11. Raja Ramlochaner Bazar

Source: Ramanath Das, *KM.*

existing English maps and directories. One—detailed in the preceding section—was: what kinds of information did he need to put on the map in order to make it useful for his intended clientele? Here, it is obvious, he was thinking of the visitor to the city, or even the temporary resident (as most residents of Calcutta were at this time, virtually everyone having a home somewhere else) who had work to get done in a government office or at the courts, or needed to buy or sell, or to locate a school or hospital, or find a lawyer or doctor. Clearly, the amount of information required was too large to be written on a map.

The other consideration was in choice of method for the identification of

Table 6.3. Bazars and commodities

1. *Teritir Bazar*
   Sitar, tanpura, violins, pictures and frames, fats of pigs, pigeons and other birds
2. *Barabazar*
   Cotton, woollen and silk *alpac,* Indian cotton cloth, woollen cloth, cloth—Indian/foreign, silk shawl, diamond, pearl, brass, brass and bell metal utensils, copper, iron, iron plates, rods, etc., cement, wooden boxes, ghee, sugar, salt, tin, paints, indigo
3. *Raja Sukhomoyer Posta*
   Mangoes, potato, spices, betel leaf
4. *Baithakkhana*
   Wooden planks (*keora*), wooden cots (*keora*), pigeons
5. *Khengrapatti*
   Tasar, *garad* material, cotton
6. *Radhabazar*
   Watches, stationery goods, survey instruments, books
7. *China Bazar/Old China Bazar*
   Tin-buckets, glass goods, chandeliers, foreign cloth, woollen, silk *alpac,* tin lanterns, trunks, old papers
8. *Pathuriaghata*
   Castor oil, brass and bellmetal idols and toys, jute
9. *Bagbazar*
   Rice: *atap*, sal-wood beams, rafters, etc.
10. *Bowbazar*
    Old iron frames, sal-wood beams, rafters, wooden frames, chairs and almirah, cement, paints of different kinds
11. *Mechobazar*
    Tarpaulin, gold
12. *Dharmatala Street*
    Low wooden seats, large wooden trays, sal-wood beams, rafters, etc., fuller's earth, salt
13. *Hatkhola*
    Jute, linseed, mustard, rice: *mugibalam*, salt, steel, steel plate, rods
14. *Armenian Street near Armenian Church*
    Yarn, old paper, umbrellas, medical instruments
15. *Battala*
    Diamond, pearl, different kinds of Bengali books
16. *Maniktala*
    Castor oil, mustard, linseed
17. *Janbazar*
    Wooden tubs, floor mats
18. *Nutanbazar*
    Brass, bellmetal utensils, items used for religious rites
19. *Lalbazar*
    Material for decorating horses
20. *Jorasanko*
    Stone images, boxes, mosquito nets, tabla, pakhawaj, castor oil
21. *Jorabagan*
    Jute, flowers

Table 6.3. Bazars and commodities (*continued*)

22.	*Sobhabazar*	Brass, bellmetal, utensils, rice: *atap*
23.	*Tallyganj*	Rice: *atap*, rice: local
24.	*Khidirpur*	Rice: *atap*
25.	*Jagannath Ghat*	Rice: *atap*
26.	*Dharmatala*	Tin lanterns, trunks, wool
27.	*Malliker Bazar*	Motor car repairers, diamond, pearls
28.	*Sibtala Street*	Dhakai saris
29.	*Bardhaman Rajar Posta*	Betel leaf, spices
30.	*Mallik Street/Cotton Street/Cross Street/Pageya Patti/Barabazar/Shyamarayer Gali*	Foreign cotton cloth, yarn, woollen cloth, shawls
31.	*Kolutola*	Shawls
32.	*West of Beadon Park*	Conch shells
33.	*Kasinath Babur Bazar*	Mosquito nets
34.	*Mirzapur Street*	Sal-wood beams, rafters, mats
35.	*Dalhousie Street*	Musical instruments
36.	*Hare Street*	Stationery goods
37.	*Beleghata*	Salt, rice: *balam*, rice: local
38.	*Halsir Bazar*	Coconut oil
39.	*Chandni Bazar*	Wool for making carpets
40.	*Banstala Street/Mission Row/Pollock Street*	Silk
41.	*Natherbagan/Benetola/Kumartuli*	Salt
42.	*Rajarchak/Mallik Ghat*	Steel, steel plates, rods, etc.
43.	*Old Court House Street*	Glass items, chandeliers, etc.

Source: Ramanath Das, *KM*.

locations. A street guide would not be very useful, because the commonly used way to locate a house or a shop was to name the locality. There were in use in Calcutta at this time a very large number of names of neighborhoods or *pāḍā*, with a complicated hierarchy: one large *pāḍā* name could encompass several smaller localities with unclear boundaries.

Ramanath needed to find a cartographic technique that would solve these two problems at the same time. He chose the method of interpolation in order to fit in the large volume of information that had to be put into the map. And he chose the grid method so as to have an abstract division of the urban space within which particular locations could be identified without having to draw the precise boundaries of localities. Although, as we have suggested earlier, Ramanath may have encountered the technique in European maps of the period, one has to admire the ingenuity of the solution to his particular problem.

In order to appreciate the cartographic problem faced by Ramanath, it is useful to compare his map with the narrative guide through the city provided by Durgacharan Ray. *Debgaṇer martye āgaman*'s section on the gods' visit to Calcutta and their walks through different neighborhoods of the city is long.[20] In more than two hundred pages of printed text, only three street names are mentioned—Chitpur Road, Bentinck Street, and Park Street, the last not as a street name but as the name of the locality where the Europeans lived. The visitors move through one *pāḍā* after another, going into offices and public buildings, looking at shops and bazars, pointing out landmarks such as prominent buildings or religious places or ponds or the banks of the Hooghly. There is, in fact, a plethora of details similar to that in *KM*, of government offices, courts, commercial houses, banks, and of the work done in each of them; of shops and markets and what was sold there; of schools, hospitals, public buildings, places of entertainment, and so forth. Being a narrative account, it also tells the histories of particular places, the life stories of prominent people associated with particular houses or institutions, advises readers on how to amuse themselves, and warns the unwary visitor of cheats, robbers, pimps, and prostitutes. But it is impossible to tell from the account which direction one is moving or which streets one must take in order to go from one place to another. Although claiming to be a travel guide, the book does not allow the reader to map the journey of the heavenly visitors through Calcutta unless that reader already knows the relative locations of the places mentioned. The guide, in other words, is not cartographic.

Ramanath Das attempted to find a cartographic solution to the problem. However, we cannot say that he was particularly successful. One indicator of this is a lack of evidence to suggest that his map was widely used. In fact, his attempt is largely forgotten. Second, his method was not replicated: it still stands out as more or less unique for Bengali maps of Calcutta. Third, although Ramanath was at pains to enable precise interpolation of directory listings with locations on the map, to make it possible to locate a doctor or medicine shop, a school or a market selling a particular commodity, one is not persuaded that this complicated exercise with the map was really the best method for finding the place.

In fact, Ramanath's failure in this regard did not represent only the failure of his individual effort. It must be said that the problem he faced was not solved at all in the process of adoption of cartography as a discipline in Bengal's modern urban culture. Although there have been many Bengali guidebooks and directories of Calcutta since Ramanath's time, some of them highly successful and widely used, the use of a map to find one's way through the city has never become a part of the urban culture. It is not simply a question of the differences in spatial perception between Indian and modern Western cultures, because such differences, we know, have been tackled in the case of other disciplines by suitable innovations and displacements. The question rather is that of the effectiveness of particular disciplinary techniques. Modern technologies of power do not, in other words, have the same application, or produce the same results, in every disciplinary field.

Notes

[The names of localities, bazars, the items in which they specialized, etc., are mentioned in the tables exactly as they appear in *KM*. They do not always tally with actual or formal names. It is possible, of course, that many of the discrepancies are the result of colloquial corruption, so that what occurs in *KM* may in fact be the names as they were used in local parlance.]

1. Gole, *India within the Ganges*, p. 84.

2. R. H. Phillimore, *Historical Records*, vol. 1, p. 267.

3. The paymaster general's proposals for surveyors' allowances in *Bengal Political Consultations,* 4 July 1768, as quoted in Phillimore, *Historical Records*, vol. 1, p. 268.

4. These were (1) plan of the territory of Calcutta as marked out in the year 1742; (2) plan of Fort William and part of the city of Calcutta by Lt. William Wells, 1753; and (3) plan of the territory of Calcutta, 1757. The area shown was mainly the old fort and its surrounding areas. The first map of this series was prepared to illustrate the defense of Calcutta against the Mahratta raids. The later maps (1756 and 1757) showed the position of the tents and huts of the "Nabob's Army" after the seige of Calcutta by the army of Siraj-ud-daulah in 1756.

5. The following maps fall within this category: (1) plan of Calcutta, reduced by permission of the commissioners of police, executed by Lt. Col. Mark Wood in 1784 and 1785, published in October 1792 by William Baillie; (2) plan of the city of Calcutta and the environs sur-

veyed by the late Major J. A. Schalch for the use of the lottery committee, etc., between 1817 and 1833; (3) plan of Calcutta from actual survey, 1847-49, by Frederick Walter Simms.

6. Phillimore, *Historical Records*, vol. 1, p. 53.

7. Phillimore, *Historical Records*, vol. 2, p. 92.

8. Jogesh Chandra Bagal, *History of Government College,* p. 7.

9. Ibid., p. 10.

10. Kamal Sarkar, "Kyālkāṭā arṭ sṭuḍior citrakalā."

11. For an analysis of the *New Calcutta Directory* of 1856 see Satyesh C. Chakraborty, "Historical Significance."

12. Gole, *Indian Maps,* p. 13.

13. Ibid.

14. Bahura and Singh, *Catalogue of Historical Documents,* Figs. 35, 36, and 37.

15. Mitra, *Bengal Atlas.*

16. Phillimore, *Historical Records*, vol. 1, p. 249.

17. Upendranath Mukhopadhyay, *Kalikātā darśak.*

18. Ramanath Das, *Kalikātār māncitra.*

19. By proclamation, the limits of the town of Calcutta were fixed on 10 September 1794. In 1857, the boundary of the town was set at the inner side of the Mahratta Ditch, and the "suburbs" were defined to include all lands within the general limits of Panchannogram. This division of town and suburbs (treated as two separate municipal towns in 1857) remained, with modification, till 1888. See for details, A. K. Ray, *Short History.*

20. Durgacharan Ray, *Debgaṇer martye āgaman*, pp. 415-630.

7 / Territory and People: The Disciplining of Historical Memory

Ranabir Samaddar

Marginal Territories

Raja Jagadish Chandra Deo Dhabaldeb, the zamindar of Jambani, had his estate headquarters in Chilkigarh, a village dominated by the Mallakshatriya caste, to which the ruling lineage belonged. To Jambani was added the estate of Dhalbhum, one railway station away from Gidni, the stop for Jambani. The Bengal Nagpur Railway line (now South Eastern Railway) cut through the Jangalmahals from Kharagpur to Singhbhum in Bihar and Sambalpur in Orissa. Jambani and Dhalbhum, the two estates of the Jambani Raj, thus formed one continuous stretch of territory (Fig. 7.1).

Dhalbhum was rich in mineral deposits. Iron could be found in nodular form in most of the hill ranges. Spangles of gold were often seen by the riverside. Copper was obtained at the foot of the hills. Nodular limestone could be found all over the estate. Two-thirds of the area was covered with forests of sal, kusum, sisu, gamar, and other trees. Forest products abounded. It was an area of 1,201 square miles with 22,124 houses, and an estimated population, as reported by Hunter, of 139,381.[1] There was one village (or rather *mauza*, the revenue equivalent) per square mile. Hunter's statistical account of the Chotanagpur division, within which the fiscal division of Dhalbhum fell, gives a detailed notice of the castes and tribes in the area. The estate was under ordinary police jurisdiction, with the regular constabulary supplemented by a large body of *ghatwali* police who were paid through

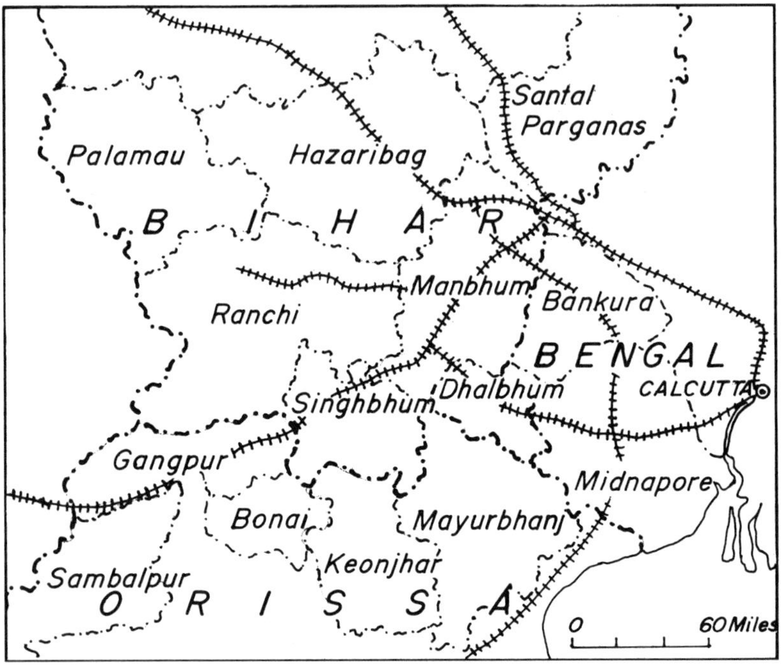

Fig. 7.1. The Jangalmahal region

land grants. The zamindar also worked through sardars, ghatwals, headmen, and similar functionaries. The ghatwali holdings were distributed throughout the estate. Hunter speaks of 23 chief ghatwals, below whom were 297 subordinate officers, with 875 *paiks* (constables) forming the rank and file of the rural force.[2] The government had nothing to do with the collection of rent, as Dhalbhum was permanently settled. The linkup of Dhalbhum and Jambani was underpinned by the fact that the fiscal division of Dhalbhum originally formed part of the district of Midnapore. In 1833, with the formation of the South-West Frontier Agency, it was transferred to Manbhum district and then incorporated into Singhbhum in 1846. The language of the area, at least as reported by Hunter, was Bengali. The zamindar paid an annual revenue of £426.14s. He received mining rents to the tune of 9,200 rupees (£920) a year. He also had in his possession the buildings and the engine of the Hindustan Copper Company, which had defaulted on its rent.[3]

The tenurial pattern in Jambani also reflected its marginal position. The forms of subtenancies and leases common in other parts of agrarian Bengal were infrequent here; prevalent were intermediate tenures such as *khargosh*, *ghatwali*, *chakran*, *brahmottar*, *debottar*, *pradhani*, *khunt katti*, and *thika*, among others. Labor was said to be abundant. Men engaged by the year got four seers (about 8 lbs.) of paddy a day with a bonus of Rs.1-8-0 (about three shillings) at the end of the year. Women obtained half this rate. Smiths got two annas daily, carpenters and bricklayers four annas. There had been a rise in prices, Hunter added, of 25 to 50 percent between 1860 and 1865. And in the famine of 1866, good quality rice was selling at Rs.6 per *maund* (about 80 lbs.), common rice at Rs.5, paddy at Rs.2.[4] According to Dr. Hayes, the deputy commissioner, grain stores were rare; surplus grain was always sold to enable the farmer to pay the cash portion of the rent and, in any case, from 1862 stocks of grain in the hands of farmers decreased. Grain-dealing *mahajans* (moneylender-traders) held back grain from the market. Relief work began in the form of road building and centers were opened for the distribution of cooked food. The total number of daily laborers employed through the district rose to 224,521.[5] Bands of destitutes began to appear, providing a preview of the sort of description that was to be written about the region a few decades later:

> Thousands of them [tribals], having become landless, wander the country seeking coolie work. The mingling of the sexes on the road, the miserable provision for their sleeping where they chance to labor, being herded together here and there amongst constantly changing companions without any of the restraint of the village organisation to which they had been accustomed, is rapidly lowering the morals of the community. Moreover this wandering life rapidly destroys any inclination they have towards patient industry. It is a feast or a famine.[6]

In other passages, the good Dr. Kennan—the British missionary author of this description—speaks of "girls full of spirits and somewhat saucy," "devoid of prudery," "men and women becom[ing] almost like animals in the indulgence of their amorous propensities" during the *Magh* feast, the "Bacchanalian festival with no restraint on their indulgence," of a "dance like a *grande galope*—a very joyous, frisky, harum-scarum scamper." Hunter, too, wrote in a similar vein: "It cannot be expected that chastity is preserved when the shades of night fall on such a scene of licentiousness and debauchery."[7]

In the colonial accounts, Jambani-Dhalbhum is an area of primitive humanity. Bands of wandering laborers starving, searching for work; a rent crisis; reclamation and resumption of land; famine; an ethic totally alien not only to Victorian individualism and prudery but also to the hierarchical archaisms of the agrarian society of the Gangetic plains. Even a hundred years ago from today, the rulers of the country thought of the Jungle Mahals as a marginal region, lying indecisively on the borders of civilization and of the rationally administered empire.

The People's Memory

But how did the people of the region make sense of the changes that were being imposed on their lives by the new order of things? One of the institutions where they were now called upon to reveal their minds was the court of law. We have a scattered collection of depositions made in various cases concerning forest rights. They make interesting reading as evocations of a collective memory. Is this memory merely one that tells us about the agrarian history of a frontier region? Or can we see in it the elements of the historical construction of a nationality? But let us not anticipate.

We can start with the deposition of a petty shopkeeper in a case over the right to forest produce being handed over by the raja to *ijaradars* (leaseholding contractors), the Midnapore Zamindari Company, and other "men of substance." Raja Jagadish Chandra was then a minor and the estate was under the custody of the court of wards. Often in these testimonies, contrast is made to practices said to have been prevalent at the time of Jagadish's predecessors, Purna Chandra and Iswar Chandra. The deposition was taken in Bengali in 1898.[8] The following is a rough English translation:

> My name is Sibaprasad Paramanik, son of late Baidyanath Paramanik. My age is forty-two. I live at Chichra, Parganah Jambani. I know all the five disputed jungles. The rule is that when the estate officials do not lease out a forest, the praja can cut the wood that year. By paying an annual cess of one rupee eight annas, they can take twenty cartloads of wood. This system runs from the time of Raja Purna Chandra. When Purna was a minor, his mother Rani Jagat Kumari allowed us such exemptions for firewood. We would then have to give one rupee and one *ārā* [a local measure] paddy each as contribution to the mandal. The mandal [headman] would hand over the money to the raja. The praja [tenants] would collect firewood after the harvest—from January to April. I cannot say what happened in earlier times. The raja does not allow cutting and collection during other months. The rain comes after Baisakh and the saplings come out. So, if cattle and men enter the jungle during that time, the saplings will be destroyed. Amla, sod, kurti, and so on are *ākāṭā* [firewood] trees. We cut these trees. But sal, piyasal, mahul, kusum, and other fruit-bearing trees are big and they are not *ākāṭā*. The forest guards protect the valuable trees like sal. If the praja need such big trees for construction of houses, they have to petition the *sadar seresta* [estate head office], pay the required cess, take leave from Dewanji or the local tehsildar. The raja looks after the big trees and sells them. The jungle at Chichra is half sal, half *ākāṭā*. Now the mandals of our village as well as of Ghutchuda have refused to pay tax to the raja.

Bhim Mahato's deposition in the same case is equally revealing:

> My age is forty. . . . Of the five jungles in dispute I know those of Bakra, Sonamukhi, and Behra. I bring firewood from those jungles. During Purna Chandra's time I was paying eight annas, then one rupee eight annas, and then during the time of Iswar Chandra I was paying three rupees for forty-eight cartloads of wood. I am a mandal. To Jagat Kumari I would pay one ārā paddy and 1 rupee as tax. By paying that amount the praja of my village as well as myself could get firewood.
>
> . . . This year I went to the jungles of Bakra, Sonamukhi, and Behra during Chaitra-Baisakh with my *munish* [laborer]. I found the jungles half empty. I don't know who had cut and carted away the wood. I did not count how many big trees had been felled. Bakra is, however, still full with big trees. I used to take one rupee and one ārā paddy each from the praja for the Chichra woods. I have not paid anything to Lal Sardar. Purna Chandra died ten or eleven years ago and the jungle cess was decided during his time, seventeen years ago. The cess was increased twice later on and printed receipts began to be given. But I have lost my receipt. However, I have with me the rent receipts of the praja submitted to the kutchery.
>
> . . . Eight years ago, the whole village of Chichra was burned down. We went to the Bakra jungle to get wood for new houses. Chichra is a big village with many people. The sal wood is costly. My munish did not cut any sal; he carted away other wood. Those jungles have piyasal, mahul, kusum, and other big trees.

Giridhar Kar gives a similar deposition:

> My house is by the side of Ghutia hat. It is on the road. The name of the jungle is written down on paper. However, sometimes we take one or two cartloads of wood from other jungles too. The reason is that if a munish is going to some other forest, we go with him and cart away one or two cartloads. Last Chaitra-Baisakh, I went through the jungle of Chichra on my way to Suliballavpur. There were two guards in Ghutiahuda forest—Debi Bauri and Arun Kamar. Previously the guards were Muba and Kina. Kina is dead and Muba has gone east. The tehsildar looks after the jungle. I pay the cess; my father does too. My father is alive. The *dakhila* [permission] is issued in my father's name. Sometimes I pay, sometimes my father. My house got burned in the fire. The dakhilas were also burned. I remember getting twenty-four cartloads of wood by paying twelve annas as cess. For cutting wood in Aswin-Kartik, we have to get special leave and the tehsildar issues the papers. Sometimes we have to go to the kutchery, sometimes the Dewan comes in person to the village to collect the taxes. In Bakra, a quarter of the forest consists of ākāṭā trees and the rest are sal. The chowkidar keeps an account of the trees.

We are listening to various depositions in case number six at the court of the subjudge, Second Court, Midnapore. The year is 1898. On 11 July, as witness number sixteen, Dewan Biswanath Satpathi corroborated the main statements of the witnesses. He agreed that the villagers used to cut only ākāṭā trees and not the valuable ones. He however could not say whether Chichra had ever been burned down. He did not know if the forest guards kept accounts regularly of trees cut and carted. He knew that the magistrate on complaint by the raja had gone to investigate the reported cutting of valuable trees. The magistrate had visited Chichra, but about Bakra he did not know.[9] When collecting taxes, the *dewan* [minister] usually waited in the house of Bhagabat Sutra, a prosperous farmer.

In the course of my fieldwork in 1990, I asked some Chichra residents of venerable age if they could remember having been told by their elders of a devastating fire burning down the whole village. They could not, although, they said, they regularly heard in their childhood of clashes over the cutting of trees. Today, Chichra has very light forest, and only memories of the once dense woods of the Jungle Mahals.

Another deposition, of Purna Dalui, in the same case corroborates those of other witnesses, and reports that he could take twenty-four cartloads of wood by paying one rupee eight annas during Purna Chandra's time. When asked if he knew the names of the twenty-four men who had cut the valuable trees in Bakra and Hatikāduā jungles, he, like the others, replied with a straight "No." Who, then, had cut the trees? Let us listen to Sital Nayek, son of Jitu Nayek, aged thirty-six, of Ghutia in Mahāl Jambani:

> I know who are the offenders. Madhu Nayek, Guri Bera, Mukunda Nayek, Jhantu Nayek, Shambhu Mahato, Biswanath Paramanik, Madhu Kuila, and others. They were seven or eight in number. Sixteen people took away wood from the Bakra jungle. They were in union and acted in consultation. They are praja and have no right to take away wood without leave and paying tax to the Raja.... They have cut even after Baisakh; I have seen them. They have no proprietary right over the jungles. I am the supervisor of the jungle. I forbade them to cut the trees. But they did not listen to me. I forbade Madhu Kuila, . . . Kanchan Giri, and others. Bhagabat's munish was also felling trees. The *pratibadis* [defendants] had cut ākāṭā trees. I am employed in my present service from last Ashadh.

The following deposition, taken on 6 June 1898, is by Durga Prasad Paramanik, who was cross-examined on 13 and 16 June:

> The wood taken away would be worth one hundred rupees.... I am the tehsildar. . . . I saw them carting away the wood. I saw Kanchan Giri and Madhu Kuila.... I look after the jungles. I know Rani Parbati Kumari.... I once again swear that they had shown me only the *dakhilas* of 1299, 1300, 1301 [B.S.—A.D.

> 1798, 1799, and 1800]. But I have not seen the particular receipts. . . . Some of the defendants can read and write. But none of them put their signatures on the back of the dakhilas and receipts. . . .
>
> . . . . They would not tell me the exact date on which they wanted to cut wood. . . . They are relatives of Jadu Mahato. Jadu Mahato is close to Parbati Kumari.

Witness number three, Gopal Pichre, supported Durga Paramanik and Sital Nayek:

> I have seen Jadu Mahato, Durga Singha, Dari Mahato and Gadadhar Mahato cutting trees illegally. I am the *morol* [mandal] of one of the Raja's villages. The four of them took away sixteen cartloads. They felled even big sal trees. We are morols for three generations. . . . I am the morol of Murakati mauza. . . . To cut wood for building houses, the praja have to take special leave. The houses in Murakati *mauza* were burned in a fire. They had to pay the raja substantial amounts for getting sal wood for rebuilding purposes.

Was this cutting of trees an organized activity and a defiance of authority? Witness number four, Pitambar Sau, deposed:

> The forest is just one shout away from my house. I saw Biswanath Paramanik, Madhu Kuila, and others cutting trees. Some had munish with them; some did the cutting themselves. . . . Biswanath, Bhagabat, Madhu and Jadu Mahato called me to Biswanath's house. Bhagabat told me of their plan there and asked me not to pay the cess to the raja. I have ten *bighas* [about thirty acres] of land. . . . I did not see that day in Biswanath's house those who have been brought here as witness.

Witness number five, Balabhadra Kulabi, was more specific:

> I know Ghutehuda. . . . I am the warden of the jungle there on behalf of the raja. Ghutehuda has five thousand bighas of land. . . . Last Agrahayan these people conspired. They were twenty-four altogether. I asked them, "Why do you want to do this?" They replied, "We have won the *fauzdari* [criminal] suit; we will now cut the trees." They took away fifty or sixty cartloads of wood. . . . I lodged a complaint against Bhagabat. . . . Nanda Bagal, Bhim Bagal were there as munish of Bhagabat. . . . I know the area and the extent of the jungle. South of it is Dhalbhum.

The seventh witness, Hari Ghosh, was the house servant of the tehsildar. His deposition was also on the same lines. Other witnesses, Gangadhar Mahato and Janardan Jana, reasserted the illegality of the action. Also significant was the deposition of an official of the Watson Company, the *ijaradar* (leaseholder) of the forests:

> My name is Sri Nritya Gopal Basu. I am forty-two. I am the *nayeb* [manager] of the Jungle Mahal concern of the Watson Company. The company has under it the entire forests of the zamindari. The Company has to pay Rs. 45,000 as rent. The zamindari has many jungles. The jungle rights are for sale for certain periods of time. The praja have no rights there. They cannot cut wood and take it away without leave. . . . Those praja who get coupons can have ākāṭā wood. They have to apply to the sahib for that. In times of rain, they are not allowed to enter the forest.

We have to remember that the lease on these forests was vacated in 1898 when they reverted back to the raja. During the period of lease, as witness number twenty-four, Kinu Mahato, said, the praja had not cut any wood. But he remembered what was the custom in the days before the lease:

> I know what used to be the norm before the ijara. During the times of Rani Jagat Kumari, the people of each village would collect firewood on payment of one ārā paddy and a rupee. The praja could get whatever firewood they needed for that payment. One ārā is equal to twenty-five seers, one maund is equal to four seers [the local maund is different from the standard Bengal maund, which is forty seers]. So an ārā is equal to five or six maunds of grain. Later on during Raja Purna Chandra's time, one would pay twelve annas for that. During Iswar Chandra's time, on payment of three rupees, we could get forty-eight cartloads of wood. However, there was no system of written permission during Rani Jagat Kumari or Purna Chandra's time. For getting sal wood, they would have to get a special permit.

In 1898, Kinu Mahato was sixty years old. He was the head of a village for thirty-five years. Here he is talking of the 1860s, of the time of Jagat Kumari, followed by that of Purna, then Purna's brother Iswar, and then Parbati Kumari. But Parbati Kumari, Purna's wife, was deprived of the estate, and it went into the custody of the court of wards after Iswar's death because Jagadish was still a minor. The main counselor of Jagat Kumari, who was supposedly leading the opposition to Jagadish Chandra, was a certain Jadu Mahato, who features in this role in the fictional account of the Jamboni Raj.[10] Finally, we have the telltale evidence of Dewan Biswanath Satpathi, from whom we heard earlier in the description of this case:

> I am Sri Biswanath Satpathi, son of Maheswar Satpathi. My age is fifty. I live in Chilkigarh. I am the dewan of Jambani Raj. I have been dewan since Raja Purna Chandra's time. I know the custom regarding the cutting of wood in the Jungle Mahals since Harihar Dhal, King Purna's father. The praja had to pay rent, but no price was charged then for cutting wood in the forest. However, they did have to pay a small amount of money and paddy. . . . Also they would give one seer *bidi kalai* [a lentil]. What the arrangement was before that, I can-

> not say. However, even then, for building purposes, the praja would pay separately. After Harihar's death, the estate went under court of wards for eighteen years from 1271 to 1288 [B.S.]. During that time, the zamindari was on ijara to the Watson Company. The jungles were under their supervision. The jungles with valuable trees were under the supervision of Watson and those with ākātā trees were in the charge of Rani Jagat Kumari. During Rani Jagat Kumari's time, the praja of each village would pay one ārā paddy and cash of one rupee. Then, in 1289, Raja Purna Chandra brought the estate under his supervision and ordered that each praja would now pay six annas annually as khajna for firewood. Then Purna hiked it to eleven annas. Subsequently this was raised to one rupee four annas and one rupee eight annas, paying which a praja could take twenty-four cartloads of wood.
>
> . . . After Iswar's death, it was again the court of wards. . . . Sal tree is not ākātā. . . . I know the accused. They are praja of the raja, but do not pay the tax. They have ganged up. They have combined to destroy the jungles. Biswanath Paramanik or Bhagabat Sui have no rights over these jungles which are within the *khas mahal* of the Raja. . . . My house is one *kosh* [two miles] away from the rajbari [palace]. I became dewan in 1288. Before that I was an assistant under Rani Lal Kumari and Rani Jagat Kumari. I knew the conditions of the estate even before 1271. The Watson Company would get three hundred rupees annually for looking after the jungles. During Purna's time, many papers were lost or destroyed. . . . I knew Bidyadhar Sarangi, dewan of Jagat Kumari. . . . No warrant has ever been issued against my name for giving false deposition.

Parbati Kumari at this time was locked in a court battle with Jagadish over the right to the estate. Jadu Mahato was close to Parbati Kumari. Parbati lost the case after incurring a huge debt. She was awarded a small part of the estate. But on default of repayment of her loans, even this property was attached.

We have an old, half-torn piece of paper that gives us the end of this story. Parbati Kumari had to go back to her native village, Fulkusma, in Bankura, after signing away all her property to Jagadish. Her houses, carriages, the mauzas, and the disputed khas jungles in her possession (where the alleged cutting of sal trees had taken place) were given over by an affidavit in 1907, the original attachment order being passed by dewani order number fifty-four in 1902 in Midnapore. I have been told by the descendants of Raja Jagadish that Parbati Kumari was given shelter in the zamindari palace in Chilkigarh in her last years, in a state of penury.

If we search these depositions for materials for an agrarian history, we get a fairly detailed picture of the Jungle Mahals toward the end of the last century. Customary rights were being curtailed. Intrafamily disputes within the zamindari household fueled popular grievances. Mahatos and other "men of substance" prosperous enough to hire laborers led the acts of disobedience. The petty officials and servants of the raja tried to keep his authority intact. Meanwhile, Kurmi, Santhal, Bagal, Tanti, Bhuniya, Kahal, Dom, Teli, Mal, Mahali, Bhumij, Dandamajhi, Lodha, Kheria, Pan, Kamar, Bauri, Hari, Ho, Munda, Oraon, and others—the great mass of the village population (all of these names occur among the accused in various cases and in the police diary)—had started to voice their discontent. The mandal's authority was being restricted. Rents and cesses were shifting from collective charges to individual payments.

This was the situation when, sometime in the early years of the present century, the survey and settlement men appeared in the jungle tract with their chains, measuring rods, topees, and troops of clerks and *gomastas* (rent collectors). The agrarian picture was one of decline, disorder, and impending trouble, and A. E. Jameson, charged with the responsibility of conducting the settlement operations in the district, knew how crucial and yet problematic his work was for the imposition of some sort of rational governability:

> Disputes as to rights in jungles and trees on tenants' holdings were numerous and except in the extreme east and southeast hotly contested; . . . it must be admitted that no class of disputes excited so deep or such widespread ill feeling between landlord and tenants as these, and it is to be feared that the settlement record is in this respect only the beginning and not the end of strife. So long as the question of abstract right was left in abeyance matters adjusted themselves easily; in the jungle tracts it is true the tenants were gradually being deprived of ancient rights, but they were accustomed to this and raised little protest and less active opposition, . . . But as soon as an endeavor was made to reduce these un-written rights within the compass of a rigid formula to be binding in all circumstances each side was up in arms and on the well known principle of demanding more than you expect to get in the hope of getting something, each made extravagant claims and supported them by trumped up evidence when in the nature of the case there could be little that was definite or conclusive. When therefore the decision was on any point in favour of the landlord it is probable that he will at the best hold fast by the letter of the law and refuse to grant concessions which he might have made in former days for fear lest advantage might be taken by the other side to base on them an attempt to get the decision set aside. On the other hand when the decision was in favour of the tenants the landlord will not let it rest there but will go to the civil court in the hopes of having it upset; indeed in several cases suits were brought immediately after *khanapuri*. In the civil court the advantages are all on the side of the landlord for apart from his more favourable monetary position the tenants have not yet learnt to combine effectively in a matter which concerns them all but does not affect anyone among them very vitally. The suits were either undefended or inadequately defended and the landlord in all cases—

> largely one imagines by means of evidence which had been rejected by the Assistant Settlement Officer on the spot but was not scrutinized with so much care by the Munsiff sitting in the artificial atmosphere of a court—got decrees. In these cases it is still less to be hoped that they will show any disposition in future to abate a jot of what has been legally declared to be theirs. Such things are inevitable in the transition from custom to contract, but it is a pity that it should be effected through the medium of courts where false evidence is a premium.[11]

Boundaries on the Ground and Boundaries on Paper

With the beginning of survey and settlement operations, troubles were bound to erupt, sooner or later; in fact, they came sooner rather than later. There were two reasons for this, the first being the switch from custom to contract, and the second the creation of villages as revenue units. We have already given an instance of the first; some light can now be thrown on the second. Indeed, while noting that the revenue survey of 1870-75 had had to leave out Binpur, Jhargram, and Gopiballavpur, since *mauzawar* survey was not possible in the jungle tracts, Jameson commented:

> Villages had to be formed *de novo*. In determining the area to be included in a village local usage was followed for the most part; in all of them the *Mandali* system either still prevailed or had died out comparatively recently. . . . a block of land was let out to a community for the purpose of reclaiming it and bringing it under cultivation. . . . The process of reclamation had not gone far enough at the time of the Revenue Survey to make it worthwhile defining isolated villages when the greater part of the area would have had to be classed vaguely as khas jungle, but since then the formation of villages has proceeded rapidly and the khas jungle areas are now only a small proportion of the whole. . . . it was often found that the locally recognised villages were of inconvenient size sometimes too large but more often too small, and in such cases they were either divided or amalgamated. . . . The only difficulty that occasionally arose was as to the exact limits of two adjoining villages when some portion was claimed by both and these were dealt with as Boundary Disputes in the ordinary way. In this manner 1,608 villages were formed in the four thanas distributed as follows: Binpur 861, Jhargram 271, Gopiballabhpur 463, Naraingarh 13.[12]

What Jameson described as the "only difficulty" actually caused much commotion. Conflicts erupted during the survey. The whole process—defining villages, denoting the boundaries of jungles, clarifying types of settlement, and locating and classifying types of land—became ridden with tension and court cases, as the following example from a survey report testifies.

The survey concerned some villages and a jungle in Jambani. The jungle on the southeast had the villages Koomree, Chaltha, Bankshole, Barasole, and

Kanimouli; on the west it had Kuldiha, Poradiha, and Sirsee. On the north there was the Kenduah jungle, which stretched across the two contiguous parganas of Jambani and Jhargram. Here again, the jungle was in dispute, and the exact boundaries of villages and the jungle had to be established. Once more we find Jadu Mahato as the defendant and Raja Jagadish Chandra as the plaintiff.[13]

How does the surveyor proceed with his work? Let us closely follow his own account. During his "sojourn at Ramchandrapur," he finds in Jadu Mahato's village, Kanimouli, six or eight saws being worked daily in making sal planks. He finds half of the big trees cut down in that portion of the forest, logs freshly cut, only the "underwood and bushes left . . . so that it appears like a garden." The whole of the jungle from north to south is "a continuous whole."[14] The surveyor finds that his chain line lies between the jungle in dispute and the jungles of the village lying to the east, belonging to pargana Jhargram. The zamindar produces a certified copy of the pargana maps to buttress his claim, but the surveyor finds them "not useful" as the "scale is too large and no fixed neighbouring trees or other objects are shown there from which I could glean a definite course." Regarding the *chithas* (records) filed by the zamindar, the "oldest men alive and mandals of the neighbouring villages" are consulted. The identity of Q2 Banka Tentul, the remnant of the stump of the tree called Dhengasol from which, according to the plaintiff, the whole jungle has derived its name, and which is situated between Y2 and Z2 stations, the asath tree at B3, the mohul tree at L3, the chaltha tree at K3 and the jora moul at Q2, and "the stones marked and unmarked" are identified.[15] But the "stone of the west bank of Kotrungi Khal" is not where it is supposed to be. Parasgeria is important, for Parasgeria is the southern point of Koomree. Yet Koomree is hard to delineate since the mango trees and the *Dhoudra Moul* forming the boundary line between villages Barasole and Chaltha are not where they are stated in the chithas. And on the other side of Koomree are Barasole and Chaltha. Only "two *Agni* trees in the middle of the jungle to the east of the village Kalimohini" are found where they are supposed to be.[16]

Village Pariharpore is separated from the disputed jungle by the intervening mauzas of Kuldiha, Poradiha, and Sirsee. The "north eastern limit of Pariharpore is marked by a *Bhand* tree which is 2245 ft from near Wa station. . . . Of the village Koomree the document filed by the defdts viz. the thika pradhani mokrari jote *pāttā* [document of proprietorship] is the only document." The plaintiff's chitha of mouza Susmi, 1289 B.S., clashes with the defendant's patta. It lies north of Koomree. The patta states that village

Gira is beyond Koomree after a tamarind tree. But here again the mauza boundary is difficult to establish; the surveyor, moving from "station Q2 *Banka Tetul* to Gira mouza of Mallabhum or Jhargram pargana," has to go through "a difficult village."[17]

He has to confess his helplessness. How is one to make sense of these conflicting versions and conclude the assignment? The chithas of Watson & Co. often intrude into Mallabhum (Jhargram). He suspects that "there is a myth" in these documents. A tree is not where it should be. In exasperation, he exclaims, "I have no such *Dha* tree. Neither could the plff or the defdts shew me any such marked or old *Dha* tree although I tried much for it. Nor could any one else of the surrounding villages shew me any old *Dha* tree as the boundary, *moul* tree is an impossible boundary."[18] Again "chita of 1271 gives as *khas* jungle, which I found to be patit only. . . . The location of the area is impossible on account of inconsistencies in the boundaries and present condition, the former occupants being dead long ago." He remarks that the "delimitation in the map is a puzzle." Mauza Barasole presents similar problems. The present defendants got *bandobust* (settlement) from Watson & Co., who were at that time ijaradars of Jambani pargana. But about one hundred bighas of forest intrude into the mauza and the zamindar has filed his chitha of 1296. According to this, the forest begins on the southern boundary of Rangavita. "Dag 26 of chita 1271 [A.D. 1770-71] of Rangavita shows no jungle included in *mouza* Rangavita. Thus where does Barasole end, the forest begin, and where is Rangavita?"[19]

The rest of the survey report runs along similar lines. Ramchandrapur has a jungle, but the chitha of 1271 shows no such thing. Dag number 122 shows a jungle of twenty bighas, but location of boundaries is impossible. Similarly indefinite is another jungle of thirty-two bighas. They fall to the west of the Jambani-Ghutia road, the yellow line on the map. But what about the southern boundary? Kanimouli and Barasole present problems. The Kend tree is displaced. There is no jora moul. Does *jora* refer to a pair of trees? The surveyor states, "I could not with the greatest endeavour possible find what is known as Jora Moul in the colloquial language of the part of the country round about the border such as I saw at Qa."[20] Similar problems arise as defendant Jadu Mahato, in possession of *jote pradhani patta* [headman's tenure] of mauza Kalimohini or Kanimouli, draws a dividing line in the disputed jungle connecting a chaltha tree, two agni trees, and the east of Kotrungi canal. He presses his claim. But how can Jadu's claim be sustained? This is evidently an "imaginary" claim, "for possession in these dense jungles can only be by continuous cutting of trees without let or hindrance."[21]

Could the forest's name, *Dhengasal,* provide a clue to its exact location? The surveyor writes:

> One would naturally think Dhengasal lies to the east of Porasigeria whereas in fact it lies to the south east at a distance of about 2000 ft from Porasigeria. In passing I may state here that during my sojourn in the disputed jungle I learnt three meanings of the word Dhengasal. The first is the tree stump between Y2 and Z2, the sense in which it was generally used by the defdts and their followers. The second is the whole jungle so called by the plff's men. The third is a mythical mouza comprising the portion of the jungle in which the tree stump stands. This is the acceptance given to the word by the chitta of 1289 of mouza Bankshole filed by the plff. It is a dense jungle and there is supposed to be situate [*sic*] the imaginary mouza Dhengasal propounded by the fertile brain of the *amin* who made the chitta.[22]

Enforcing Agencies

One consequence of the switch from custom to contract and the transformation of villages from solidarities to settlement units was the decline of the institution of the mandal. Mandals were the pillars of the agrarian economy in the frontier region. They helped reclamation, extension of agriculture, the management of the inflow of labor, management of village affairs, the use of the surplus, and settlements with the zamindar. This institution was clearly being eroded by the last decades of the nineteenth century.

The Rent Law commission, in its report of 1883, had surmised that a mandal was a substantial *raiyat* (tenant) who in the Jungle Mahals was granted wasteland by the zamindar and who then, by his own family labor and partly by inducing other raiyats to settle under him, would, after reclamation, establish a village on the land. He would give a stipulated lump sum as rent to the zamindar and, as head of the settlement, would be the mandal, or headman. The terms of the bargain between mandal and zamindar would be adjusted from time to time. The settlement proceedings of 1839 had declared them as having only *sthani* rights; in other words, they were *khudkasht* raiyats—tenants, not rentiers—and were not entitled to any profit. The mandali right was also thought to be transferable by custom. The land allotted was somewhat vaguely specified without actual measurement; the rent was not exorbitant, and the community founded had full rights to reclaim as much or as little as it liked, with the headman being in no way different from other members except that his superior social position allowed him to retain a larger area for himself.

In the 1918 settlement report, Jameson reported the existence of such a system in Jambani: "Similarly in Jambani according to a patta of 1261 in which money rents were fixed, the Mandal was allowed a deduction of Re. 1 from his own rent as profit but was expressly forbidden to realize from the other members more than the fixed assessment."[23] Jameson also noted variations:

> In Pargana Jambani, which is not now under the Midnāpur Zamindāri Company although they were ijaradars of it for a time, the conditions are similar though homesteads were found to be included in the Mandals' agreements and not to be the property of the landlord.[24]

The stages by which the mandali right had been transformed were not traceable, said Jameson, but he made a guess: mandals might have tried to enhance their rights, with ensuing breakup of the institution from within the community. Or possibly the zamindars had tried to increase their share, and the mandal had simply become an ordinary raiyat. In the meantime, the mahajans had made an appearance, "only to make maximum of profit and caring little or nothing for the ancient rights of the community."[25] The original mandals were sometimes ejected.

Thus, there was a combination of factors: there were challenges to rights in jungles and to mandali rights, a crisis in tenures, and a rent crisis, and together these produced the political crisis in the Jungle Mahals, particularly in Jambani. The report concluded that "opening up the country for railways" and restricting the hitherto "unrestricted right to cut jungles" were certainly causes.[26] But by themselves they would not have caused a political breakdown on such a scale.

I will cite here another case: suit number seventy-eight of 1909, the plaint filed on 16 February 1909 in the subjudge's court, First Court, Midnapore. Again, the suit was for damages on account of violation of jungle rights, the claim laid at Rs.3400. The proceedings show how the mandali was facing a crisis of legal recognition: the judge refused to recognize the institution and a customary practice failed to get translated into a legitimate reality. The case is between Trailokya Pal, by caste Sadgop, a substantial landowner as well as a lawyer, and Jagadish Chandra Dhabal Deb and Durga Rakshit, the two defendants.[27]

Again the case is entangled in the dispute within the zamindar's family. Rani Parbati Kumari had claims to the rent of four *mauzas*: Dhaniapal, Tetelapal, Kendua, and Berha. After the death of Purna Chandra, Parbati's husband and Purna's brother Iswar became the zamindar. Parbati Kumari fought a court battle for possession of the four mauzas. She got partial possession in a court verdict, the other half going to the other wife, Rani Radha Kumari.

But Parbati had taken on a heavy loan from the plaintiff, Trailokya Pal, under a registered mortgage. There being a default in repayment, Trailokya took possession of the four mauzas along with the forests that they contained. Jagadish meanwhile became the zamindar, following Iswar's death, and Durga Rakshit was a tenant under Rani Parbati, at an annual *jama* of Rs.498-13-9 for 963 bighas-8 cottas-9 chattaks of cultivable land. The defendants cut jungles of nearly a thousand bighas in the Kendua and Dhaniapal mauzas. Hence the damage suit.

The question was, did the plaintiff have any right in the jungle? Was not the second defendant the possessor of the jungle in suit? The verdict, the reversal of the verdict on appeal, and other details are not of interest to us in the present context; our interest centers on the mandali and its significance in determining the suit. The second defendant, Durga Rakshit, by caste Tamli, maintained that the jungles were in his khas possession and that he was a mandal. The subjudge, Prabhas Chandra, dismissed the arguments of the plaintiff and the suit. Among other things he said:

> The deed of relinquishment propounded by the plaintiff . . . cannot affect the defendant's rights to the jungle; . . . the defendant is a permanent tenure holder mandal of the disputed mouzahs and is not a common tenant, and the plaintiff is entitled to nothing more from him except his fixed rent, and the jungle which existed in the mouzahs is covered by the defendant's patta.[28]

The judge argued that the contention of the plaintiff that Durga Rakshit was mandal and hence just a tenure holder, with no rights to the jungle, was unsustainable. He dismissed the assertion also that in "Purgana Jambani '*jote mandale*' and a right to cut down trees are inconsistent and cannot go together." Referring to cross-examination of a witness who had reported "some two-hundred or two-hundred-fifty *mandals* in Purgana Jambani" and mandals having no settlement in the jungles, whereas permanent tenants with registered leases may have such rights, the judge observed,

> The plaintiff has tried to use a generic word in a specific and special sense which it does not bear at all. From the evidence it appears that the word *mandal* is used in the case of tenancies of various nature and it is not inconsistent with a right to jungles.[29]

The judge further referred to *8 Calcutta Weekly Notes, 117,* where tenancy was described as *jote* and argued that it was a tenure and not a holding and thus the name given to a tenancy was not important, but the *terms of contract* were. Still the question remained: Why did most pattas in Jambani have the words *jalkar*, *falkar,* and *matsyakar,* but never *bankar*? Two opinions surfaced in the proceedings. One referred to the jungles being always the khas possession of the landlord; the other argued that jungles generated no special right and therefore *bankar* needed no special mention. In any case, the judge opted for an evasive course. He skirted the controversy, concentrated upon the terms of patta, and said, "I have not the slightest doubt that the defendant [Durga Rakshit] was granted a permanent *mokurari mourasi* tenure with full rights to the jungles in the mouzahs."[30]

The case went to the court of the district judge, J. Cornes, where the decision was reversed. Again, the judgment and details of the verdict do not concern us; we shall see only how the argument went on the *jote mandali* issue. According to Cornes, the phrase *jote mondali right* ran through the whole lease. The lessee was in possession of *hak hakuk* [all rights] of these mauzas and rents had been enumerated as "jalkar, falkar, matsakar"; but the important term *bankar* was absent. But what was meant by *hak hakuk*? The Englishman Cornes feels trapped:

> This leads to a consideration of a very important clause in the document—"You will, *purgana pratha anusware*, have interest in all trees and jungle, etc., which are now in existence and which will grow in future." The expression *purgana pratha anusware* is rendered by the learned subordinate Judge "as that is the custom of the purgana." Appellant would render it "subject to the custom of the purgana." I am extremely diffident to attempt to arbitrate on the meaning of an expression in a foreign language. . . . It is to be remembered that the lease was not drawn up by a skilled draughtsman.[31]

So was the mandali a jote? What rights did such a jote entail? Was it something like tehsildar or the ijaradar in the Jungle Mahals? Evidently, here was a mandal backing Raja Jagadish in his attempt to grab the property of another man of substance. But in most other cases, mandals largely went against the raja since they were being reduced to ordinary tenants and divested of their customary role of representing the community. The court of law and the settlement officers—both were confused. In any case, the transition from custom to contract entailed a decline of the institution of the mandal. In my interview with Bhavani Rana, the octogenarian former estate official of the raja told me that mandals took the lead in the agrarian unrest in the ensuing decade.

In the private papers of the raja, I found many affidavits like this one in which Avinash Sui, a Khandait peasant, of the village of Ghutia, hands over 239 bighas in four mauzas, expressing his helplessness over unpaid rents up to 1322 B.S. and his inability to collect rents from the praja. He appeals to the raja for commutation of the rent to be paid by him and hands over all the lands to the raja to be distributed and settled afresh by him according to his will. The affidavit is dated 8 April 1915. Again, affidavits are found where disputed jungles change hands.[32] Mahatos supporting Rani Parbati become special targets; their property and the land settled with them are claimed back by the raja.[33] We also find several applications by the raja for registration and mutation of names in respect of revenue-paying and revenue-free portions of mauzas.

To the historian grappling with the problem of collective identity, the court cases, raise the possibility of a different theme. Formally, the depositions seem to be one more source for a standard agrarian history. But as texts of a history of the rise and growth of a people, these depositions show how the people of Jambani memorized the past, brought back their memories, and presented them as *evidence*, in fact as *historical* evidence, of how their social order was being unjustly changed. Could we suppose that these submissions, which the disciplinary gaze both of the colonial revenue official and of the nationalist historian would turn into the materials of an agrarian history of a frontier region, might become *real* elements in a historiographical project of constructing the identity of a people? In creating a sense of nationality?

Cases, and depositions in court, we must remember, showed only the tip of the iceberg. After all, only "men of substance" could afford to go to court with their grievances. A "List of Properties Purchased During the Khas Management of the Rajah and during the Management by the Encumbered Estates Department" gives a somewhat better idea of the range of people who were robbed of their land. This list, which I found among the private papers of the Jambani family, contained 107 names—Dandapats, Mahatos, Laiks, Sardars, Mundas, Santhals, Majhis, and so on. They were persons belonging to nearby villages of Chilkigarh and the purchases refer to the years 1894-95 and 1896-97.

The raja, for all we know, was oblivious to the storm that was brewing. In 1917, Raja Jagadish was writing to Bijay Chand Mahtab, the maharaja of Burdwan, addressing him as the "organ voice of the landholders of Bengal":

> It is very gratifying to note that Maharajadhiraj Bahadur . . . has considered it fit to know the opinion on the proposed Amendment of the B.T. [Bengal Tenancy] Act of his constituents.
>
> I beg to submit in the following lines my views on the Bill i.e., I have full sympathy for the object of the Bill. Money lenders, taking advantage of illiteracy and ignorance of aboriginals their debtor, may compel them to part with their valuable property for their small dues. There is no doubt that this sort of

> practice will be stopped by the operation of the proposed Act. But at the same time there is a dark side of the matter. Even at a time of urgent necessity, they will not be able to farrow a single pice from a nonaboriginal to remove their want at the same time there are very few aboriginal money lenders.
>
> . . . Regarding Sec.49A. I beg to state that it is not stated who will come under the category of the term "Aboriginal." If all the cultivators of backward tribes be included in this term the proposed Bill if passed will curtail unnecessarily to a regrettable extent the vested rights of the landlords.[34]

When trouble came, in 1923, it struck like a tornado.

Memories of Insurgency

It is said that structure determines events. Perhaps structure also determines the memory of events. The Brahmins of Dubra, the leading high-caste village in Jambani, three kilometers away from the raja's kutchery and one kilometer from the police station, had supported the praja in the uprising of 1923. In 1990, when I asked Shambhu Nath Sarangi, the oldest man in the village and writer of a genealogy of the Dhabaldebs, I found him clearly unwilling to talk on the subject. He remembered other things, but on *deshgaro* he would not speak. Even in his fictive history of the Jambani raj, he wrote virtually nothing about the unrest.

The descendants of Raja Jagadish, however, well remember the atmosphere of siege in the palace. The lathials, sepoys, police, the men with bows on guard day and night. They remembered the panic most of all. They could not say why there was unrest. It must have been the nayeb, they said, the estate manager whose highhandedness had infuriated the praja. They remembered the nayeb being sacked after it was all over.

Some of the Mahatos I talked to knew of *deshgaro*, but the memory was not particularly vivid and did not evoke any emotions. In folklore, of course, the memory survives. *Deshgaro*, meaning *deshe graha,* or unrest in the country, is a known word in the area and does signify an event that took place some sixty or seventy years ago. But apart from this historical reference, not much is remembered by the people; only members of the Dhabaldeb family remember well because they heard graphic accounts of the event in their childhood.

We cannot say when exactly the mobilizations, the siege of the kutchery, the looting, the felling of trees, began. The raja in the meantime had sworn loyalty to the British Empire and had promised to deliver recruits for the army. In this, he did not meet with much success.[35] The noncooperation movement also started around that time. People in Jambani told me of one Rai Charan Dhal, of Ambikanagar, near Jambani, who went to prison at the time for political offenses. We have two interviews by Satcouripati Roy and Anil Baran Roy that talk of nationalist activities in the Jhargram-Binpur-Bankura region. National schools were set up, and Satcouripati Roy mentions the influence of Biren Sasmal, the most well known Congress leader of Midnapore. A noncooperation activist, Sailajananda Sen, took shelter in Jambani.[36] And a "leading Santhal agitator" referred to Satcouripati when asked of any possible influence on their agitation. The additional magistrate of Midnapore noted in the same report that "activities of non cooperation party [were] very common."[37] We know that in Manbhum, too, there was this coincidence of nationalist activities and peasant unrest.

Yet it is difficult to establish any direct connection of nationalist politics with the peasant unrest in the Jungle Mahals. Citing the same government report, Sumit Sarkar has argued that the linkage with nationalist politics was a crucial factor in subaltern awakening in Bengal in those days. It is true, of course, that Birley, in his report to the divisional commissioner in Burdwan, observed that in Gopiballavpur, bordering Jhargram, Jambani, and Nayabasan, the Santhals had claimed that the "chaukidari tax had been abolished by Gandhi Maharaj's order" and that hat looting had taken place in Jhargram and Silda amid shouts of "Gandhi Maharaj ki Jai."[38] But there is no clear evidence, apart from a few surprised comments, such as "there was panic in Jhargram town" or that "outbursts were continuing even after Non Cooperation had been called off," that nationalist politics was the catalyst of civil unrest in the Jungle Mahals.

Sarkar's observation is intriguing on another point. On the unrest in Jambani-Silda, he writes:

> Yet for the resistance to develop, a change for the worse in the conditions of exploitation is often less important than rumours of breakdown of the second type: Santals of Jhargram and Bankura after all had been losing their forest rights for decades. Within the concept of breakdown of authority, I think it is useful to distinguish further between a less and a more extreme form. In the first the rumour is that of a conflict among the superiors: the *zamindars* or the *babus* have quarrelled with the government, the latter's officials consequently would be more sympathetic toward our grievances (or conversely the immediate superior would help us in our struggle). The more extreme variety is that all existing authority is collapsing, usually through the emergence of a new symbolic power-centre like the Gandhi raj of 1921-22.[39]

But surely, "rumours of breakdown" do not explain subaltern militancy; on the contrary, they only beg the question: Why were the people ready to lend credence to these rumors? The answer, it seems to me, must be sought not in some external breakdown, but rather in the process of erosion of authority within the community. In Sarkar's analysis of the conditions and nature of subaltern militancy, the community does not receive adequate theoretical or political importance.

Even Swapan Dasgupta, who has attempted the most detailed historical account so far of the unrest in Jambani, has focused principally on the combination of tribal people with a substantial minority of low-caste Hindus on agrarian issues against the zamindar-sahukar-colonial raj. His main argument is that land alienation went to extreme lengths in the Jungle Mahals. The mandali system had been destroyed; commercialization of forest rights increased discontent. Intralandlord conflicts fueled the disturbances. "What comes across from these acts of apparent fearlessness and solidarity is an alternative conception of justice born out of fundamentally different sets of values. . . . They believed in the morality of their struggle and asserted their 'natural' rights through traditional communal activity such as fishing, now undertaken as tank looting in support of insurgency."[40] Despite this assertion of "morality" and "alternative conception of justice," one is unable to find in Swapan Dasgupta's account any sense of a threat to the solidarity of the community that could have provoked such a violent reaction.

During my visits to Jambani, I found that only two questions survive in the memory of the people: encroachment on forest rights and the notorious manager Manoranjan Ray, "who gave the Raja a bad name." Even nationalist agitation has not left much trace in popular memory.

The reaction of the colonial administration to the sudden turn of events in Jambani was one of surprise and perplexity over how the "law abiding," "merry making," "obedient" Santals could take to public agitation. There need not have been this surprise if the administration had been alive to the possible consequences of the settlement operations. We get a glimpse of the surprise and shock in the fascinating tour diary of the additional district magistrate of Midnapur, James Peddie.[41]

Peddie reached Chilkigarh on 27 April 1923. He found "discomfort prevailing among Santhals over jungle rights." He wrote back: "The area extends for at least 20 miles north to south and 6 to 12 miles east to west thick jungles. . . . They can easily assemble and disperse—without enough police I can't do much." Peddie reported further of thirty cases of looting; in Chilkigarh he arrested ten people. "Santhals are assaulting people [who are] helping police. One [is] injured badly, he will not survive." There was an attack on the subinspector of Jambani. Peddie found not merely looting and illegal fishing, but open defiance of authority. "Santhals can fire arrows 80 to 90 yards and do a lot of damage while remaining out of gunshot range themselves." He sent a message for an additional superintendent of police with summary powers to relieve the superintendent. An additional first-class magistrate on immediate temporary deputation was also needed. He found "each house full of wood. . . . There was attack upon [my] car." There were also attacks on the property of a mining company near the Dhalbhum border and of the Midnapur Zamindari Company in Silda. Peddie felt that his arrival had never been more needed than now, and he hoped for "success of mediation between the Raj and the tenants." Tenants have legitimate grievances. But "they cannot spoil jungles by cutting them indiscriminately. They should not be allowed to fish tanks. Civil courts should be suitably directed." After his arrival, "there was one further looting case—in Alampur."

Peddie, however, did think that the peasants' grievances were justified. He seemed to take up where earlier government reports on that part of the Jungle Mahals had left the matter.[42] "There was a reasonable case against the manager." Upon Peddie's persuasion, it seems, "the proprietor of the Raj has consented to send him on leave." In Silda, however, the situation was more serious. "Active prosecution should be pursued" there. "People are too clannish to furnish evidence" in connection with the assault on government officers. Peddie reported the spread of looting from Jambani to Silda. He was aware that there were similar grievances in Malda and Dinajpur, but "this cannot be an imitation" of what had happened there. Clearly local grievances had made the situation ripe for an outbreak, and "Pratap [had] merely utilised the unpopularity of the manager."

We continue with Peddie's field jottings. Santhals were looting near Chakulia, which showed that the unrest was spreading in Dhalbhum, too. Peddie held an urgent mediation meeting in Parihati. He reported appointing headmen as special constables. Mandals were consulted and claims of tenants were discussed. The strategy employed by Peddie was clear enough: consultation, mediation, empowerment of village bosses such as headmen and mandals, a display of armed force while at the same time meeting a few minor demands halfway. Peddie reported an attempt to loot the Chilkigarh palace on 22 and 23 April, where "people came from distant places like Singbhum and Mayurbhanj."

The district magistrate, Graham, wrote to A.W. Cook, the divisional commissioner: "I quite agree with Peddie that it is necessary to overawe the area at once."[43] Cook accordingly recommended immediate dispatch of the Eastern Frontier Rifles.[44] Cook interpreted the events largely in terms of popular grievances against the manager. "There is an agitation against the Manager. I have made enquiries, but I cannot find anything against him that would not be found against the average zamindari manager." But Cook was aware of the need for an appropriate strategy for suppression. "Satpatis [the Jambani brahmins] are crucial. . . . Pressure should be brought upon them to throw influence on the side of law and order." Mandals were leading the tenants, so "all the headmen and influential raiyats" should be consulted.

In a letter dated 22 April 1923, Cook reported "the opposition of raiyats of the west of Midnapur District to the jungle rights claimed by the zamindars." He mentioned the "efforts by Mr. Pyne, late SDO, to bring the parties together. The zamindar [Jagadish Chandra] however does not believe that his manager is troublesome and throws the blame on mischief makers who are instigating the tenants against him. . . . Police has been despatched to Kalibund where fish has been looted from zamindary tanks." Graham had written to Cook two days earlier that it was "not a hat looting case, but fish were taken by force from a tank [a large pond]. The trouble will probably subside as soon as the leaders of those concerned in earlier outrages are in *hajat* [custody]."[45] Graham wrote further of the looting of thirty tanks and expressed the apprehension that appointing special constables was not producing much effect. "The Santhals," Graham wrote to the deputy commissioner of Singhbhum, "were in great excitement," and Cook talked of "considerable depredations."[46] Cook reported later that Peddie had written to him of "trouble due to non cooperation."

The raja of Jambani had earlier presented the genealogy of the raj to the government.[47] He had contributed financially to the war effort and now promised to draft recruits from the local population for the war effort. The response was, however, lukewarm:

> By beat of drums, a public meeting was convened. . . . Babu Upendra Nath Maity was requested to attend. . . . Pandit Gnanendra Chandra Chatterjee, Lecturer, Midnapur College and some other gentlemen attended the meeting. [I announced] I shall give 10 Bighas of land without rent or remit rent for 15 Bighas of land for life.

Members of the audience said that they would think over the matter.[48] While noting the loyalty of the raja, the chief secretary commented in 1921 that "Trailokya Nath Satpati of Dubra was not cooperating with the Raja." Graham was trying to convince the Santhals through local officers that the "theory of no private property in water," which Santhals in Malda were advocating, "was mistaken."[49] Cook mentioned obstruction to settlement operations and "proposed actions against [such] obstructions in the Birbhum

District."[50] The settlement officer, F. W. Robertson, had reported that surveyors were in danger there.

Hari Gupta was the deputy superintendent of police in Midnapur. He camped at Parihati in Jambani on 19 April and wrote to the SP: "Agreeably to your orders I left Midnapur by early morning train. Reached Kalibund. There was news of Santhal mobilisation. . . . I reached the spot." The Santhals had meanwhile left. "I am trying to apprehend the stragglers." As usual, the police force was inadequate. Gupta reported "a mob of 5,000, [which] attempted to burn Parihati Kutchery." They tried to rescue the arrested. The deputy superintendent asked for reinforcements.[51] It was after Hari Gupta's report that Peddie was sent on a pacifying mission. Peddie wrote:

> In the estate certain persons hating Jagadish Babu's family bitterly have seen that by stirring up the simple Santhals and other uneducated peoples of the jungle, by holding meetings and by organising opposition to the zamindar, they can cause the latter a great deal of annoyance and worry. . . .
>
> They have been successful. . . . The zamindar has lost total control . . . servants cannot go to village for fear of being beaten and his manager's life is in danger were he to be caught by a mob of refractory tenants. . . .
>
> Satpatis and Mahatos are hereditary enemies of the estate.[52]

Peddie was reasonably successful in restoring order in Jambani by following the strategy outlined in his diary. But unrest spread. Gurusaday Dutt, at the time the district magistrate of Bankura, was evidently alarmed, as his messages to Cook suggest. A telegram from him (date not specified in the file) reads: "Trouble believed agrarian, not political."[53] Dutt wrote a letter to Cook on 25 May 1923, and Cook was appreciative of Dutt's efforts. "Mr. Dutt appears to have tackled the situation with energy. . . . I think we should say the same about Mr. Peddie."[54] Cook had also requested provision of additional police forces in Silda,[55] reporting looting in Lalgarh and Belpahari and referring to the "affair of Jambani." Cook's request was evidently granted. The Dacca commissioner tersely informed him: "150 military police leave Dacca for Burdwan Division." They were to "go straight to Gidni," the railhead in Jambani.

Gurusaday Dutt had earlier camped in Raipur and on 7 May reported on the looting of the Raj *bandhs* (tanks).[56] Now he referred to possible connections with the local self-government agitation, reporting that "the unrest [is] agrarian and economic in character" and adding that it appeared to be "directed against the owners of tanks and jungles in general." However, Dutt claimed to know the peasants intimately and was sure that "the attitude of local Santhals towards Government Officers, although at first somewhat sullen, has been on the whole one of confidence and of appeal to them for the removal of their supposed grievances in respect of jungle rights." He admitted that the price of wood "was going up," referring also to high prices "charged from tribals"—two measures of rice for every rupee paid as rent to the landlord: "Ijaradars were charging the tribals, zamindars withholding jungle rights of villagers." Zamindars were settling "customary rights" with the Midnapur Zamindari Company. Interestingly, Dutt echoed the suspicion that the "movement [was] spreading from Dinajpur and Malda." Binpur was reported as the trouble spot; ten Santhals had been arrested there and looting prevented.[57]

In both Peddie's tour diary and Gurusaday Dutt's dispatches, the agrarian character of the discontent is recognized. What is left out is the particular role of the settlement operations. They place the emphasis on the violation of customary rights over jungles and tanks. One is tempted to remark that colonial officials in these frontier regions knew a thing or two about the theory of "moral economy." What is significant, however, is that Peddie and Dutt speak only of Santhals: it is a Santhal unrest, Santhal mobilization, Santhals looting property, and so on. Yet, even at the time, there was no evidence to show that it was only a Santhal unrest. The great divide between Santhals and Mahatos had still not come about. Mahatos, too, participated in large numbers, as did Kamars, Bagdis, Bagals, and others. Possibly because of official memories of the Santhal rebellion seventy years earlier and the Munda uprising at the turn of the century, the archetypal image of the docile, fun-loving tribal who has suddenly run amuck dominated the perceptions of officials. Perhaps for this reason—that it was "merely" an agrarian tribal unrest—despite the note of urgency in the messages, a patent confidence shows through them: it was the confidence of a modern state sure of its ability to put down protests of this type.

Another point of interest is the fact that "outside agitators," "troublemakers," and "budmashes" are rarely mentioned by name in these messages: the emphasis is placed largely on "angry mobs." Individual conspirators, organizers, nationalist activists, and the like would certainly have been mentioned had Peddie or Dutt come to know of any. Perhaps the major weakness of the agitation was that it was not sufficiently linked either with the nationalist movement (as would happen later in Manbhum) or with Bengal's dominant peasant politics of the time. Not surprisingly, for contemporary administrators as well as later historians, the politics of the Jungle Mahals remained a fringe affair, apparently not sufficiently integrated with the larger arenas of politics to deserve its own narrative. To this we now turn.

The Territoriality of Historical Memory

I have said before that the people of Jambani use the word *deśgāro* when referring to the unrest of the 1920s. After inquiries, I figured out what *gāro* meant: *graha*, unrest, turbulence, hazard. I did not think much about *deś*, which, rather naively as I later realized, I took to mean "the country," i.e., Jambani. But the more I heard about events in Bankura and other areas, the more I grew suspicious. Balak Dehri and Sasadhar Roy, two of the oldest Cho dancers of Jambani, and Kishori Malla, a wise old man distantly related to the family of the raja, first awakened me to the possibility that *deś* might mean the whole region—all of the Jungle Mahals, a single landmass extending from Mayurbhanj across Jambani to Bankura, Barabhum, and Manbhum and finishing with the Chotanagpur region that spreads from Ranchi and meets Jambani via Dhalbhum. The more I thought about the stray speculations of colonial officers on whether the unrest might have been caused by events in Malda or Dinajpur or Birbhum, the more I felt that *deś* must have signified something wider.

I was faced with an obvious difficulty. No historian has ever recorded the events over such a wide region as constituting a single political narrative. Swapan Dasgupta, Sumit Sarkar, even K. S. Singh—all have recorded the unrest piecemeal. Could I say that these events constituted a rebellion in that whole *deś*?

We have already noted that the unrest had spread to Silda in Midnapur and Raipur in Bankura. Let us speculate for a while on the possibility that *deśgāro* may imply a movement engulfing the whole of the Jungle Mahals. I must repeat that this story of the unrest has not yet been written as history. But could it be, some day, perhaps by a future historian of the Jharkhand people?

Silda was a pargana, with its center in a village named Jhatibani, on the bank of the River Tarafeni. It was very much a part of the Jungle Mahals, densely wooded. Today it is on the western side of Binpur thana in Medinipur district. My attention was drawn to it by a local chronicle, "Śildār kathā o kāhinī" written by Amarendranath Majumdar.[58] The chronicler writes of a poet, Satish Mukherjee, who had composed songs on the oppression and unrest in Silda. One song speaks of the indigo planters of the 1870s and 1880s, the time of the zamindars Gangaram Datta, Rani Durga Kumari, and Bamasundari, when intrafamily quarrels flared up and the Robert Watson company became ijārādar of a large part of the pargana. The same company, we may remember, was also ijārādar of Jambani. The Watson lease passed into the hands of the Midnapur Zamindari Company in 1906. Both companies engaged extensively in indigo cultivation, and the ruins of the *nīlkuṭhi* can be seen at six places in Silda: Silda, Belpahari, Tamajuri, Shyamnagar, Dharmapur, and Mohanpur. The local peasants called them the *ḍipughar:* depot. Tamajuri was later a major center of unrest. The dipughar symbolized forcible incarceration and torture. If any one dared protest against the misdeeds of the company, he or she was forcibly sent to the Duars of Bengal and Assam. A *jhumur* (local folk) song goes:

I thought I'd go to Assam,
And sleep under a fan hanging from the ceiling;
Instead the sahib gave me a spade to dig with.
Who were you to me
That you should sell me off for money,
And write the names of my forefathers
In your record book?

We know that between 1906 and 1922, both exactions and coercive measures increased rapidly. In Silda, too, court cases increased. Nayeb Aftabuddin encouraged the company and its manager, Muirhead, to impose taxes (e.g., a dust tax, which had to be paid if bullock carts raised dust in front of his bungalow; various forest levies; a cess on cowsheds and on certain plants and flowers, and also on temple land; there was even a cess on homestead land). On land that was in the direct possession of the company, indigo was cultivated forcibly. Grazing cattle were picked up and added to Muirhead's stock. Amarendranath tells the story of Nilmani, five of whose cows were taken away in this manner. Nilmani dressed up as a shaman, went into Muirhead's cowshed, and did a dance, shouting: "Today I will set free Mother Cow!" The ropes were untied, Nilmani went away dancing, as though in ecstasy, while the guards stood by, dumbfounded.

As it did elsewhere in the Jungle Mahals, the message of noncooperation arrived in this area. Congress workers of Midnapur came to Binpur. The company's orders began to be openly flouted. The *hāt* at Belpahari was stopped. Trees in Silda were felled. Peasants refused to cultivate indigo. Satish Mukherjee, the poet chronicled by Amarendranath, was at that time a cook in the house of Adhar Pal, the munshi at Belpahari. Satish sang:

Daulat Khan and the forester went to Krishnapur
To sow the blue crop.
They only got a hiding and had to run away.
They came back and said, "O great sahib,
The Shyamnagar tenants have gone beyond all control.
We've had enough of working for you.

Good-bye, and let us go."
Ganguli thought for a while
And said to the tehsildar,
"Let's not wait a while longer, now's the time to run."
They took half their clothes with them,
And half were left hanging from trees.

Amarendranath tells us that this song is incomplete: he had not been able to collect the rest of it. In any case, he does give us the testimony of Satish Mukherjee, who tells us that Adhar Pal had to flee from Belpahari in his "sahib's taxi." Birley, the additional magistrate, advised that Muirhead be replaced as manager by another Englishman, named Peter. "Seven hundred" mandals were consulted and peasants were granted the right to cut trees or plants of up to nine inches in diameter. According to Amarendranath, in Silda and Lalgarh parganas alone, the praja had to pay punitive taxes amounting to Rs.60,000. Up to 1927, Silda remained unquiet; ponds continued to be looted, the magistrate was attacked, and the company was resisted. Policemen were stoned, "miscreants" were arrested, and the pattern of unrest in the Jungle Mahals continued.

We learn these things from what Amarendranath has saved of Satish's compositions—songs that reflect all that had happened in neighboring Jambani, too. It is interesting to note, again, how memory acts selectively as an appropriating process. All parts of the Jungle Mahal remember very well the story of the Chuār revolt of the early nineteenth century; indeed, it is a matter of collective pride, even more so because "men of substance" had led that revolt. The heritage of a particular section of rural society that later became the dominant force in the region could be transformed into a collective heritage. Thus *Bhairab raṅkinī māhātmya* narrates in verse the legendary history of Silda[59] from the time when Bhairab, the god of thunder, first visited Silda from the temple of Rankini in Ghatshila to the time of the Chuār revolt and the subsequent establishment of the Malla Rai and Datta zamindari.[60]

But there is no such trace in the collective memory of the peasant unrest of the 1920s. The only possible answer is that whereas the earlier revolt was indeed a communitarian one, the later one split the community. The contract between the rulers and the ruled was broken. A collective legend giving shape to a collective memory is simply not possible here.

The *nīlkuṭhi* (indigo factories) and the English ijārādar companies remain vivid in the songs that have been rescued. They signify the identification of the zamindar and the colonial authorities by the agitating peasants of the Jungle Mahals. Rothermund has argued that much of the developments of the region can be explained by what he calls the "enclave economy." The zamindars welcomed the new tenure holders—the British companies—because they provided them with a large rental income. Timber stockyards, lime and copper yards, the railway stations from Jhargram to Ranchi, with sheds and go-downs, provided a striking contrast to the verdant forests and the "thatched huts and green rice terraces." The enclave economy was common to the whole area of Jhargram, Ghatsila, Chotanagpur, Manbhum, and even Mayurbhanj. The agrarian system, the ecology, the land utilization pattern, the managing agency system, recruitment of labor—all these presented a common picture. Rothermund refers to three types of captivity in this region: the agrarian system was based on the captivity of the peasant who owed his lord rent and services; the managing agency system operated in a captive market, where supply and demand did not freely respond to each other but had to be manipulated; and the labor recruitment system depended on the captive worker, who was bound by contract, indenture, and advances and thus deprived of mobility. These three types of captivity, concludes Rothermund, formed an interdependent pattern that made it a subsystem of the colonial system.[61] These features were present in the entire frontier region.

Even without taking recourse to a political-economy argument of the Rothermund type, my inclination to look at the events in the Jungle Mahals from the second decade of this century as constituting a single movement stems primarily from a cultural argument. If cultural silence explains why we do not find a vivid evocation of the struggle in the popular memory of the region, there is the opposite phenomenon of cultural literacy, too—in songs and other oral traditions. If the present-day Jharkhand activists tend to treat the events as a single movement constitutive of the history of the Jharkhand people, I find little reason to dismiss it as an unauthentic "invention of tradition." Rather, such a phenomenon shows how the disciplining of historical memory has always been a question of power.

In 1917, Mayurbhanj witnessed a violent peasant movement, of Santhals and Kurmis, known as *medi* (unity, *meli*). The government had attempted to raise a labor corps for the war in France. Peasants who had so long allowed themselves to be recruited as coolies for tea gardens in the Duars now resisted transportation across the seas. The sahibs, they said, were facing the wrath of the German God and were now seeking help from the villagers. But imperial power had collapsed; suddenly, the desire for freedom came into the open. The railway line was cut in May 1917; bazars were sacked. After an assembly of Santhals and Mahatos, "robbery" and "murders" were committed. Rairangpur became the center. Order could be restored only with regular troops. Four peasants were sentenced to death and were hanged: Hridu Kolkamar, Kanka Mahato, Kalia Majhi, and Rameswar Singh Munda. Out of 1,118 persons tried, 977 were convicted and 33 were transported for life. K. S. Singh has commented that this was the biggest trial of its kind involving tribals.[62]

Again the issues were similar, the region broadly the same, and the circumstances of emerging subaltern militancy almost uniform. If events in Mayurbhanj preceded those in Jambani by a few years, they soon followed in Manbhum. There, agrarian disturbances started from the mid-1920s in a milieu of activism among the Kurmi-Mahatos. During the 1880s and 1890s, the average number of rent suits per year increased by 117 percent and 79 percent in Ranchi and Manbhum, respectively. Jambani experienced a similar increase.[63]

The Chotanagpur Tenancy Act failed to stop land alienation, and in Manbhum, as Sifton observed during the survey and settlement operations of Barabhum and Patkum, land owned by ghatwals was systematically passed on to the Watson Company, and subsequently to the Midnapore Zamindari Company, for indigo plantation. As in Gidni, Salbani, and Ghatsila Birendranath Sasmal had attempted to bring the Santhals, Mahatos, and Lodhas into the larger political and cultural world of Midnapore, so in Manbhum did Nibaran Chandra Dasgupta. The fissures in the prevailing structure of popular solidarity appeared around this time. It happened the same way in Mayurbhanj, where local Mahato leaders like Niranjan Mahato fought desperately to avoid being appropriated by the hegemonic politics of Harekrushna Mahatab, Nabakrishna Choudhury, and Madhusudan Das.

Today's Jharkhand activists accuse the landlords, the high-caste gentry, the colonial state, the industrialists, and the present Indian state of having done such a thorough job of suppression that the people do not even remember their "true" history. There is undoubtedly much truth in this. And that is precisely the polemical ground on which it becomes feasible to conceive of these events as a process of formation of a popular identity, as the historiographical material of a new history of a people and of a nationality.

Revenue history, landlordism, local power structures, the colonial state, community politics, and the emerging nationalist movement—these are the elements of Jambani's history recounted here. I have argued that these elements were present in similar events that took place in neighboring areas at around the same time. The question is thus posed: Did not the events in Jambani in 1923 form a part of a wider movement in the Jungle Mahal region? In trying to answer this question, we have made two passages: one, from the history of survey and settlement operations to a bigger political history, and the other, from the background of the Jungle Mahals to that of Jharkhand. The first is the connection between agrarian history and mass political mobilization that is routinely made in all nationalist historiography but held in abeyance for a "frontier" region such as the Jungle Mahals. The second passage—a change of names—is actually a fundamental historiographical operation that puts the stamp of legitimacy on the identification of a territory with a people.

The elements are all here for the history of a modern solidarity—as yet unwritten, but waiting for its historian. Perhaps some day this same material, which now seems to have vanished into the depths of popular memory, will be routinely recounted from popular literature and school textbooks as the historical memory of a people.

Notes

I am grateful to Nirmalesh Chandra Dhabaldeb and Pasupati Mahato for their generous help in the collection of materials for the writing of this chapter.

1. Hunter, *A Statistical Account,* p. 34.
2. Ibid., p. 121.
3. Ibid., p. 103.
4. Ibid., p. 85.
5. Ibid., p. 97.
6. From a letter written by the Rev. A. L. Kennan, dated 31 July 1906, attached with the petition of the Santhals of Midnapore to the government, cited by McAlpin, *Report on the Santhals,* para 195.
7. Hunter, *Statistical Account,* p. 49.
8. Case no. 6, subjudge, Second Court, Midnapore, 1898. I found the deposition papers among heaps of torn and scattered documents relating to the Jamboni raj. The private papers of the raj, uncared for since the abolition of zamindari, are not of much help in the construction of the history of the Jambani-Dhalbhum estate.
9. M. Datta, as commissioner appointed by the court, had indeed gone there, as shown by his petition to the judge at Midnapore on 22 January 1902 in civil suit 19, 1900. In this appeal, he asks for full payment of his fee, Rs.1,100, of which he had been paid Rs.600 by the plaintiff, and also for the reimbursement of his travel expenses and his assistant's fee. He speaks of how he had to "calculate the number of trees cut," measure "the girths of these trees" for valuation, survey the jungle "with compasses and a Gunther's chain 100 ft. long." Disputes over forest products featured prominently when the survey and settlement operations were in progress in the 1890s and the first decade of this century. Mention may be made of cases like Raja Jagadish versus Srinivas Satpathy (1899), Raja Jagadish versus Jadu Mahato, Rupchand Mahato, Harekrishna Mahato, and others (1902), Taraknath Adhikari and others versus Dwarka Nath Satpati and others (T.S. no. 278, 1908). There is again an interesting report on a dispute over boundaries, between village Kadamdiha and village Hijli, written by G. H. W. Davis, assistant superintendent of survey at Camp A, case no. 43, 31 January 1913. Santhal *ryots* and laborers were brought as witnesses by both sides.
10. I have written in detail about this in "Reflections in Another Mirror."

11. Jameson, *Final Report on Survey and Settlement Operations,* 1918 (hereafter *SSR*), para 130, pp. 150-51.

12. *SSR*, para 113, pp.131-32.

13. The report is twenty-four pages long and was filed in the court of the subjudge, Second Court, Midnapore, on 10 January 1902. The surveyor's signature is illegible. The copying clerk put the date 22 January 1902 at the end of the report. I have maintained the spellings of the report here. Today, the jungle between Jambani and Jhargram (now two separate police stations) has almost vanished. Hereafter we will cite this report as the Jambani-Jhargram Jungle Survey Report (*JJSR*). However, nowhere in the report is the jungle referred to by a name.

14. *JJSR*, pp. 1-2.

15. Ibid., p. 4.

16. Ibid., pp. 5-6.

17. Ibid., p. 8.

18. Ibid., p. 13.

19. Ibid., pp. 17-18.

20. Ibid., p. 20.

21. Ibid., p. 56.

22. Ibid., pp. 9-10. We find similar remarks by the first subjudge in Midnapore in suit number 245 of 1894 in the case Tarak Adhikari versus Jagadish Chandra Dhabaldeb (minor) and his guardian Rani Chura Kumari, a case that concerned the boundary between village Jamnasole and Bankasole—a boundary that was within a disputed forest. Evidently Tarak Adhikari was a "man of substance." Another such report concerns the case of Dinanath Adhikari versus Biswanath Satpaty that opened on 10 January 1893 and continued to 17 January 1907 (subjudge, Second Court, Midnapore).

23. *SSR*, para 29, pp. 41-42.

24. Ibid., para 30, p. 43.

25. Ibid., para 30, p. 42.

26. Ibid., para 52, 53, pp. 50-60.

27. The details of the case are found in printed form: *Burdwan Group No. 10, Appeal from Appellate Decree No. 72 of 1911 (Midnapore) from a Decision of J. Cornes Esq. District Judge of Midnapore, dated the 30th November 1910, Reversing a Decision of Babu Prabhas Chandra Singha, Sub-Judge 2nd Court of Midnapore, dated the 28th February 1910* (prepared and proof compared by J. Ainslie—10.4.13). I could not get the printer's name; the last page was missing.

28. Ibid., p. 9.

29. Ibid., p. 18.

30. Ibid., p. 20.

31. Ibid., p. 25.

32. This document is not dated, but was found among the papers of 1890-1910. It describes how to classify the land in a mauza. For such classification, see also *SSR*, para 123, pp. 142-43. From an ecological viewpoint, it is interesting to note that only 66 percent of the land was cultivated and thus conflicts over *paikan* land, *chaukidari chakran* land, and *jamabandi* estates were intense. See Bhubaneswar Sanyal, *Minor Settlement Operations,* para 8.

33. Ibid., pp. 3-4.

34. Letter 194, *Correspondence Book of the Jambani Estate, 1917-1918,* dated 1 November 1917.

35. Letter 59, ibid.

36. Oral history transcript, Nehru Memorial Museum Library (hereafter NMML), nos. 58 and 267.

37. GOB Home Poll. (Conf.), 317/1921, 181/1923 (NMML); L. Birley, additional magistrate, Midnapore, GOB Home Poll. 181/1923 (NMML).

38. Sumit Sarkar, "Conditions," pp. 300-301; Birley to Cook, divisional commissioner, Burdwan, 1 February 1922, GOB Home Poll. 1/22 (NMML).

39. Sarkar, "Conditions," pp. 306-7.

40. Swapan Dasgupta, "Adivasi Politics," pp. 134-35.

41. The entire tour diary was submitted as a government report. GOB Home Poll. 181/1923 (NMML).

42. These reports are found in GOB Home Poll. 317/1921 (NMML).

43. Hubert Graham to Cook. D/O 115C, GOB Home Poll. 181/1923 (NMML).

44. Cook to Birley, chief secretary. D/O 153C, GOB Home Poll. 181/1923 (NMML).

45. Graham to Cook, 20 April 1923. GOB Home Poll. 181/1923 (NMML).

46. D/O 162C, GOB Home Poll. 181/1923 (NMML).

47. GOB Home Poll. 235/1916 (NMML).

48. "Investment in Govt. Securities and Contributions to War Loans," letter 636, 20 June 1918; letters 199 and 200 from Raja Jagadish to W. A. Marr, D.M. Midnapore; letter 66, 2 Aswin 1325 (B.S.) from raja to Marr; letter 34, 9 September 1917 from raja to Marr, *Correspondence Book of the Jambani Estate, 1917-1918.*

49. GOB Home Poll. 155/1921 (NMML).

50. Letter dated 29 November 1921, GOB Home Poll. 347/1921 (NMML).

51. GOB Home Poll. 181/1923 (NMML).

52. Peddie's tour diary, p. 12. GOB Home Poll. 181/1923.

53. OH 14/10 (00076); GOB Home Poll. 181/1923 (NMML).

54. Cook to chief secretary, letter 188C, 14 May 1923. GOB Home Poll. 181/1923 (NMML).

55. Cook to chief secretary, letter 182C, 10 May 1923. GOB Home Poll. 181/1923 (NMML).

56. G. S. Dutt to Cook, letter from Camp Raipur, 7/8 May, 1923, D/O 163 T/B. GOB Home Poll. 181/1923 (NMML).

57. G. S. Dutt to Cook, 7 June 1923. GOB Home Poll. 181/1923 (NMML).

58. In *Taruṇer ḍāk* (Silda), 1, 1 (1962), pp. 49-57. I am grateful to Pasupati Mahato for lending me his copy of this journal.

59. Binay Ghosh made extensive use of this text in *Paścimbaṅger saṃskṛti.* It is a fictive genealogical account much like the ones I have discussed in "Reflections in Another Mirror." It narrates the story of the deity Sri Sri Bhairab Jeu, whose temple is in the village Orhganda.

60. The legend chronicles the time from Vijay Singha (1524), covers Medini Malla Ray (1524-66), Mangaraj Malla Ray (1556-1623), Gaudachandra (1623-91), Balaram (1691-1711), Mangovinda (1724-87), Kishormani (1787-1848), Srinath (1848-59), and Subarnamani (1859-61), after which begin the family quarrels and the entry of the Datta family and the English ijaradars.

61. D. Rothermund, "Tenancy Legislation for Chotanagpur: The Emphasis on Executive Protection," in Rothermund and Wadhwa, eds., *Zamindars, Mines and Peasants*; also Rothermund, "The Coal Fields: An Enclave in a Backward Region," ibid.

62. Cited in Pasupati Mahato, "Socio-Political Movement," p. 203. K. S. Singh's source is India Office Library, L/P & J/6/1488. But even Pasupati Mahato's account is cryptic. Though the event is placed in the context of the emerging activism of the Mahatos, there is no answer to the question of why it has attracted so little historiographical attention.

63. Mahato, "Socio-Political Movement," pp. 169-70.

Bibliography

Bengali-language Sources

Abanindranath Thakur. *Bhārat śilpa* (Calcutta: Hitabadi Library, 1909).

———. *Priyadarśikā* (Calcutta: Bharat Mihir Press, 1921).

———. *Bāgeśvarī śilpa-prabandhābalī* (Calcutta: University of Calcutta, 1941).

———. *Abanīndra racanābalī*, vol. 1 (Calcutta: Prakash Bhavan, 1973).

Alok Ray. *Rājendralāl mitra* (Calcutta: Vagartha, 1969).

Amarendranath Basu. *Śiśumaner bikāś-o-bikār* (Calcutta: Sribhumi, 1984).

Amarendranath Majumdar. "Śildār kāthā o kāhinī," *Taruṇer ḍāk* (Silda) 1, 1 (1962), pp. 49-57.

Anandachandra Mitra. *Kabitākusum*, vol. 1 (Calcutta, 1871).

———. *Prācīn bhārat o ādhunik iyorope sabhyatār bhinna mūrtti* (Mymensingh: Bharatmihir Press, 1876).

———. *Helenākābya*, vol. 1 (Mymensingh: Bharatmihir Press, 1876).

———. *Byabahār darśan*, vol. 1 (Calcutta: Roy Press, 1878).

———. *Bhāratmaṅgal* (Calcutta: Brahmo Mission Press, 1894).

———. *Mitrakābya* (3rd ed., Calcutta: Nabyabharat Press, 1898).

Annadacharan Khastagir. *Pāribārik susthatā* (Calcutta: East Bengal Association, 1885).

Arunkumar Mitra, ed. *Amṛtalāl basur smṛti o ātmasmṛti* (Calcutta: Sahityalok, 1982).

Arunkumar Mukhopadhyay. *Bāṅlā samālocanār itihās* (Calcutta: Classic Press, 1965).

Asim Bardhan. *Śiśu kena "śiśu"* (Calcutta: West Bengal State Book Board, 1989).

———. *Kiśor-kiśorīder youna samasyā* (Calcutta: West Bengal State Book Board, 1991).

Asitkumar Bandyopadhyay. *Samālocanār kathā* (Calcutta: Modern Book Agency, 1971).

Balendranath Thakur. *Citra o kābya* (Calcutta: Brahmo Samaj Press, 1894).

Bankimchandra Chattopadhyay. *Baṅkim racanābalī*, vol. 2 (Calcutta: Sahitya Samsad, 1983).

Baradakanta Datta. "Citrabidyā o prakṛtijñān," *Bhāratbarṣa*, Magh 1322 (1915-16).

Barunkumar Mukhopadhyay. *Bāṃlā mudrita granther itihās*, vol. 2 (Calcutta: University of Calcutta, 1985).

Bhudeb Mukhopadhayay. "Pāribārik prabandha," in Pramathanath Bisi, ed., *Bhūdeb racanāsambhār* (Calcutta: Mitra and Ghosh, 1969).

Binay Ghosh. *Paścimbaṅger saṃskṛti* (Calcutta: Pustak Prakasak, 1957).

———. *Bāṃlār bidvatsamāj* (2nd ed. Calcutta: Prakash Bhaban, 1978).

Binaybhusan Ray. *Uniś śataker bāṃlāy bijñān sādhanā* (Calcutta: Subarnarekha, 1987).

Brajendranath Bandyopadhyay. *Saṃbādpatre sekāler kathā*, vol. 1 (Calcutta: Bangiya Sahitya Parishat, 1983).

Brajendranath Bandyopadhyay and Sajanikanta Das. *Sāhitya-sādhak-caritmālā*, vol. 4 (Calcutta: Bangiya Sahitya Parishat, 1946).

Charuchandra Nag. *Citrabidyā*, part 1 (Calcutta, 1874).

Chittaranjan Bandyopadhyay. "Aślīlatā nibāraṇ āin" in *Saṃskṛti o granthāgār* (Calcutta: General Printers, 1963).

———, ed. *Dui śataker bāṃlā mudraṇ o prakāśan* (Calcutta: Ananda, 1981).

Dineschandra Sen. *Baṅgabhāṣā o sāhitya* (reprint Calcutta: West Bengal State Book Board, 1991).

Durgacharan Ray. *Debgaṇer marttye āgaman* (1886; reprint Calcutta: Dey's, 1984).

Durgaprasad Bhattacharya and Rama Deb Ray, eds. *Bāṃlā bhāṣāy arthanīti carcā (1818-1947)* (Calcutta: Socio-economic Research Institute, 1983).

Haraprasad Sastri. *Haraprasād śāstrī racanā saṃgraha*, vol. 2 (Calcutta: West Bengal State Book Board, 1981).

Indubhusan Sen. *Pāribārik cikitsā* (Calcutta: Erenda, 1927).

Jatindramohan Bhattacharya, ed. *Bāṃlā mudrita granthādir tālikā*, vol. 1: 1743-1852 (Calcutta: A. Mukherjee, 1990).

———. *Mudrita bāṃlā granther pañjī 1853-1867* (Calcutta: Paschim Bangla Academy, 1993).

Jnanendramohan Das. *Bāṅgālā bhāṣār abhidhān* (2nd ed. 1937; reprint Calcutta: Sahitya Samsad, 1991).

Jogeschandra Bagal. *Hindu melār itibṛtta* (Calcutta: Maitri, 1968).

Kamal Chaudhuri and Parimal Chaudhuri, eds. *Kalkātā chāpākhānā* (Calcutta: Naba-yuvak Sangha, 1978).

Kamal Sarkar. "Kyālkāṭā ārṭ sṭuḍior citrakalā," paper presented at centenary anniversary of the Calcutta Art Studio, November 1978.

Madhusudhan Mukhopadhyay. *Suśīlār upākhyān*, reprinted in *Kalej sṭrīṭ* (September-October, 1986).

Manmathanath Bandyopadhyay. *Caritra gaṭhan* (Dhaka: Jnanadaini Press, 1933).

Manmathanath Chakravarti. "Barṇa-citraṇ," *Śilpa o sāhitya*, 1312 (1905) and 1315 (1908-9).

Nagendrabala Dasi. *Nārīdharma* (Calcutta: Kalika Press, 1902).

Nilkanta Goswami. *Āmi tomāri* (Calcutta: Saraswat Press, 1864).

Nripendranath Seth. "Cheler asukh o mātār jñātabya," *Svāsthya* 2, 3 (1898).

———. "Mātṛstanyapāyī śiśur pālan bidhi," *Svāsthya* 2, 6 (1898).

———. "Āmāder śiśu," *Sakhī* 1, 3, Caitra 1307 (1900).

———. "Śiśu pālan," *Sakhī* 1, 8-9 Bhādra Āśvin 1308 (1901).

Nrisinghachandra Mukherjee. *Arthanīti o artha-byabahār* (Calcutta: New School Book Press, 1874).

Pankaj Datta. *Racanā bicitrā* (Calcutta: Debu Prakashani, 1992).

Prasannatara Gupta. *Pāribārik jīban* (Calcutta: Kuntaleen Press, 1903).

Pratapchandra Majumdar. *Strīcaritra* (Calcutta: Nababidhan, 1891).

Rajsekhar Basu. *Calantikā* (Calcutta: M. C. Sarkar, 1966).

Ramanath Das. *Kalikātār māncitra* (Calcutta: B. P. M. Press, 1884).

Ramgati Nyayaratna. *Bāṅgālābhāṣā o bāṅgālāsāhitya biṣayak prastāb: A Treatise on the Bengali Language and Literature*, parts 1 and 2 (Hugli: Bodhaday Press, 1872; reprint Calcutta: Supreme Book Distributors, 1991).

Ramkamal Vidyalankar. *Sacitra prakṛtibād abhidhān* (6th ed., Calcutta: B. Banerjee, 1911).

Ramkrishna Ray Chaudhuri. *Artha-byabahār* (Calcutta: Sanskrit Press, 1875).
Saradaprasad Hajra Chaudhuri. *Saṃsār-dharma o bisaykarma* (Calcutta: Abasar Press, 1906).
Saratchandra Deb. *Gārhasthya prasaṅga* (Calcutta: Grihastha Publishing House, 1923).
Saratchandra Dhar. *Abalā bāndhab* (Dhaka: Students Library, 1912).
Sarojini Debi. *Āryasatī* (Dhaka: Madhusudan Press, 1917).
Satischandra Chakrabarti. *Santāner caritra gaṭhan* (1912; reprint Calcutta: Sahitya Sanstha, 1989).
———. *Nabayuger āhvān* (1916; reprint Calcutta: Sadhanasram, 1952).
Shobhon Shome and Anil Acharya, eds. *Baṅlā śilpasamālocanār dhārā: Śyāmācaraṇ śrīmāṇi, balendranāth ṭhākur, sukumār rāy* (Calcutta: Anustup, 1986).
Shyamacharan Srimani. *Sūkṣaśilper utpatti o āryajātir śilpacāturi* (Calcutta: Roy Press, 1874).
———. *Siṃhal-bijay-kābya* (Calcutta: Sanskrit Press Depository, 1875).
Sibaji Bandyopadhyay. *Gopāl-rākhāl dvandvasamās: upanibeśbād o bāṅglā śiśusāhitya* (Calcutta: Papyrus, 1991).
Sibnath Sastri. *Gṛhadharma* (Calcutta: Sadharan Brahmosamaj, 1881).
———. *Ātmacarit* in *Śibnāth śāstrī racanāsaṃgraha* (Calcutta: Saksharata Prakashan, 1979).
———. *Rāmtanu lahiḍī o tatkālīn baṅgasamāj* (1904) in *Śibnāth racanāsaṃgraha* (Calcutta: Saksharata Prakashan, 1979).
Srikumar Bandyopadhyay and Praphullachandra Pal, eds. *Samālocanā-sāhitya-paricay* (Calcutta: University of Calcutta, 1960).
Sripantha [Nikhil Sarkar]. *Yakhan chāpākhānā elo* (Calcutta: Banga Sanskriti Sammelan, 1978).
Sukumar Sen. *Baṭtalār chāpā o chabi* (Calcutta: Ananda, 1989).
Upendranath Mukhopadhyay. *Kalikātā darśak* (Calcutta: New Calcutta Press Depository, 1890).

European-language Sources

Alison, Alexander. *The Future; or, The Science of Politics* (London, 1852).
Amos, Sheldon. *The Science of Politics* (London: Kegan Paul, Trench, 1883).
Anderson, Benedict. *Imagined Communities: Reflections on the Origins and Spread of Nationalism* (London: Verso, 1991).
Ariès, Philippe. *Centuries of Childhood: A Social History of Family Life,* trans. R. Baldick (New York: Knopf, 1962).
Arnold, David. *Colonizing the Body: State Medicine and Epidemic Disease in Nineteenth-Century India* (Berkeley: University of California Press, 1993).
Bagal, Jogesh Chandra. *History of the Government College of Art and Crafts, 1864-1964* (Calcutta: Government College of Arts and Crafts, 1966).
Bagchi, Amiya Kumar. "Wealth and Work in Calcutta 1860-1921," in Sukanta Chaudhuri, ed., *Calcutta: The Living City,* vol. 1 (Calcutta: Oxford University Press, 1990), pp. 212-23.
Bagchi, Jasodhara. "Representing Nationalism: Ideology of Motherhood in Colonial Bengal." *Economic and Political Weekly,* 25 (1990), 42-43, pp. WS65-WS71.
———. "Socialising the Girl Child in Colonial Bengal." *Economic and Political Weekly* 28 (1993), 41, pp. 2214-19.
Bahura, Gopal Narayan and Chandramani Singh. *Catalogue of Historical Documents in Kapad Dwara,* vol. 2, Maps and Plans, (Jaipur 1990).
Bala, Poonam. *Imperialism and Medicine in Bengal: A Socio-historical Perspective* (New Delhi: Sage, 1991).
Basu, Aparna. *The Growth of Education and Political Development in India, 1898-1920* (Delhi: Oxford University Press, 1974).
Basu, B. D. *History of Education in India under the Rule of the East India Company* (Calcutta: Modern Review, 1922).

Bethune Society, *The Proceedings of the Bethune Society for the sessions of 1859-60, 1860-61* (Calcutta: Baptist-Mission Press, 1862).

Bhabha, Homi. "Signs Taken for Wonders: Questions of Ambivalence and Authority under a Tree Outside Delhi, May 1817," *Critical Inquiry* 12 (autumn 1985), pp. 144-65.

———. "DissemiNation," in Bhabha, ed., *Nation and Narration* (London: Routledge, 1990).

Blumhardt, J. F. *Catalogue of the Library of the India Office*, Vol. 2, part 4; Bengali, Oriya and Assamese Books (London: Eyre and Spottiswoode, 1905).

Bolton, C. W. "Reports on Publications Issued and Registered in the several Provinces of British India during the year 1878." *Selections from the Records of the Government of India,* Home Revenue and Agricultural Department No. LIX (Calcutta, 1879).

Bose, D. M. *J. C. Bose's Plant Physiological Investigations in Relation to Modern Biological Knowledge* (Calcutta: Bose Research Institute, 1948).

Bose, Jagadis Chunder. *Researches on Irritability of Plants* (London: Longmans, Green, 1913).

———. "Plant Autographs and Revelations," *Annual Report of the Smithsonian Institution* (Washington: Government Printing Office, 1915), pp. 421-43.

———. *A Manual of Indian Botany* (London: Blackie, 1920).

———. *The Physiology of Photosynthesis* (London: Longmans, Green, 1924).

———. *Growth and Tropic Movements of Plants* (London: Longmans, Green, 1929).

Brass, Paul R. "Politics of Ayurvedic Education: A Case Study of Revivalism and Modernization in India," in Susanne Hoeber Rudolph and Lloyd I. Rudolph, eds., *Education and Politics in India* (Cambridge, Mass.: Harvard University Press, 1972).

Busteed, H. E. *Echoes from Old Calcutta* (Calcutta, 1882).

Chakrabarti, Dilip K. *A History of Indian Archaeology up to 1947* (New Delhi: Munshiram Manoharlal, 1988).

Chakrabarty, Dipesh. "The Deference-Deferral of (a) Colonial Modernity: Public Debates on Domesticity in British Bengal," *History Workshop* 36 (Autumn 1993), pp. 1-34.

Chakraborty, Satyesh C. "Historical Significance of the Geographer's City: Calcutta of 1856," Noh Commemoration Volume, Institute of Geography, Tohoku University, Sendai, Japan, 1975.

Chandra, Pramod. *On the Study of Indian Art* (Cambridge, Mass.: Harvard University Press, 1983).

Chartier, Roger. *The Cultural Uses of Print in Early Modern France* (Princeton: Princeton University Press, 1987).

Chatterjee, Partha. "A Religion of Urban Domesticity: Sri Ramakrishna and the Calcutta Middle Class," in Partha Chatterjee and Gyanendra Pandey, eds., *Subaltern Studies VII* (Delhi: Oxford University Press, 1992).

———. *The Nation and Its Fragments: Colonial and Postcolonial Histories* (Princeton: Princeton University Press, 1993).

Chattopadhyay, Goutam, ed. *Awakening in Bengal in Early Nineteenth Century (Select Documents),* vol. 1 (Calcutta: Progressive Publishers, 1965).

Choudhuri, Keshab. *Calcutta: Story of Its Government* (Calcutta: Orient Longman, 1973).

Cole, H. H. *Catalogue of the Objects of Indian Art Exhibited in the South Kensington Museum* (London: South Kensington Museum, 1874).

Coomaraswamy, A. K. *Essays in National Idealism* (Madras: G. A. Natesan, 1909).

Cotton, H. E. A. *Calcutta Old and New* (1909; Calcutta: General Printers, 1980).

Craig, John. *Elements of Political Science,* 3 vols. (Edinburgh: William Blackwood, 1814).

Dasgupta, Swapan. "Adivasi Politics in Midnapur," in Ranajit Guha, ed. *Subaltern Studies IV* (Delhi: Oxford University Press, 1985).

deMause, Lloyd, ed. *The History of Childhood* (New York: Harper, 1975).

Donzelot, Jacques. *The Policing of Families,* trans. Robert Hurley (New York: Pantheon Books, 1979).

Dorfman, Ariel. "Childhood and Underdevelopment," in his *The Empire's Old Clothes* (New York: Hoffman, 1983).

Dove, P. E. *The Science of Politics* (London: Johnstone and Hunter, 1850).

Dutt Gupta, Bela. *Sociology in India: An Enquiry into Sociological Thinking and Empirical Social Research in the Nineteenth Century with Special Reference to Bengal* (Calcutta: Centre for Sociological Research, 1972).

Febvre, Lucien, and Henri-Jean Martin. *The Coming of the Book: The Impact of Printing 1450-1800* (London: Verso, 1976).

Fergusson, James. *Illustrations of the Rock-cut Temples of India: Selected from the Best Examples of the Different Series of Caves at Ellora, Ajunta, Cuttack, Salsette, Karli and Mahavellipore* (London: J. Weale, 1845).

———. *Picturesque Illustrations of Ancient Architecture in Hindostan* (London: J. Hogarth, 1848).

———. *The Illustrated Handbook of Architecture, Being a Concise and Popular Account of the Different Styles of Architecture in All Ages and Countries* (London: John Murray, 1855).

———. *On the Study of Indian Architecture: Read at a Meeting of the Society of Arts on Wednesday, 19th December 1866* (reprint Varanasi: Indological Book House, 1977).

———. *A History of Architecture in All Countries: From the Earliest Times to the Present Day,* 3 vols. (London: John Murray, 1873-76).

———. *History of Indian and Eastern Architecture* (London: John Murray, 1876).

Forbes, Geraldine Hancock. *Positivism in Bengal* (Calcutta: Minerva Associates, 1975).

Foucault, Michel. *The Archaeology of Knowledge,* trans. A. M. Sheridan Smith (London: Tavistock, 1972).

———. *The Birth of the Clinic: An Archaeology of Medical Perception,* trans. A. M. Sheridan Smith (New York: Vintage, 1975).

———. *Discipline and Punish: The Birth of the Prison,* trans. Alan Sheridan (New York: Pantheon, 1978).

———. *The History of Sexuality,* vol. 1, trans. Robert Hurley (New York: Vintage, 1980).

Fruzzetti, Lina, Ákos Östör, and Steve Barnett. "The Cultural Construction of the Person in Bengal and Tamilnadu," in Ákos Östör et al., eds. *Concepts of Person: Kinship, Caste and Marriage in India* (Delhi: Oxford University Press, 1992).

Gole, Susan. *India within the Ganges* (New Delhi: Jayaprints, 1983).

———. *Indian Maps and Plans from Earliest Times to the Advent of European Surveys* (New Delhi: Manohar, 1989).

Guha-Thakurta, Tapati. "The Ideology of the 'Aesthetic': The Purging of Visual Tastes and the Campaign for a New Indian Art in Late 19th/Early 20th Century Bengal," *Studies in History*, 8, 2 (July-December 1992).

———. *The Making of a New "Indian" Art: Artists, Aesthetics and Nationalism in Bengal, 1850-1920* (Cambridge: Cambridge University Press, 1992).

Gupta, Samita. "Theory and Practice of Town Planning in Calcutta, 1817 to 1912: An Appraisal," *Indian Economic and Social History Review* 30, 1 (January-March 1993), pp. 29-55.

Havell, E. B.. "Some Notes on Indian Pictorial Art," *The Studio,* 15 October 1902.

———. "British Philistinism and Indian Art," *The Nineteenth Century,* February 1903.

———. *Indian Sculpture and Painting* (London: John Murray, 1908).

———. "Art Administration in India," *Journal of the Royal Society of Arts,* 4 February 1910.

———. *The Ideals of Indian Art* (London: John Murray, 1911).

Humphreys, E. R. *Manual of Political Science, for the use of schools and more especially of candidates for the civil service* (London: Longman, Brown, Green, and Longmans, 1855).

Hunter, W. W. *A Statistical Account of Bengal,* vol. 17 (London, 1877; reprint Delhi: Concept, 1976).

Imam, Abu. *Sir Alexander Cunningham and the Beginnings of Indian Archaeology* (Dhaka: Asiatic Society of Pakistan, 1966).

Jameson, A. K. *Final Report on the Survey and Settlement Operations in the District of Midnapore, 1911 to 1917* (Calcutta: Bengal Secretariat Book Depot, 1918).

Jenkins, Ian. *Archaeologists and Aesthetes in the Sculpture Gallery of the British Museum, 1800-1939* (London: British Museum, 1992).

Kane, P. V. *History of Dharmaśāstra,* vol. 3 (Poona: Bhandarkar Oriental Research Institute, 1973).

Karlekar, Malabika. "Kadambini and the Bhadralok: Early Debates over Women's Education in Bengal," *Economic and Political Weekly* 21 (1986), 17, pp. WS25-WS31.

Kejariwal, O. P. *The Asiatic Society of Bengal and the Discovery of India's Past 1784-1838* (Delhi: Oxford University Press, 1988).

Kesavan, B. S. *History of Printing and Publishing in India: A Story of Cultural Re-awakening,* vol. 1 (New Delhi: National Book Trust, 1985), pp. 179-229.

Krishna, V. V. "The Emergence of the Indian Scientific Community," *Sociological Bulletin* 40, 1-2 (March-September 1991), pp. 89-107.

Lasch, Christopher. *Haven in a Heartless World* (New York: Basic Books, 1977).

Lewis, Jan. *The Pursuit of Happiness* (Cambridge: Cambridge University Press, 1983).

Long, J. *A Descriptive Catalogue of Bengali Works* (Calcutta: Sanders, Cones, 1855).

———. "Returns relating to Publications in the Bengali Language in 1857," in *Selections from the Records of the Bengal Government,* no. XXXII (Calcutta: General Printing Department, 1859).

McAlpin, M. C. *Report on the Condition of the Santhals in the Districts of Birbhum, Bankura, Midnapore and North Balasore* (Calcutta: Bengal Secretariat Press, 1909; reprint Firma K. L. Mukhopadhyay, 1981).

McCully, Bruce Tiebout. *English Education and the Origins of Indian Nationalism* (New York: Columbia University Press, 1940).

Madan, T. N. "The Hindu Family and Development," *Journal of Social and Economic Studies,* 4 (1976), 2, pp. 211-31.

Mahato, Pasupati. "Socio-Political Movement of the Kurmi Mahatos of Purulia and Neighbouring Areas of Bihar and Orissa," unpublished report, Anthropological Survey of India, Calcutta, 1991.

Messer-Davidow, Ellen, David R. Shumway, and David J. Sylvan, eds. *Knowledges: Historical and Critical Studies in Disciplinarity* (Charlottesville: University of Virginia Press, 1993).

Mills, W. T. *Science of Politics* (London, 1888).

Mitra, Rajendralal. *The Bengal Atlas: Series of Original and Authentic Maps of the Districts Included in the Lieutenant Governorship of Bengal* (Calcutta, 1871).

———. *The Antiquities of Orissa,* vol. 1 (Calcutta: Wyman, 1875); vol. 2 (Calcutta: Wyman, 1880).

———. *A Scheme for the Rendering of European Scientific Terms into the Vernaculars of India* (Calcutta: Thacker Spink, 1877).

———. A. F. Rudolf Hoernle, and P. N. Bose. *Centenary Review of the Asiatic Society of Bengal from 1784 to 1883* (1885; reprint Calcutta: Asiatic Society, 1986).

Mitter, Partha. *Much Maligned Monsters: History of European Reactions to Indian Art* (Oxford: Oxford University Press, 1977).

Mukhopadhyay, Tarun Kumar. *Hicky's Bengal Gazette: Contemporary Life and Events* (Calcutta: Subarnarekha, 1988).

Nandy, Ashis. *Alternative Sciences: Creativity and Authenticity in Two Indian Scientists* (New Delhi: Allied, 1979).

———. "Reconstructing Childhood: A Critique of the Ideology of Adulthood," in Nandy, *Traditions, Tyranny and Utopias: Essays in the Politics of Awareness* (Delhi: Oxford University Press, 1992).

Nurullah, Syed, and J. P. Naik. *A History of Education in India (during the British Period)* (1943; 2nd ed. Bombay: Macmillan, 1951).

Okakura, Kakuzo. *The Ideals of the East* (London: John Murray, 1903).

Panikkar, K. N. "Indigenous Medecine and Cultural Hegemony: A Study of the Revitalization Movement in Keralam," *Studies in History* 8, 2 (July-December 1992).

Phillimore, R. H. *Historical Records of the Survey of India* (Dehradun: Survey of India, vol. 1 1945, vol. 2 1950).

Prakash, Gyan. "The Modern Nation's Return to the Archaic," unpublished ms., Department of History, Princeton University, 1993.

———. "Science Gone Native in Colonial India," *Representations* 40 (Fall 1992).

———. "Science Between the Lines," in Shahid Amin and Dipesh Chakrabarty, eds. *Subaltern Studies IX* (Delhi: Oxford University Press, 1995).

Ray, A. K. *A Short History of Calcutta, Town and Suburbs: Census of India, 1901, Volume VIII, Part 1* (1902; reprint Calcutta: Riddhi-India, 1982).

Ray, Prafulla Chandra. *A History of Hindu Chemistry from the Earliest Times to the Middle of the Sixteenth Century, A.D.,* 2 vols. (London: Williams and Morgate, 1902-9).

Raz, Ram. *Essay on the Architecture of the Hindus* (London: Royal Asiatic Society of Great Britain, 1834).

Rothermund, D. and D. C. Wadhwa, eds. *Zamindars, Mines and Peasants* (Delhi: Manohar, 1978).

Roy, Sourindranath. "Indian Archaeology from Jones to Marshall," *Ancient India* 9 (1953).

Samaddar, Ranabir. "Reflections in Another Mirror: Fictional Genealogies of Chilkigarh," *Indian Economic and Social History Review* 29 (1992), 1, pp. 77-102.

Sanyal, Bhubaneswar. *Final Report on the Minor Settlement Operations in the District of Midnapore, 1907-13* (Calcutta: Bengal Secretariat Book Depot, 1916).

Sanyal, Rajat. *Voluntary Associations and the Urban Public Life in Bengal (1815-1876)* (Calcutta: Riddhi-India, 1980).

Sarkar, Nikhil. "Printing and the Spirit of Calcutta," in Sukanta Chaudhuri, ed., *Calcutta: The Living City,* vol. 1 (Calcutta: Oxford University Press, 1990), pp. 128-36.

Sarkar, Sumit. "The Conditions and Nature of Subaltern Militancy: Bengal from Swadeshi to Non-cooperation, 1905-22," in Ranajit Guha, ed., *Subaltern Studies III* (Delhi: Oxford University Press, 1984).

Sarkar, Tanika. "Nationalist Iconography: Images of Women in 19th-century Bengali Literature," *Economic and Political Weekly* 22 (1987), 47, pp. 2011-15.

———. "The Hindu Wife and the Hindu Nation: Domesticity and Nationalism in Nineteenth-century Bengal," *Studies in History* 8 (1992), 2, pp. 213-35.

Seal, Anil. *The Emergence of Indian Nationalism: Competition and Collaboration in the Nineteenth Century* (Cambridge: Cambridge University Press, 1970).

Seal, Brajendranath. *The Positive Sciences of the Ancient Hindus* (London: Longmans, Green, 1915).

Shah, A. M. "Changes in the Indian Family: An Examination of Some Assumptions," *Economic and Political Weekly* 3 (1968), annual number, pp. 127-34.

———. *The Household Dimension of the Family in India* (Berkeley: University of California Press, 1973).

Sinha, Pradip. *Calcutta in Urban History* (Calcutta: Firma KLM, 1978).

Tagore, Surendranath. "Kakuzo Okakura," *Visvabharati Quarterly,* August-October 1936.

Uberoi, Patricia. "Family, Household and Social Change," in Patricia Uberoi, ed., *Family, Kinship and Marriage in India* (Delhi: Oxford University Press, 1994), pp. 383-92.

Viswanathan, Gauri. *Masks of Conquest: Literary Study and British Rule in India* (London: Faber and Faber, 1990).

Wenger, J., compiler. "Catalogue of Sanskrit and Bengalee Publications printed in Bengal." *Selections from the Records of the Bengal Government,* no. XLI (Calcutta, Bengal Central Press, 1865).

Contributors

Pradip Kumar Bose is professor of sociology at the Centre for Studies in Social Sciences, Calcutta. He is the author of *Classes in a Rural Society: A Sociological Study of Some Bengal Villages* (1984) and *Classes and Class Relations Among Tribals of Bengal* (1985).

Partha Chatterjee is professor of political science at the Centre for Studies in Social Sciences, Calcutta, and has held visiting appointments at St. Antony's College in Oxford, the Australian National University in Canberra, the New School for Social Research in New York, and the University of Michigan at Ann Arbor. He is the author of *Nationalist Thought and the Colonial World* (University of Minnesota Press, 1993) and *The Nation and Its Fragments: Colonial and Postcolonial Histories* (1993).

Keya Dasgupta is a fellow of the Centre for Studies in Social Sciences, Calcutta. Her published papers are mainly on the historical geography of Assam.

Tapati Guha-Thakurta is a fellow of the Centre for Studies in Social Sciences, Calcutta, and has been a visiting fellow at the Shelby Cullom Davis Center for Historical Studies at Princeton University and at Wolfson College, Cambridge. She is the author of *The Making of a New "Indian" Art* (1992).

Tapti Roy teaches history at Maharani Kashiswari College, Calcutta, and has been a fellow of the Centre for Studies in Social Sciences, Calcutta, and Charles Wallace Fellow at the School of Oriental and African Studies, London. She is the author of *The Politics of Popular Uprising: 1857 in Bundelkhand* (1994).

Ranabir Samaddar is a senior fellow of the Maulana Azad Institute of Asian Studies, Calcutta. He is the author of *Workers and Automation: The Impact of New Technology in the Newspaper Industry* (1994). His full-length study of the ecology, politics, and culture of the forest regions of Bengal, Bihar, and Orissa is forthcoming.

Index

Germany, 67, 93, 101, 195
Ghatshila, 194, 195
Ghosh, Kaliprasanna, 54
Ghuri, Muhammad, 113
Gidni, 167, 190
Goldighi, 43
Gole, Susan, 149-50
Gopiballavpur, 177, 186
Goswami, Nilkanta, 59
Gothic, 86
Government Art Gallery, 6
Government House, 3, 6
Government School of Art, 6, 64, 65, 66, 76, 78, 79, 80, 149, 152
Graeco-Bactrian, 68
Graeco-Roman, 83
Graham, H., 188-89
grammar, 38, 40, 41, 114
Greek, 21, 23, 56, 67, 70, 74, 75, 83, 85, 94, 99. *See also* Graeco-Bactrian; Graeco-Roman
gṛha-lakṣmī. See lakṣmī
Guha-Thakurta, Tapati, 26
Gupta, Hari, 190
Gupta, Iswarchandra, 43
Gupta period, 86

Halhed, Nathaniel Brassey, 30
Hardwar, 151
Harihar, Raja, 174-75
Hastinapur, 70
Hastings, 4
Havell, E. B., 77-79, 80, 83, 85, 88, 89
headman. *See* mandal
Hebrew, 67
Helen of Troy, 94
Hicky, James Augustus, 30, 60n.3
High Court (Calcutta), 3, 6, 114, 156
Hindi, 21
Hindu: art, 73, 75, 85, 86-87; bride, 81; law of inheritance, 106-7; orthodox, 5; period, 69, 71; system of courtship in, 36. *See also* Hinduism; temple
Hindu College, 13, 14, 43
Hindu Mela, 66, 73
Hinduism, 33, 35, 41, 84, 126. *See also* Brahman; Hindu
Hindustan Copper Company, 168
history, 27, 35, 38, 40, 52, 56, 94, 113, 195-97; agrarian, 170, 175-77; 184; of art, 63-89; Indian, 68, 72; nationalist, 73, 86-87, 104; natural, 6
home, 21, 81. *See also* family
Hooghly, 41
Hooghly (river), 4, 146, 155, 164
hospital, 18, 156, 164
Howrah, 2, 4, 155
Howrah bridge, 2, 3
Hunter, W. W., 167-68
Huxley, T. H., 16
hybridization, 20-22, 72, 83

ijaradar, 170, 173-74, 181, 191, 192, 194-95
Iliad, The, 94, 99
Imperial Art School (Tokyo), 84
Imperial Library, 49
Imperial Secretariat Building, 6
India: ancient, 55-56, 63, 68, 69, 70, 73, 74, 75, 80, 86-87, 110, 112-16; condition of, 94; medieval, 72, 87; northern, 69, 112, 151; northwest, 150; printed books in, 49; southern, 69, 70, 150; toleration in, 110; western, 67, 150
India House Library. *See* India Office Library
India Office Library, 37, 49
Indian Agricultural Service, 16
Indian Association for the Cultivation of Science, 19
Indian Forest Service, 16
Indian Medical and Bacteriological Service, 16
Indian Munitions Board, 16
Indian Museum, 6
Indian National Congress, 112, 186, 193
Indians: in art teaching, 65-66; as privileged subjects of knowledge, 73-74, 77; in scientific research, 12, 16, 19
indigo, 90n.15, 192-95, 196
Indology, 12, 74, 143n.6. *See also* Orientalism
Indra, 2-3, 6
Indraprastha, 70, 110
Indus (river), 110
industry, 8, 25, 30, 34, 93
insurgency, 185-97
International Children's Year, 120
Irish, 16
Islamic. *See* Muslim
Iswar Chandra, Raja, 170, 171, 174, 175, 181, 182
Italy, 93